Better Broadcast Writing,
Better Broadcast News

Greg Dobbs

PEARSON

Boston • New York • San Francisco
Mexico City • Montreal • Toronto • London • Madrid • Munich • Paris
Hong Kong • Singapore • Tokyo • Cape Town • Sydney

Series Editor: Molly Taylor
Series Editorial Assistant: Michael Kish
Senior Marketing Manager: Mandee Eckersley
Production Editor: Won Jang
Composition Buyer: Linda Cox
Manufacturing Buyer: JoAnne Sweeney
Cover Administrator: Kristina Mose-Libon
Electronic Composition: Publishers' Design and Production Services, Inc.

For related titles and support materials, visit our online catalog at www.ablongman.com.

Library of Congress Cataloging-in-Publication Data

Dobbs, Greg
      Better broadcast writing, better broadcast news / Greg Dobbs.
         p. cm.
      Includes index.
      ISBN 0-205-35994-9 (pbk.)
      1. Broadcast journalism—Authorship.   2. Reporters and reporting.   3. Report writing.
      I.   Title.

PN4784.B75D63 2005
808'.06607—dc22

                                                                                      2004040105

Printed in the United States of America
10   9   8   7   6   5   4   3   2   1   09   08   07   06   05   04

Photo Credits: Photos on pages 26 and 76–79 are courtesy of ABC News; photos on pages 65, 150, 212, and 215 are courtesy of KCNC-TV; photos on page 187 are from iStockphoto.com; photos on pages 47, 94, 116, and 192 are courtesy of Greg Dobbs.

Contents

15   *A Picture Is Worth a Thousand Words*   **182**

PART V • *It's All Part of the Show*   **195**

16   *If the Shoe Fits, Write It*   **197**

17   *Fitting It All In*   **209**

18   *Even More Ways for Radio*   **221**

Preface

Back when I was a student like you, I often wondered how a professor analyzing Shakespearean plays could tell me why Shakespeare wrote as he did. How could the teacher be so *sure* about what Shakespeare meant if Shakespeare didn't tell him? I wanted to know what ran through *Shakespeare's* mind, not just the professor's. Impossible though it was, I wanted to hear from the writer himself.

That's why I decided to write this textbook about writing for broadcast news. No, the writing in my news stories wasn't like Shakespeare's (which might be a blessing for audiences that just want straightforward explanations of stories); it's neither as incisive nor as complex. But at least I can use it in examples throughout the book, and explain why I wrote something the way I did—sometimes effectively, sometimes not. Therefore, though unconventional for a textbook, much of it is written in the first person.

Sure, there are already lots of good textbooks about broadcast news out there, but from the first day I taught a journalism course at the Medill School of Journalism at Northwestern University, then later at the School of Journalism and Mass Communication at the University of Colorado, I couldn't escape one unavoidable flaw common to almost all the textbooks I considered using: they were about someone *else's* work. By and large, their authors could only analyze someone else's news stories—whether well or poorly produced—secondhand. Just like my longing back when I studied Shakespeare, I wanted to take their analyses a step further, and ask the journalists themselves why they wrote and produced broadcast news stories the way they did.

You're going to get those answers here. Most of the writing examples throughout this book are from my own career, mostly as a correspondent for ABC News. Some won awards (including two Emmys, and the Distinguished Service Award and Bronze Medallion from the Society of Professional Journalists), some are embarrassingly bad, and in one way or another demonstrate pitfalls I hope you'll learn to avoid. But all serve a couple of purposes: first and most important, to demonstrate not just the difference between good and bad writing and good and bad production, but also to give you insight into the reasons why something was good and something else wasn't.

The other purpose? To show you how exciting the news business can be. This book isn't a personal memoir, but it has some of the elements of one, because instead of just giving you examples of stories and how my colleagues and I covered them, I want to give you some background too: the fun, fulfilling, silly, stupid, challenging, crazy, adventurous, dangerous things you sometimes have to do to get your story. I can't think of another career in which I'd have gotten to pet an African lion, *and* fire a machine gun, *and* ride around the track before the Indy 500, *and* follow the Tour de France in a helicopter, *and* climb around the face of Mt. Rushmore and out on the girders of the Eiffel Tower, *and* break bread with the Defense Minister of Saudi Arabia, *and* observe the worst oil spill in history, *and* see the inside of an Afghan jail, *and* meet presidents and dictators alike.

For many who cover the news—whether writing, editing, producing, recording, or transmitting—it's not a nine-to-five job; on the contrary, the hours can be long and irregular. And despite the fortunes paid to some of the big personalities in broadcasting, the pay for most broadcast journalists is modest. Other rewards make it worth your while. Whether covering city hall or the nation's capital, fatal head-on collisions or fatal earthquakes, you are on the periphery of history. You get to deal firsthand with issues and events that everyone else learns secondhand when they hear the news in their cars or watch it on TV or read it in the newspaper.

Of course, you're the one who gives it to them. But you'll only keep that privilege if you do it honestly and effectively. That's why it's important that you pay attention to what you learn in this book. It's mainly about writing, but in broadcast news, it takes more than good writing to produce a good story. It takes good researching, good reporting, good interviewing, good organizing, good pictures, and good sound—all of which are worthless without good ethics.

This book is about both television and radio news. For the most part, although the bulk of examples throughout the book apply to television coverage, a lesson for one medium (TV) can apply to the other (radio). Sure, a few things, particularly technical points about production and format, are specific to only one medium or the other. But I deliberately did not divide the whole book into separate sections about each, because the principles of good journalism apply to both.

One of the most innovative figures in the history of broadcast journalism was a man who started his career in broadcast sports before moving into news: Roone Arledge, the President of ABC News during most of my twenty-three years there. When he first took over our news division, most of us who already called ourselves veterans were skeptical. We expected every news broadcast would be packaged like the Super Bowl. But we were pleasantly surprised, never more than when he articulated a mission statement for news coverage that ended up being quoted by a competitor from CBS News at Arledge's funeral: "If a story breaks, you send the best people you can find out to see what's happening, then tell the rest of us whether we need to worry about it." Be the best, and you'll have the privilege of telling the rest.

Acknowledgments

Most of the people I should thank are those who helped me learn my profession along the way—producers, editors, directors, and camera, sound, and light artists. If any of you read this, please know I'm grateful.

Specifically for this book, special thanks to a few individuals who helped keep it contemporary: News Directors Angie Kucharski of KCNC-TV, Byron Grandy of KMGH-TV, and Dick Kelsey of KNRC Radio, correspondent Lee Frank of CBS Radio News, Managing Editor Dave Green of KMGH-TV, reporter Cheryl Preheim of KUSA-TV, and producer/reporter Chris Taylor of KWGN-TV and KOA Radio. Also, thanks to Brent Green for invaluable ideas and to technical genius Phil Lauter, who taught me the techniques I needed to scan photos and artwork before publication . . . and then when I got it all wrong, taught me again.

And the whole idea of the book—how to get started, how to get it done—is thanks to a couple of deans from the School of Journalism and Mass Communication at the University of Colorado: Steve Jones and Meg Moritz.

As much as anything, I owe a huge dose of gratitude to ABC News, past and present. ABC News *past* opened the door to a life of learning and adventure, enduring my shortcomings, and encouraging my attributes. ABC News *present* opened the door to this book, allowing me to use scripts from stories that are, for now and evermore, the property of the network. In the process of evaluating the manuscript for this purpose, Kerry Marash, Vice President of Editorial Quality for ABC News, took the trouble to read the whole thing, for which I owe her a particular note of thanks, for she already has her college degree and probably thought textbooks were only a part of her past. ABC News didn't have to bestow upon me ownership of my scripts; my compensation came in countless other forms.

Thanks to Molly Taylor and Michael Kish at Allyn and Bacon, who kept me organized and on track, as well as thanks to production editor Won Jang and the especially capable and careful eye of copyeditor Karen McClure. Otherwise, this book might never have reached you, and if it did, without these professionals it might have come with faulty punctuation and on a million random scraps of paper.

And many thanks to the following reviewers for their time and input: Don A. Grady, Elon University; Peter Hunn, Oswego State University; William L. Knowles, The University of Montana; Gary W. Larson, University of Nevada, Las Vegas; Sam Lovato, University of Southern Colorado; Thomas J. McHugh, Luzerne County Community College; George M. Plasketes, Auburn University; Jeffrey Porche, Sam Houston State University; James E. Reppert, Southern Arkansas University; Keith Swezey, University of Central

Oklahoma, Doug Underwood, Central Missouri State University; and A. Randall Wenner, Syracuse University.

Finally, but most importantly, my family's sometimes involuntary contributions were critical. In their younger years, my sons Jason and Alex grew up with an often-absent dad. And that meant that my wife Carol had to be a single mother. If she hadn't tolerated my news career—my myopic attitudes, the unpredictable absences, the mortal dangers—I couldn't have had it as long I did, and collected the experiences that distinguish this book.

I don't have it any more, which is good for Carol, but also good for me. There's not a single experience I would trade, but just as surely, I cherish the merit of mid-life change. That is the first lesson in this book. Maybe it ought to be the last.

Greg Dobbs
July 2004
Evergreen, Colorado

I

How to Write the Right Words and Sentences

1

The Right Words, The Right Stuff

A few broadcast stories depend strictly on pictures, a few strictly on sound. But the rest? They depend mainly on words. Words you understand. Words everyone understands. So that's where this book will start. The right words. The right stuff.

Probably by the time you're in high school and certainly when you're in college, you walk into a new course and the teacher hands you a syllabus. You read it, you discuss it, hopefully you abide by it, and maybe you even tell friends who will be taking the course the following semester about it. But does anyone ever actually explain the word "syllabus," let alone define it? No one did when I was in school.

That's why, when I started teaching journalism and a dean asked me to "prepare a syllabus," I wasn't really sure what to do, because I wasn't really sure what it meant. I had seen and used plenty of syllabi (that's even worse; at least "syllabuses" is a more acceptable plural form of "syllabus"), but nothing in life had ever forced my brain to instinctively understand the word.

This leads me to the whole point of this chapter: when you're writing for a news broadcast (and this is a good rule for newspaper writers too), don't use words your audience wouldn't use in normal conversation. Don't use words they may not be able to envision. Don't use words they won't easily understand. And don't use words that sound judgmental, because that's not your job. It obstructs the process of communication, when you're supposed to enrich it. How can you avoid these pitfalls? By using the shortest and simplest words possible. Short, simple, unambiguous, descriptive, active, fair, everyday English.

This chapter is simply about words you ought to use, and others you shouldn't. Simple, huh?

The Never Ending Story

One of the ongoing features of this first section in *Better Broadcast Writing, Better Broadcast News* is the Never Ending Story, a news report that starts out written about as poorly as a news report can be written. It'll appear twice in each chapter that deals with the style and mechanics of writing: first at the beginning and again at the end. Your job at the beginning is to simply read it (and review the corrections you should have made in the last chapter), then at the end, to clean it up. Don't make every conceivable correction though; just make changes based on that chapter's lessons.

For instance, in this chapter, "The Right Words, The Right Stuff," your only task is to find specific words that should be improved or eliminated, which you should be able to do by the end of the chapter. Don't peek ahead though, because the next chapter, "The Wrong Way to Write It," will open with the improved version that you should have produced (although it still will be packed with other kinds of flaws). In each chapter that follows in this section of the book, those flaws will be more obvious to you, so that at the end of each, you'll be able to find and correct them. By the end of the section, you ought to have a news report that can be read on the air!

In a place where a rear-ender traffic mishap's usually the most consequential event of the day there's been a huge occurrence with a terrible impact on each and everyone. Tonight the lives of three persons were tragically claimed by a bomb, which set off a 3-alarm blaze that raised temperatures to almost 200° Fahrenheit at a garment store at 3645 Main Street, in the heart of Ft. Stutter, Miss., the police said. No group took credit for the horrific blast, but forensics experts are combing the scene of the senseless attack tonight and in case there's more danger there, a hazmat team's dispatched to the scene. In order to explain why there wasn't an admonition, the police chief of the city of Ft. Stutter, Jazibeauz Perez, claims there was definitely no indication that the explosive device was going to detonate, then he said, "Everyone wishes to God we'd known this was going to transpire." The police dept. hasn't asked the FBI for help the chief said. The deceased includes Jason J. Jones, 29, Sally S. Smyth, 24, and Greg G. Goldstein, who died at 22. None were employees at the bombed store. Two unidentified men are in critical condition, meaning they might die too. Everyone in Ft. Stutter is absolutely petrified now to go out on the street, and city officials admit increased protection will cost the population of Ft. Stutter a lot of wampum, $6.1-million. There isn't a date set for a decision about expending that aggregate of money, but the mayor can't be back in the community by Tues., which isn't early enough for her critics. Whether such an expenditure'll really be beneficial remains to be observed.

Short Is Better than Succinct

Here is an example of a sentence where the writer uses a sophisticated, less conversational word, instead of a simple one:

The automobile crashed into the house.

It's straightforward, it's accurate. But it's not as short and simple as possible. What would be?

The car crashed into the house.

As a speaker and writer of the English language, you have a heavier burden to bear than journalists who work in any other language on earth. Why? Because the English language has more words—616,500 of them, according to the Oxford English Dictionary—than any other language on earth. There are remote (and disappearing) languages in Asia and Africa whose entire word count is only in the tens of thousands. Writers in these languages don't have to grapple with the burden of choosing between "vessel," "boat," or "ship." You do.

Eventually in your journalism career, choosing the shortest and simplest words in our language (or any language) will be second nature, but until it is, consciously ask yourself whether you are using the shortest, simplest words in the sentences you write. When you are proofreading, make this one of the tasks on your checklist.

Why is it important? Because in a TV or radio news story, the audience hears your words only once. The fewer complexities you throw at them, the more easily they'll absorb everything they hear. Think about the following pairs of sentences that might appear in news stories, and about which version—after simplifying a single word—seems better. Read them all *aloud*; the differences will be even more transparent:

> *He said he didn't comprehend why his wife killed herself.*
> *He said he didn't understand why his wife killed herself.*

> *The councilwoman says she wants to revise the speed limit.*
> *The councilwoman says she wants to change the speed limit.*

> *The attorney is charged with contempt.*
> *The lawyer is charged with contempt.*

> *Police apprehended the suspect.*
> *Police caught the suspect.*

> *She was murdered outside her residence.*
> *She was murdered outside her home.*

And here's the best example to test what you've learned so far:

> *The student saw the syllabus and decided to drop the class.*
> *The student saw the course outline and decided to drop the class.*

See which one works better? The second one, every time. In fact in the last example, more (slightly more) is best, if more is simpler.

What's the Point?

Although there are exceptions, the basic principle here is as true with individual words and phrases as it is with whole sentences (which you will read about later in the book): shorter and simpler almost always is better. In other words, although you want to avoid the un-structured nature of spontaneous conversation (such as repetition, putting your own words into parentheses, pronouns without reference), write the way you talk!

Learn These, for a Start

Here are two lists of words. The list on the left has words most people probably understand, while the list on the right has words that are undoubtedly shorter and simpler and understood by all. Almost without exception (yes, like most rules, there are exceptions), the words on the right side are the ones you should use in news stories.

For Example . . . Words to Live By

aid	help	lacerations	cuts
altercation	argument	lawful	legal
apprehend	catch	male	man
attorney	lawyer	manufacture	make
automobile	car	mishap	accident
beverage	drink	obfuscate	confuse
blaze	fire	observe	see
cognizant	aware	occur	happen
commence	start	pass away	die
compensate	pay, pay back	persons	people
comprehend	understand	physician	doctor
conduct	do	presently	now
deceased	dead	prior to	before
determine	decide	produce	make
endeavor	try	reside	live
exacerbate	make it worse	residence	home
examination	test	revise	change
expound	talk	subsequent to	after
extricate	pull out	terminate	end
female	woman	transform	change
incarcerated	in jail	transpire	happen
indisposed	sick	vehicle	car, truck, whatever!
inferno	fire	vessel	boat, ship, whatever!!
initiate	start	utilize	use
intoxicated	drunk	youth	girl or boy
juvenile	child	youthful	young

This list isn't even close to complete. The purpose here is not to memorize the shorter, simpler version of every longer, more complex word or phrase in the English language. It is to think about the words you write—especially nouns and verbs—and get yourself into the habit of choosing the best ones.

By the way, several of the words on the left side of the box—words like "apprehend," "deceased," "female," "intoxicated," and so forth—are used in everyday speech by people in law enforcement. (Wouldn't the word "police" probably work better than "people in law enforcement" at the end of that sentence?) But just because they use them, doesn't mean you have to.

What's the Point?

Besides being a communicator, think of yourself as a translator. Once again, the lesson is to write the way you talk.

Translating English into Better English

Here's an example of the type of explanation you might hear from a police officer at the scene of an accident. It employs (wouldn't "uses" be better than "employs"?) words from the left side of the box you just studied. Read the explanation aloud, and see what you would change:

> *Several persons observed the male driver weaving between lanes in the blue vehicle. Subsequent to apprehending him, officers conducted a sobriety examination and determined that he was inebriated. The driver, who is presently incarcerated, resides at 123 Main Street. The deceased youth in the red vehicle has not yet been identified.*

If you want to convey it precisely but come up with better words for the audience to absorb, here's a rewrite that works. Here are corrections for all the word flaws you should have caught:

> *Several people saw the man in the blue truck weaving between lanes. After catching (or stopping) him, officers did a sobriety test and decided he was drunk. The driver, who lives at 123 Main Street, is now in jail. The dead boy in the red car has not yet been identified.*

Okay, that is easy enough to translate. But what do you do when someone in law enforcement—or someone in what's known as "public safety"—lays a sentence like this on you:

> *The chemicals spilled from the truck when it overturned, but we have a hazmat team on its way.*

A "hazmat team?" Maybe *you* know what that means—do you?—but many in your audience probably don't have a clue, unless they work in public safety or journalism. Yet words and phrases which insiders understand often get written into news stories, which means outsiders only get confused. "Hazmat," for example, is verbal shorthand for "hazardous materials," so a "hazmat team" means the people who, among other things, know how to clean up chemical spills.

But as soon as you use "hazmat" in a story, your audience is distracted. All over your viewing or listening area, people are thinking, "Hmmm, I wonder what 'hazmat' means?" As soon as they start thinking that, they are no longer thinking about anything else you're telling them. In other words, once you've given the audience a distraction, you've lost them and may not get them back for the duration of the story.

The same problem can come up with other kinds of "insider" words and phrases, the kinds of things you might have heard a million times but don't really know or understand. If you're covering a fire and you're told that it started in the "tool and die" department, do you know what that means? Probably not. If you don't, neither will the audience (it's where new tools are forged). Likewise, when covering a plane crash, don't just report that investigators suspect a problem with the "ailerons." If you don't know what ailerons are, find out and explain them in your story. If you do know, explain them anyway, because you're in the minority.

What's the Point?

Make sure you don't use words or phrases that you don't understand. And even if you understand them, make sure that you and your information source aren't the only ones who do!

Translating Other Tongues into English

It's great if you speak a foreign language, but it's awful if you write foreign words for an English language audience, just because you understand and maybe even use them yourself. Unless your whole audience speaks the foreign language at least as well as you do—which of course it doesn't—people simply won't understand what you're trying to tell them.
　　For example:

> *Her* nom de plume *is Julie Jupiter.*

Or:

> *They declared a* jihad *on Americans.*

There's not a broadcast audience in America in which everyone understands those foreign words. What's more, because the words are a distraction, you may lose the audience's attention. More often than not, writers intent on showing off (and inadvertently distracting their audience) use French words and phrases, perhaps because French once was the world-wide language of diplomats.
　　Even Latin, a dead language from the past, is alive and well in written and spoken English. It's especially popular with lawyers and churchmen, but sometimes it's popular with journalists too. It shouldn't be. Examples of foreign words in English language news stories are endless, but below is a handful that I've heard in stories, without any explanation to clarify their meaning for the audience:

> *nom de plume*
> *ad hoc*
> *gestalt*
> *tete a tete*
> *jihad*
> *que sera sera*
> *quid pro quo*
> *soiree*
> *in toto*
> *Cinco de Mayo* (okay, it's the name of a well-known Mexican holiday, but I've also
> 　　heard it out of context, even though most English speakers probably don't know
> 　　it means "May 5th")

I'm not going to translate these, or any others, for you. Why not? Because then you might think it's okay to write sentences like these:

Her nom de plume, *or "pen name," is Julie Jupiter.*

They declared a jihad, *a "holy war," on Americans.*

If you want to tell your audience what her pen name is, or what the radicals have declared, just do it, short and sweet and unadorned:

Her pen name is Julie Jupiter.

They declared a holy war on Americans.

You don't have to totally discontinue your use of foreign words. In fact, we have adopted plenty of foreign words into English, and they are perfectly okay to use. Most of us probably don't even consciously remember that words like *rendezvous* and *chauffeur* are French! We know what a *sombrero* is, and we wouldn't know any way but the German way to refer to the third *Reich*. So when words like these are the best ones to convey meaning in an English language sentence, by all means use them. But think. Think about the difference between foreign words we all use in English, and those we don't.

What's the Point?

You're not writing for an audience so you can show off. You're writing so you can show them the elements of a story in language they'll understand.

Be Dynamic When You Can

You're also writing so you can "involve" your audience in the story you're reporting. This means a few things:

1. Whenever possible, the present tense is better than the past tense.
2. Whenever possible, active voice is better than passive voice.
3. Whenever possible, a descriptive word is better than a dull word.

Here's what each of these points means.

Don't Get Tense over the Tense

Let's start with the tense of your main verb. Which of these two sentences, both telling the same story, sounds more active, more immediate, more dynamic, more alive? (Read them *aloud* and you'll get a better sense of the right answer.)

The mayor said he didn't take a bribe.
The mayor says he didn't take a bribe.

Sure, the news conference at which the mayor made his statement is over; the story may be half-a-day old. But is there anything wrong with the second version? No. Why not? First, if you were to go back and ask the mayor the same question right now, his answer (presumably) would be the same. Secondly, it's part of an ongoing news story. Perhaps yesterday you reported the charge against the mayor; today you report the mayor's response to the charge; tomorrow you'll report some other angle of this continuing story. "The mayor says. . ." will be accurate until and unless he changes his tune!

This leads to a quick review of a lesson you first learned years ago: the three tenses you're likely to use (four, if you count the future tense, which we won't bother with in a discussion of news stories).

- Present tense is used for something that's happening right now, or at least hasn't stopped happening.
- Present perfect tense is used for something that is over by the time you say (or write) it, but which does not imply any particular time, or something which might still be happening.
- Past tense is used for something which has ended, and only can be considered in the past.

So read (aloud) the following pairs of sentences, and see if you agree that even though the past tense is not inaccurate, whenever possible the present tense, or present perfect tense, is better:

There were six survivors from the plane crash.
There are six survivors from the plane crash.

Rain soaked the baseball field.
Rain has soaked the baseball field. (present perfect)

The announcement of a tax increase angered some congressmen.
The announcement of a tax increase angers some congressmen.

None of this means the past tense should be relegated to the past. Sometimes the present tense simply doesn't work. For example, if the president is on an overseas trip and arrived eight hours ago in India as you're writing your story, the present tense in this sentence doesn't make sense:

The president lands in India.

Neither does this one:

The president is landing in India.

But does that mean you are only left with the past tense? If so, then your only choice is:

The president landed in India.

Well, that's accurate but it's *not* your only choice. You may not remember the strict meaning of "present perfect tense," but here's how—and where—you use it:

The president has landed in India.

Now, reread aloud the last two examples, and see which one you think makes the sentence more active, more dynamic, and more alive:

The president landed in India.
The president has landed in India.

There's no contest, is there? By using the present perfect tense rather than the past tense, you are telling your audience that while the action isn't still going on, it hasn't been superseded by something else.

Of course, there are times when the past tense is the only tense you should use. Here are a few examples:

The coastline was destroyed by last year's hurricane.

This is better than:

The coastline has been destroyed by last year's hurricane.

The Broncos lost the 1986 Super Bowl.

Rather than:

The Broncos have lost the 1986 Super Bowl.

She slipped on a banana peel.

This certainly makes more sense than:

She is slipping on a banana peel.

While this book isn't long enough to cover every possibility, here are a few more examples for you to read aloud and think about. Think of them all as stories that are happening as you are writing. Your job as a writer is to decide when you can accurately use the present tense, when you can't use the present tense but the present perfect tense is okay, and when you must use the past tense.

The ship rams the dock.
The ship has rammed the dock.
The ship rammed the dock.

A car is hitting a bike.
A car has hit a bike.
A car hit a bike.

Miss Smith is winning the election.
Miss Smith has won the election.
Miss Smith won the election.

Every flower is blossoming.
Every flower has blossomed.
Every flower blossomed.

It's not so easy, is it? In the third and fourth examples, you really have to decide between the first (present tense) and second (present perfect tense) sentences. They both work, but that's what makes your job as a writer so tough: you have to choose the one that works best, the one that dynamically but accurately tells the audience what's happening right now!

So although the audience doesn't stop and consider the implications of the tense you choose for every verb, the choice you make does send a message. It tells viewers and listeners whether the action in a story is ongoing or finished. And because it affects the dynamic sound of your story, it can determine whether people pay close attention or not.

Active versus Passive

What's the difference between active and passive voice? The answer to this question also helps determine the audience's attention level. Go back to a few examples from the last section.

Instead of, *the mayor says he didn't take a bribe*, would you write, *no bribe was taken by me, the mayor says*?

No, of course not. The first version is active (do you remember "subject, predicate," etc., from those early grammar lessons in school?). The second is passive, as well as awkward.

But how about a slightly less obvious contrast: *rain has soaked the baseball field*, versus *the baseball field has been soaked by rain*? Neither is awkward, but still, the first version is more *active*, not to mention shorter and to the point.

Exceptions? Sure, as always. If a president gets shot, you don't write, *somebody has shot the president*, which follows the rules of good grammar. No, you write it the other way—*the president has been shot*—because in this hypothetical case, the object (the president) is the most important thing in the sentence.

Descriptive versus Dull

Here's a perfectly decent sentence from a news story:

The sheriff knocked down the front gate, went quickly into the house, and took possession of the counterfeit bills.

Decent, but not very exciting, is it? Wouldn't this be better?

> *The sheriff rammed the front gate, rushed into the house, and seized the counterfeit bills.*

Of course, a word like "rammed" has a pretty narrow definition. You shouldn't use it if it isn't accurate in the context of your story. But if it is, then isn't it more dynamic, more colorful, and more descriptive than "knocked down?" The same is true for "rushed," which tells the audience so much more than the earlier words, "went quickly." And "seized," if it's a fair description of what the sheriff did, tells us much more about the speed and intensity of the sheriff's actions than "took possession."

The trouble is, sometimes writers use dynamic words for the purpose of creating a picture in the viewer's or listener's mind, but the viewer or listener doesn't have any idea what kind of picture he should see. For example:

> *The senator stalked out of the room.*

Excuse me? She "stalked" out of the room? Does that mean she "slithered?" If it does, what exactly is "slithered?" Does "stalked" suggest movement that's blistering, belligerent, dispirited, or something else? Words matter, and with the burden of so many words to choose from an English language dictionary, you must go to pains to choose words that are descriptive, yet accurate.

But don't automatically reject a colorful word. We can conjure up a better version of a foreign government's harshness, assuming it's accurate, if we write that its army "smothered" a revolution, rather than that it "put down" the revolution. "Smothered" works because everyone who hears it understands it. On the other hand, if you write that the army "asphyxiated" the revolution, even though "asphyxiate" and "smother" are synonymous, it doesn't convey the same meaning. For that matter, "asphyxiate" is used seldom enough in everyday conversation that some of the audience might take so long to process the word that they stop absorbing whatever follows. That's instant death in a broadcast news story.

Judgmental Verbs May Be Accurate, But Wrong

What will people think if they hear the following sentence in a newscast?

> *The city controller claims he doesn't know who put the money in his safe.*

There's a "nod-nod-wink-wink" quality to the word "claims." It's as if the reporter is saying, "Look, he *claims* he doesn't know, but nod-nod-wink-wink, you and I know better!"

Or think about this sentence:

> *The councilwoman concedes that she met with the local crime boss.*

Here too, what will the audience infer? "Well, if she now *concedes* that, she must have been lying before." (By the way, learn the difference between "infer" and "imply." They are often confused. If you "infer" something, it means you figure it out from someone else's words. If you "imply" something, it means you intend to convey a message with your own.)

[handwritten margin note: infer imply]

Once again, words matter, because the words you use as a reporter can make the difference between the appearance of stating a fact and the appearance of stating an opinion. Look at the two examples above; the words can be unjustly harmful. If you know in the first example that the city controller is lying, then "claims" is a perfectly appropriate word for you to use. But if you don't know, then it would be better to use a word like "insists" or even the safe but dull old standby, "says." If you don't definitely know that the city controller is lying, "claims" is unfair.

Likewise in the second example, instead of "concedes," you could substitute a word like "confirms," or of course, "says." Now, read each sentence again, with each of the two substitutions that take the judgment out of the hands of the writer and put it into the hands of the audience:

> *The city controller insists he does not know who put the money in his safe.*
> *The city controller says he does not know who put the money in his safe.*
>
> *The councilwoman confirms that she met with the local crime boss.*
> *The councilwoman says that she met with the local crime boss.*

Less judgmental, more fair. Isn't that part of every journalist's ethical obligation? You bet it is! (You'll read a lot about your obligations as a journalist in the chapter entitled, "Holding onto Your Ethics," about ethics and their impact on good news writing.)

For Example, Words to Choose From, Carefully!

"Says" always works, but it can sound dull and, when used too often, repetitive. Here are alternatives, but think about what they imply before you use them. Also bear in mind that since every synonym for "says" can carry a different meaning, some news directors frown on any alternatives at all:

The councilwoman . . .

acknowledges	demands
admits	exclaims
asserts	implies
charges	insists
claims	observes
concedes	protests
confesses	remarks
confirms	reports
declares	suggests

Judgmental Adjectives and Adverbs Are Usually Dreadfully Unnecessary

If you're writing a story about a murder, does the audience learn anything valuable if you add an adjective and describe it as a "*senseless* murder"? Of course not; all murders are senseless.

Or are they? If someone had gotten to Adolph Hitler and killed him before he finally killed himself, it might have been murder but it hardly would have been "senseless." To the contrary, it would have almost universally been praised as a justifiable act, and depending on when it happened, it might have saved the lives of millions and therefore been quite sensible, rather than senseless.

See how words matter? Even something seemingly as obvious as using "senseless" in front of the word "murder" may itself be senseless!

And how about the "reckless driver" we hear so much about in newscasts? When you see the damage a driver caused as she careened from parked car to parked car, it's hard to conclude anything else. But aren't there other plausible explanations? Maybe she was having a heart attack. Maybe she was having an argument. Maybe she was repaying her neighbors for setting fire to her house. Who knows? Sometimes at least, the answer to the question, "Who knows?" is, "Not us."

This is not to say that there is no such thing as a "reckless driver," but it is to say that until a journalist knows without question that a driver was completely cavalier and uncaring about the consequences, the word "reckless" may not be accurate, and therefore should not be used. Let the audience decide. They probably won't have much trouble.

Adverbs can be just as troublesome, and put you in the position of making unethically judgmental observations. What's wrong if you write this sentence?

The governor dressed sloppily and came to the news conference.

Who appointed you as the guardian of good fashion? Does "sloppily" mean the same thing to everybody as it means to you? There are some people who think it's sloppy if your pants are wrinkled or your shoes are scuffed. Others think that unless you have tomato stains smack dab in the middle of your shirt, you look perfectly neat, thank you very much! Is a polka dot necktie on a paisley shirt sloppy, or just ugly? (See, that's my own value judgment! Not everyone would agree.)

Now let's look at one more example of a judgmental adverb, one with potentially serious consequence if it's indiscriminately used:

The vice president carelessly pushed the dog out of his way as he came into the meeting room.

If you write that, the vice president loses the animal lovers' vote for sure! But is that fair? Maybe he just didn't want the dog in the room and so he pushed it out, but what's "careless" to some might be "gentle" to others. Anyway, what is the audience to conclude? That the vice president pushed out the dog with his hands or with his feet? Did he give it a forceful but gentle push, or a swift kick? What's more, maybe the vice president did whatever he did because he didn't want to take the chance that someone would step on the dog's paws. That would be more like "lovingly" than "carelessly."

The big picture is, aside from purely factual adjectives and adverbs—"the *blue* car ran off the road," or, "he drove *quickly* to the police station"—you're better off keeping them out of your stories. I won't say they serve no purpose, but I will say that the only purposes they usually serve are to inject bias into a story that doesn't need it, and to expose the writer's bias to the audience.

Your job is to be objective. And to give the appearance of objectivity. If through a bad choice of words you fail on the second count, it means the audience believes you have failed on the first.

What's the Point?

You can write almost entirely without judgmental adjectives and adverbs. You can certainly write without judgmental verbs. Your job is to let people in the audience reach their own conclusions, not to hit them over the head with yours.

Exercises to Hone Your Word Skills _____

1. The Never Ending Story
   Here it is again, the Never Ending Story. Rewrite it now by substituting better words for bad, and removing words that don't belong at all. Don't make any other corrections; they're for later chapters.

   In a place where a rear-ender traffic mishap's usually the most consequential event of the day there's been a huge occurrence with a terrible impact on each and everyone. Tonight the lives of three persons were tragically claimed by a bomb, which set off a 3-alarm blaze that raised temperatures to almost 200° Fahrenheit at a garment store at 3645 Main Street, in the heart of Ft. Stutter, Miss., the police said. *has taken* No group took credit for the horrific blast, but forensics experts are combing the scene of the senseless attack tonight and in case there's more danger there, a hazmat team's dispatched to the scene. They're driving three separate emergency vehicles to get there. In order to explain why there wasn't an admonition, the police chief of the city of Ft. Stutter, Jazibeauz Perez, claims there was definitely no indication that the explosive device was going to detonate, then he said, "Everyone wishes to God we'd known this was going to transpire." The police dept. hasn't asked the FBI for help the chief said. The deceased includes Jason J. Jones, 29, Sally S. Smyth, 24, and Greg G. Goldstein, who died at 22. None were employees at the bombed store. Two unidentified men are in critical condition, meaning they might die too. Everyone in Ft. Stutter is absolutely petrified now to go out on the street, and city officials admit increased protection will cost the population of Ft. Stutter a lot of wampum, $6.1-million. There isn't a date set for a decision about expending that aggregate of money, but the mayor can't be back in the community by Tues., which isn't early enough for her critics. Whether such an expenditure'll really be beneficial remains to be observed.

2. The Ever-Improving Story

Remembering the "Words to Live By," write a better broadcast version of the following sentences (your instructor may want you to read each version aloud in the next class, for everyone to hear the difference between each set of versions):

The ministers engaged in discourse that [...]

- The two politicians expounded about the high crime rate.
- Three of the deceased were children.
- He communicated his feelings to his girlfriend.
- The man said he had so many lacerations from the accident that he will tell his attorney to sue.
- The boss promised to utilize more non-union help in the factory where the furniture is manufactured.
- The bill passed through both of the two houses of Congress.
- The man fired the weapon at his wife, who was hit in the stomach.
- The woman told the judge that presently her compensation is $1,000 a week.
- The young reported that his residence is just south of the city.
- Prior to the altercation, the male suspect had consumed several alcoholic beverages, and after he was apprehended, he endeavored to escape.
- Four persons passed away before a physician arrived in his automobile and administered medicine to the survivors of the blaze.

3. The Ever-Less-Confusing Story

Write a better broadcast version of the following sentences:

- Authorities believe the boat overturned when the jib sail got stuck.   *front triangular*
- The councilman says the contract is just a pro forma part of the deal.
- No one was hurt when the car's catalytic converter caught fire.
- The actress showed a certain panache by wearing that dress to the show.   *dash/verve*
- The cowboy said adios to his horse, jumped on his hog, revved the engine and headed home.
- Because the murder happened at a soiree where many guests were high on drugs, the charge was reduced to manslaughter.

4. The Much-More-Active Story

Write a better broadcast version of the following sentences:

- All three planes landed safely tonight.   *have landed*
- After the fire was extinguished, arson experts discovered that three bombs exploded.   *firefighters put the fire out*
- The commissioner said he wants to fix the county's worst roads.   *has said*
- Every car on the track finished this morning's race, and every driver paid compliments to the organizers.   *has finished / has paid / complimented*
- The organizer promised that all state senators will be repaid for their airfare.   *has promised*

5. The Rewritten Story

Write a better broadcast version of the following stories:

- The vehicle company Ford, may be confronted with another recall. A California judge made a preliminary determination on Tuesday to recall 300 models that were manufactured subsequent to 1982 but prior to 1995. If Ford is compelled to recall those vehicles, it could cost them a tremendous aggregate: somewhere in the range of 70 million to 250 million dollars.

- The Senator strongly claimed to us that he wasn't responsible for the embezzlement of the funds. Then he very quickly turned around in the other direction and stomping on the floor with each step, initiated his embarrassing departure from the room. His aide says he bumped into a wall on the way out.

6. In case you thought you'd get away without knowing what an aileron is (in the example earlier in the chapter), write the definition of "aileron."

2

The Wrong Way to Write It

(handwritten margin notes: abbreviations, contractions, grammar, numbers, symbols, commas—words, emphasis—words, pronunciation—words, time)

What You'll Learn

The basic lesson of the last chapter was don't use words in a news story that are so arcane, exclusive, or complicated that you wouldn't use them in a conversation with your mother, your roommate, or your best friend. The lesson of this chapter is don't use anything in a script you're preparing for someone else that you wouldn't want in a script that you might have to read, *live,* on the air.

What's the difference? Simple. When you have a personal talk with someone you know—on the phone or across a coffee table—you probably don't give a moment's thought to how you look, how you sound, how long you take to state your point or how you form your sentences.

On the air though, no one has that casual and careless luxury. No matter who's doing the reading, it has to be flawless: no unintelligible explanations, no tripping on the tongue. The script has to be clear and clean. But this is more easily said than done. Why? Because the anchorwoman has a lot more to do than simply read the script.

If she's on TV, she's also trying to watch the studio floor manager giving her a silent countdown with his fingers so she hits the tape package the very moment she's supposed to, while she's also trying to absorb the words of the producer in her earpiece who's telling her to skip the next story in the script because the show is running too long, while she's also trying to watch the monitor concealed in her anchor desk to make sure she's looking into the right camera lens, while she's also trying to do what the audience wants her to do: look cool and comfortable and completely in charge. If she's on the radio, she doesn't have to think about eye contact, but in addition to all those other things, she probably has to personally cue up the next audio sound bite and be prepared to push the right button to play it, all while reading her script with confidence and certainty. So when the anchorwoman, especially on television, works hard to look and sound authoritative (meaning she wants the audience to believe she knows the story intimately, and needs only briefly to even consult the script she holds in her hands), she's going to be mighty embarrassed if some small visual flaw *you* allowed to make it onto the teleprompter causes her to bungle her words and have to start the sentence again. It just doesn't look professional, does it?

What you'll learn in this chapter, "The Wrong Way to Write It," is how to minimize those embarrassments, and perhaps any threats to your job security if you're responsible! You'll learn when to abbreviate (almost never), when to use contractions (almost never), when to use perfect grammar (*almost* always), and how to deal with numbers, symbols, commas, words you want to emphasize, words you *don't* want mispronounced, and references to time.

The Terms of the Story

As you read through this book, mostly in later sections about production, you'll come to terms you probably haven't seen before, usually terms exclusive to broadcasting. In chapters where they show up, there'll be a glossary, here near the top of the chapter, defining these terms. That way, when you come to them, you'll already know what they mean.

In this chapter, there are just a couple:

Sound Bite   The parts of a story in which we hear someone or something other than the reporter.

Teleprompter   A mirror device that hangs below the lens of a television camera and reflects the script (scrolled electronically by an operator in the control room) onto a piece of glass directly in front of the lens, so the anchorperson can appear to be talking directly to the viewer without frequently referring to the printed script in his hands.

The Never Ending Story

As you read in the first chapter, one way *Better Broadcast Writing, Better Broadcast News* teaches you how to write for radio and TV is recurring versions of the Never Ending Story, which is deliberately written as poorly as possible. At the end of the last chapter, your job was to improve the words in the story (but nothing else); your improvements more or less should match what you see below.

Yet this "improved" version of the Never Ending Story still is not even close to being good enough to read on the air. Your job now is to review your improved version and compare it to this one (and if you missed any major corrections, think about why you did).

Then at the end of this chapter, your job will be to correct the additional errors you've learned to recognize here—errors that could twist the anchorwoman's tongue into the shape of a pretzel and embarrass her on the air—but remember, you should make changes based only on this chapter's lessons. Don't peek at the *next* chapter yet, because the version at the beginning of that chapter will show the improvements that you should have learned to make in this chapter. Slowly but surely, you're going to turn this poorly written news report into something worth reading on the air!

In a place where a rear-ender traffic ~~mishap's~~ **accident's** usually the ~~most consequential~~ **biggest** event of the day there's been a huge ~~occurrence~~ **event** with a terrible impact on each and everyone. Tonight the lives of three ~~persons~~ **people** ~~were~~ **have been** tragically claimed by a bomb, which set off a 3-alarm ~~blaze~~ **fire** that raised temperatures to almost 200° Fahrenheit at a ~~garment~~ **clothing** store at 3645 Main Street, in the heart of Ft. Stutter, Calif., the police ~~said~~ **say**. No group ~~took~~ **has taken** credit for the horrific blast, but forensics experts are combing the scene of the senseless attack tonight and in case there's more danger there, a ~~hazmat~~ **hazardous material** team's dispatched to the scene. They're driving three separate emergency vehicles to get there. In order to explain why there wasn't ~~an admonition~~ **warning**, the police chief of the city of Ft. Stutter, Jazibeauz Perez, ~~claims~~ **says** there was definitely no ~~indication~~ **sign** that the ~~explosive device~~ **bomb** was going to ~~detonate~~ **explode**, then he said, "Everyone wishes to God we'd known this was going to transpire." The police dept. hasn't asked the FBI for help the chief ~~said~~ **says**. The ~~deceased~~ **dead** includes Jason J. Jones, 29, Sally S. Smyth, 24, and Greg G. Goldstein, who died at 22. None were employees at the bombed store. Two unidentified men are in critical condition, meaning they might die too. Everyone in Ft. Stutter is absolutely ~~petrified~~ **scared** now to go out on the street, and city officials ~~admit~~ **say** increased protection will cost the ~~population~~ **people** of Ft. Stutter a lot of ~~wampum~~ **money**, $6.1-million. There isn't a date set for a decision about ~~expending~~ **spending** that ~~aggregate~~ **amount** of money, but the mayor can't be back in the ~~community~~ **town** by Tues., which isn't early enough for her critics. Whether ~~such an expenditure'll~~ **it'll** really be ~~beneficial~~ **helpful** remains to be seen.

Don't Abb.

"Abb." can be an abbreviation for "abbreviation." Did you fail to recognize "abb." for "abbreviation"? Did you mistake it for something else? Or didn't you even have a clue? That's why you shouldn't abbreviate.

Here's a fairly obvious example: you are writing about a flood in Missouri, and in keeping with how we address envelopes, your script says it's in "Ft. Lupton, MO." Unfortunately, your anchorman doesn't know whether "MO" is Missouri or Montana. But you're smart enough to recognize that. So you think "Well, I'll make sure there's no mistake. I'll make the abbreviation longer." You change the script to read, "Ft. Lupton, Miss."

Whoops. Is that Missouri or Mississippi? You may know, but will your anchorman? Maybe not. Don't abbreviate and it won't be a potential problem. That includes "Ft. Lupton" too. Make it "Fort Lupton" and there will be no mistake.

How general is this rule for broadcast scripts? Almost absolute. This is the kind of thing that can trip up an author who leaves something out, but I've checked with colleagues, and all agree that the only exceptions to the "no abbreviation" rule are the following five abbreviations, four of which are personal titles:

Mr., Mrs., Ms., Dr., and *St.*

Why these five titles? Because we're all more accustomed to seeing them abbreviated than fully written out. "St. Peter's" looks more familiar than "Saint Peter's." "Missus" still looks like a term from *The Adventures of Huckleberry Finn.*

But that's it. Don't abbreviate anything else. Not states, not months, not organizations. Not even common abbreviations like "gov't." or "int'l." Nor when the abbreviation seems obvious, like "N.Y." Put yourself in the shoes of an anchorwoman and ask yourself, which of the following script lines is less fraught with risk?

The plane blew up over Grand Junction, Co.

Or:

The plane blew up over Grand Junction, Colorado.

This leads to another warning: when a proper name is known by its letters—for example, the F.B.I.—think of those letters as words. In the case of the F.B.I., the name therefore is three words: "F," "B" and "I." So when you write it in a script, you don't write "FBI" or even "F.B.I."; you treat it as three separate words and separate them with dashes, this way: "F-B-I."

[handwritten margin note: treat common abbreviations as 3 words]

Therefore the huge transport aircraft flown by the U.S. Air Force isn't a "C5A" in a script; it's three words: a "C-5-A." Likewise, the chief executive officer of a company isn't the "CEO," at least not in a script, because while the possibility may seem remote, your anchorperson might be so busy paying attention to everything else happening in the studio that she glances quickly at the script in front of her which says "CEO Jean Jimenez" and on the air accidentally says something like "Seeoh Jean Jimenez." So on a script you'd write, "C-E-O Jean Jimenez."

Is there an exception? Yes, as always. The United States, commonly abbreviated "U.S.," gets abbreviated just that way: "U.S." That's how we're used to seeing it, so that's how we write it on a script.

One last lesson about abbreviations. Acronyms are not abbreviations! Therefore, the name of the space agency in the United States, NASA (the National Aeronautics and Space Administration), isn't read as four words, "N," "A," "S" and "A," because it isn't said that way. It's one word: "NASA." So we write it that way. No dashes. This rule applies to all acronyms that are pronounced as a word rather than as separate letters.

What's the Point?

Abbreviations can trip up a reader on the air. So avoid them. Learn the few exceptions above, then in all other cases, don't abbreviate.

I Can't Hear You

Imagine yourself in your car, listening to a radio newscast. Think of all the sounds competing with the radio for your attention: other passengers talking, the rough surface of the road, another driver honking, a loud truck accelerating, the ventilation fan blowing, and the cell phone ringing, not to mention the possibility of just plain lousy reception.

It's the same with the TV. While you're trying to hear a newscast, noise may be intruding from other people in your home, a ringing telephone, a ringing doorbell, a buzzing microwave, a humming air conditioner, music in the next room, sounds on the street outside, and again, the possibility of lousy reception.

The lesson? When writing a broadcast news script, you can't use contractions. Why not? Well, pretend you're in one of those noisy situations and someone says from your TV screen, "You can't use contractions." With all the distractions, you aren't sure you heard it right. You wonder, "Did he say you CAN use contractions or you CAN'T?" Particularly with competing noise, they can sound confusingly alike.

If you need me to hit you over the head with this, pretend the guy on TV makes it even more definitive: "You can't use contractions. And there isn't a single exception to this rule. I wouldn't tell you this if it weren't true." Now pretend there's a baby crying and a telephone ringing in the background. Did he say "there IS" or "there ISN'T?" "I WOULD" or "I WOULDN'T?" "If it WERE true" or "if it WEREN'T?"

Sure, there's a big difference between how we hear "I won't" and "I will," but there are too many contractions where the differences are subtle. Mistakes can be made, like "have" versus "haven't." Say them aloud, particularly with a lot of competing noise, and you'll hear what I mean.

Of course, this contradicts the earlier rule about writing the way you talk. So be it. It's one of those lessons you'll find often in this book, that every rule is made to be broken. In this case, it's broken for a reason.

So play it safe. Avoid contractions in a script. If you write something like, "You cannot use contractions, there is not a single exception to this rule, I would not tell you this if it were not true," then despite the competing sounds of a ringing phone and a crying baby, no one is likely to mishear it.

What's the Point?

A contraction is unmistakable to the eye, but not to the ear. Don't take the chance that someone hears it wrong. Avoid contractions altogether.

Turning Numbers into Words

There is a simple rule about how to write numbers on a script. From 1 to 11, spell them out.

In other words, if this were a script instead of a page in a textbook, you'd write that line this way:

From one to eleven, spell them out.

Some journalists and journalism teachers think it ought to be just one to ten. I choose to go up to eleven for a simple reason: the purpose of the rule is to minimize the chance that with all the other distractions in the studio, the anchorman misreads the digit. Seen quickly, especially if the printer needs new ink, a seven might accidentally be read as a one or vice versa. A three might look like an eight. Therefore an eleven is as easily misread as a one.

Is there a rule of thumb for when a number is too small to generalize and too big to be specific? Not really. Just depend on your own sense of (1) what the audience needs to know, and (2) what the audience will absorb and remember.

This always raises good questions: "If I have, say, a death toll of 108 people, how do I write it in a script?" Here's how:

one-hundred-eight

How about a baseball team passing the million mark in attendance when the total number of tickets reaches 1,032, 209?

> *one-million, 32-thousand, two-hundred-nine*

Of course a good script wouldn't give the whole number. If the story is about the team passing the million mark, then "more than a million" is the best way to say it.

And telling the time? Again, if it's the part of a story that says, "They found the body at 8 o'clock," write it this way:

> *They found the body at eight o'clock.*

This is true for everything from "one o'clock" through "eleven o'clock." You can use the number 12 in "12 o'clock" because of the "write them out from one through eleven" rule, but if it's "12 o'clock," you're probably better off with either "noon" or "midnight."

Turning $ into Dollars

Once again, put yourself in the shoes of the anchorwoman. Think about how quickly she has to glance at the script while dealing with all the other distractions. Because of this, you should not use symbols on a script. Instead, write them out. Here are the most obvious.

Write It Out

Write	*Not*
dollars	$
cents	¢
percent	%
and	&
degrees	°
point	.

If this still isn't clear, here's an example of each, wrong and right. You probably can see which one is easier to read. If you can't, read them all *aloud.* Then it will be obvious.

> *The new plane costs $32,000,000.*
> *The new plane costs 32-million-dollars.*
>
> *The man killed his friend for 90¢.*
> *The man killed his friend for 90 cents.*
>
> *The government says the unemployment rate dropped to 4%.*
> *The government says the unemployment rate dropped to four percent.*
>
> *Senator Allard & Governor Owens went to Washington.*
> *Senator Allard and Governor Owens went to Washington.*

The record for this date is 97°.
The record for this date is 97 degrees.

The damage estimate reached $18.5 million.
The damage estimate reached 18-point-five million dollars.

What's the Point?

Play it safe. Why take the chance that an anchorperson glances too quickly at a symbol and either misses or misreads it, when typing it out makes it obvious?

Sounding Smart, Saying It Right

One of the best ways to sound stupid is to pronounce a word that the audience—even just a single person in the audience—knows is wrong.

During the initial American attacks on Afghanistan at the start of the war on terrorism in 2001, for example, newspaper and magazine reporters could just write the names of places in Afghanistan and Pakistan that they never had heard of before: Herat, Kandahar, Peshawar, Quetta, Mazar-e-Sharif, even the capital, Kabul.

I say "even the capital, Kabul," because while it's fairly well known, it's commonly pronounced two different ways, which I'll put phonetically here, with the syllable that's meant to be accented or emphasized in ALL CAPS (all capital letters): "KAH-bool" and "kah-BOOL." Read them aloud right now so you hear the difference. It's easy for print reporters to write about Kabul or any of those other places because for their readers, pronunciation isn't necessarily an issue. Does Kabul have an accent on the first ("KAH-bool") or the second ("kah-BOOL") syllable? Is Peshawar "PESH-uh-were" or "pesh-OW-were"? Do you use a "w" sound in Quetta to pronounce it "KWEH-tuh" or ignore it and say, "KEH-tuh?" Print reporters don't really have to know. All they have to do is spell it right.

Broadcasters don't have that luxury. Broadcasters have an obligation to get it right, because the way they pronounce a place name or a person's name is the way the audience learns it. So how do you insure against mistakes? Easy. Type questionably pronounced names in the script, then in parenthesis beside it or above it, put a "pronouncer," which means the word is shown phonetically, separating the syllables with hyphens and putting the emphasized syllable in ALL CAPS.

You already have seen how to write a pronouncer for "Kabul." If it's part of a script line, it should end up looking this way (with the phonetic pronouncer either typed or handwritten in parenthesis beside or above the script line itself):

American planes have dropped ten bombs on Kabul (kah-BOOL).

Let me show you how the other Afghanistani place names would be handled, not because you'll ever have to pronounce them yourself, but because the technique I use to make them readable is the technique you should use, no matter what the word, or what the language. Simply come up with the most easily recognizable phonetic spelling, so that everyone who sees it says it the same way.

> *In Herat (Hair-AHT), there was no electricity.*
>
> *Three targets in the provincial capital of Kandahar (KAHN-duh-har) were destroyed.*
>
> *Refugees from Mazar-e-Sharif (mah-zahr-ee-shah-REEF) reported fires throughout the city.*

By the way, the best way to phoneticize a syllable is to use a real word if you can, a word everyone recognizes and says the same way, like the word "hair" for the first syllable in "Herat."

Of course it doesn't do you or anyone any good if you put pronouncers next to words that need them *but you don't actually know if they're correct.* Good journalism demands that every time you come to a name and you're not positive how to pronounce it, or there's simply more than one way to pronounce it, you check.

If it's a city, check the atlas. If that doesn't help and it's in the United States, call Directory Assistance and ask the local operator how to say it. Or get the number of a local shop and call there. If it's overseas, call the Washington D.C. embassy for the country in which the place is located and ask someone there.

If it's a person rather than a place, go to the same trouble. If it's someone in a crime story, ask the police. If it's someone in business, call the company. If it's someone in politics, call the political body with which she is associated. The point is, don't guess. Call!

The trouble is, while a place name like "Mazar-e-Sharif" may obviously need a pronouncer, there are plenty of names where it's not so clear. For instance, if a major league shortstop is named Jose Perez, how does he say Perez: "pear-EHZ" or "PEAR-ehz"? If you don't know, you absolutely must find out.

You *don't* need phonetics if you're working with a name we all recognize. But what if the name of a spokeswoman for the Air Force is Helene Goldstein? Now you have two challenges. Is her first name said as "Helen" or "hell-EEN"? And how about her last name? The first syllable is always emphasized in Goldstein, but is it "GOLD-steen" or "GOLD-stine"? If a last name is "Smyth," is it a long or short "I"?

See the problem? See why it's important to check? See why it's important to get it right?

Finally, here is a picture of the first page of a script I wrote from Iran, about a month after fifty-two Americans were taken hostage by militants loyal to the new fundamentalist Islamic government there (and held for 444 days). The script is pretty sloppy, but it does illustrate "pronouncers."

As you see, I had to say two names that were unfamiliar to me. So I tried to write them phonetically. The fact is, according to the very lessons I impart above, I didn't do a great job of it (no one told me that someday I'd be teaching this kind of thing), but it served its purpose, which simply means I didn't stumble and get them wrong.

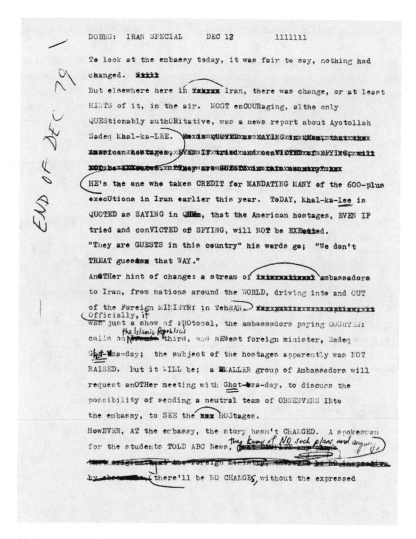

Make it simple: phoneticize.

What's the Point?

If a name is mispronounced on the air, someone's going to know (maybe a lot of "some-ones"). That puts your credibility, as well as the anchorperson's, on the line, and people's perceptions of your responsibility is shot.

English 101, Revisited

If you tell me, "I have never used a split infinitive," I have to respond, "You have just now used one . . . and so have I." Corrected to eliminate the split infinitive (where the adverb was placed in the middle of a present perfect verb), your statement should be, "I never have used a split infinitive." Mine should be, "You have used one just now."

But this textbook is not written for a course in English; it is written for a course in journalism. What that means is, I'm not going to give you chapter and verse about correct versus incorrect grammar. It also means that while there is a clear difference in English between right and wrong, it's more of a grey area in journalism, especially when the emphasis is on broadcasting. Why? Because the whole principle of writing for broadcast is that you should write the way you talk—and when we talk, we use split infinitives all the time.

So the only rule I'll lay down here is this: use good grammar unless it sounds stuffy. Unless it sounds contrived. Unless it sounds unnatural. The following sentence comes from a feature story I wrote about a new health care clinic in the Alaskan Arctic:

> *Nearly the whole professional staff here has recently been imported.*

Read the above sentence aloud, then read the sentence below aloud too. You'll hear that the first one—split infinitive and all—sounds conversational, the other one doesn't.

> *Nearly the whole professional staff here recently has been imported.*

But later in the same script, the following sentence, which obeys the rules (meaning no split infinitive), sounds perfectly fine:

> *They always have had a hands-on therapeutic kind of care.*

What's the Point?

Use proper grammar whenever possible. But if you have to choose between proper and colloquial, go with the latter. Write the way you talk.

English 101, Revisited Yet Again

It is easy, because of the work it takes to avoid them, especially when you're in a hurry to make a deadline, to write with a lot of dependant clauses, which help define what you're trying to describe.

Have you caught on to my tricks by now? That sentence you just finished reading is riddled with dependent clauses. It doesn't have to be. Try it this way, and see whether it's less clear or more clear:

> *Because of the work it takes to avoid them, it is easy to write with a lot of*
> *dependent clauses, especially when you're hurrying to make a deadline. They help*
> *define what you're trying to describe.*

See? By splitting one sentence into two and rearranging the phrases, it's already better. But can we improve it even more? Of course, by reworking a couple of words and creating three sentences:

It is easy to write with a lot of dependent clauses. They help define what you're trying to describe. It takes work to avoid them, especially when hurrying to make a deadline.

Personally, I used to use too many dependent clauses myself. I didn't appreciate the beauty of short, sharp, simple sentences. I do now.

So in the spirit of "before and after," here are some sentences straight from my scripts, followed in each case by what I *should* have written.

(from a story about the presidential campaign of Colorado Senator Gary Hart)

Hart made it official Tuesday by filing in New Hampshire, but that flurry of publicity, thanks mainly to his celebrity, is really about all he has.

Hart made it official Tuesday by filing in New Hampshire. That flurry of publicity, thanks mainly to his celebrity, is really about all he has.

(from a feature about a new bank especially for children)

It's a real bank, but kind of a huge piggybank that opened here, one that caters to a special age group, one whose customers seem to really understand the current value of the dollar, one where the signature card is a brand new experience.

It's a real bank, but kind of a huge piggybank that opened here. It caters to a special age group. Its customers seem to really understand the current value of the dollar. For them, the signature card is a brand new experience.

(from a story about a medical funding crisis in Oregon)

With two-year-old David's life on the line with leukemia—he still needs a bone-marrow donor—his mother left home behind and uprooted from Oregon to Washington state, which helps pay for life-saving transplants.

Two-year-old David's life is on the line with leukemia. He still needs a bone-marrow donor. So his mother left home behind and uprooted from Oregon to Washington state. Washington helps pay for life-saving transplants.

(from a feature about avalanche control)

While safety officials fight a perennial war against avalanches, trying here for instance to provoke one under control, they're the first to admit, with 14-million acres of forest service land alone, that their procedures are far from foolproof.

Safety officials fight a perennial war against avalanches. They're trying here for instance to provoke one under control. But with 14-million acres of forest service land alone, they're the first to admit that their procedures are far from foolproof.

(from a story about a hijacked Kuwaiti Airlines 747 that ended up in Algeria)

About an hour after the Kuwaiti plane pulled up, so did a private jet, the Algerian president's jet one of my sources tells me, which immediately got stocked with food and fuel, and this matched everything we had heard about the hijackers' plans, although those reports were only second hand.

About an hour after the Kuwaiti plane pulled up, so did a private jet. One of my sources tells me it was the Algerian president's jet. It immediately got stocked with food and fuel. This matched everything we had heard about the hijackers' plans, although those reports were only second hand.

What's the Point?

As you have read several times now, keep your sentences short, sharp, and simple. Keep dependent clauses to a minimum. The other point is be careful how sloppily you write scripts because, like me, someday you might have to put them on display in a textbook!

When Time Doesn't Matter

Here's a rule that's simple to state but harder to follow: Never start or end a sentence with a time reference.

So this is inferior:

This morning there was a three-car crash that stopped traffic on I-80.

And so is this:

There was a three-car crash that stopped traffic on I-80 this morning.

This is superior:

There was a three-car crash this morning that stopped traffic on I-80.

Why are the first two examples inferior and the last one superior? Not because the first two are grammatically incorrect, but because the time of the crash and the traffic tie-up isn't the most important fact in the story. Sometimes it is even irrelevant. If you're reporting it, it's implicit at least that it's *today*. What *is* most important? Obviously the crash, and the tie-up. That's why you should bury the time—"this morning," "tonight," "yesterday," "tomorrow," "next week," "last month," etc.—somewhere in the middle of your sentence.

There's another reason for the rule too. A good story, like a good newscast, begins and ends with something that has an impact on the audience, something you want them to remember about the day's news. Well, guess what! A good sentence begins and ends that way too. What most likely has that kind of impact? What should the audience carry away from your reporting? Certainly not the time the story happened. No, you want them to remember the story itself.

Just to make sure you know the difference, read (aloud) and think about the following examples. Which ones deliver more impact from the most important facts?

The Dow Jones Industrials rose 120 points today.
The Dow Jones Industrials today rose 120 points.

Next week the president will fly to Moscow to negotiate arms reductions.
The president will fly to Moscow next week to negotiate arms reductions.

The Yankees' star pitcher will sign for thirty-million-dollars-a-year tomorrow.
The Yankees' star pitcher tomorrow will sign for thirty-million-dollars-a-year.

Last night 180 people died in a plane crash.
180 people died last night in a plane crash.

Like I said, it's an easy rule to state, harder to follow. So here's one more way to think about it: if you have to include a time reference in a sentence, write it so that if you removed the time reference from the middle, the sentence still would tell the basic story. And although there are exceptions, here's an easy way to apply it: try to put the time reference as close a possible to the verb.

Is this the first rule of the book that has no exceptions? Of course not! Sometimes the time something happens (or will happen, or has happened) is the most critical fact. For instance, if a murderer whose crime and trial have been well covered by the media finally is due to be executed tomorrow, then "tomorrow" is the big news. Thus:

The man who killed four children in his backyard a decade ago will be executed
tomorrow.

Or, needing no explanation:

Today the world will end.

Need I say more?

What's the Point?

Despite the example above, the world will *not* end today. Almost always, bury the time reference.

The Important Thing, About Commas

Stop thinking about commas as commas. In broadcast newswriting, practically speaking, commas can serve an entirely different—and more important—purpose than however you used to use them. This might not turn up in other broadcast newswriting textbooks, but trust me, it can help: from now on, don't think of commas as commas, think of them as pauses. They just look like commas.

For instance, take a look at this paragraph, from a documentary I did about dangers in the American workplace. For once, do not read it aloud; just look, and see how many grammatically incorrect commas you spot.

> *The Veterinary School at the University of Florida is a classic, sick building. Erected in this age of energy conservation, it is deliberately sealed, to the outside. This means everyone inside depends on a mechanical ventilation system for the very air, they breathe. Sounds safe! But what inspectors found in the system here, was a sickening mold growing, in the ducts. What they found elsewhere, sounds even worse.*

Did you spot an unnecessary comma or two, or six? Well yes, there are six unnecessary commas if you think of them as commas. But think of them instead as something else: *pauses.* Think of them as a sign to you, or to whoever is reading the script, to stop for a dramatic beat—some might say a "pregnant pause"—to let something sink in. Now, here's the same paragraph. Instead of looking, read it aloud, pausing where those "commas" appear to be.

> *The Veterinary School at the University of Florida is a classic, sick building. Erected in this age of energy conservation, it is deliberately sealed, to the outside. This means everyone inside depends on a mechanical ventilation system for the very air, they breathe. Sounds safe! But what inspectors found in the system here, was a sickening mould growing, in the ducts. What they found elsewhere, sounds even worse.*

Everyone's reading style is different. Yours may not be anything like mine, which means you might not place commas where I place them, or you might not pause where I pause. This isn't practiced in every broadcast newsroom, but it might be useful in *yours* to know that a comma no longer has to be a comma in a broadcast news script; it can be a pause.

Sometimes, however, this is more easily said than done. If you work in the print media and want to write about "Omaha, Nebraska," you write it precisely that way, with a comma between the city and the state. But in broadcast news, you don't pause between the two like this:

> *Two trains have collided head-on in Omaha, Nebraska.*

Therefore, you do not insert a comma; write it instead like this:

> *Two trains have collided head-on in Omaha Nebraska.*

When you proofread your script, add the concept of "commas-as-pauses" to the list of things for which you must be alert. If there's a comma there that shouldn't be there, the anchorperson probably will pause and sound silly. If there's no comma where there ought to be one, well, the result could be the same. Don't let it happen. Put in commas where you want pauses, and take them out where you don't.

What's the Point?

A script is your road map. That's why the purpose of every piece of punctuation, like all other markings, is to make it easy to read. The commonplace comma can have a new role in your life.

Giving It Some Punch

Sometimes you really want to punch a word. In other words, emphasize it. Say it louder than the other words in the sentence. Or longer. For example, in the first sentence of the paragraph you're reading right now, if you're reading it aloud you want to emphasize the word "really." So here's the easiest lesson in this book. When you want to punch a word, either underline it or type it in ALL CAPS. Therefore:

> *Sometimes you <u>really</u> want to punch a word.*

Or:

> *Sometimes you REALLY want to punch a word.*

This helps the anchor or the reporter finesse the sentence when reading it into the microphone. But this can be overdone. I've been as guilty as anybody. I used to isolate specific syllables I wanted to emphasize. Not whole words, just *syllables*. When I'd send a script to ABC News in New York, the producers made fun of my typing style. Here's how a typical sentence looked:

> *By this MORNing, most homeless surVIvors, it appEARS, have at least CANvas overhead, food and WATer in their STOMachs.*

My bosses in New York loved this particular story, but sent back a response dripping with visual satire. It looked something like this:
"SuPERB. . . CLASSy. . . SENsitive. We were VEry PROUD."

What's the Point?

If you want to make sure the right words get the right emphasis, make it clear on the script. But save it for the really important words, not every syllable. Too much, and it looks silly.

Exercises to Hone Your Writing Skills _____

1. The Never Ending Story
    Here it is again, the Never Ending Story, just like what you saw at the beginning of this chapter but this time, the lessons of the first chapter have been applied. Your job now is to rewrite it again, applying the lessons of this second chapter—avoiding contractions, clari-

fying pronunciation, checking for commas, eliminating extraneous information, and so forth. As before, don't peek yet at the next chapter, because that will show the improvements that you should have made in this chapter.

In a place where a rear-ender traffic accident's usually the biggest event of the day, there's been a event with an impact on everyone. Tonight the lives of three people have been claimed by a bomb, which set off a 3-alarm fire that raised temperatures to almost 200° Fahrenheit at a clothing store at 3645 Main Street, in the heart of Ft. Stutter, Calif., the police say. No group has taken credit for the blast, but forensics experts are combing the scene of the attack tonight and in case there's more danger there, a hazardous material team's dispatched to the scene. They're driving three separate emergency vehicles to get there. In order to explain why there wasn't a warning, the police chief of the city of Ft. Stutter, Jazibeauz Perez, says there was definitely no sign that the bomb was going to explode, then he said, "Everyone wishes to God we'd known this was going to transpire." The police dept. hasn't asked the FBI for help the chief says. The dead includes Jason J. Jones, 29, Sally S. Smyth, 24, and Greg G. Goldstein, who died at 22. None were employees at the bombed store. Two unidentified men are in critical condition, meaning they might die too. Everyone in Ft. Stutter is scared now to go out on the street, and city officials say increased protection will cost the people of Ft. Stutter a lot of money, $6.1-million. There isn't a date set for a decision about spending that amount of money, but the mayor can't be back in town by Tues., which isn't early enough for her critics. Whether it'll really be helpful remains to be seen.

2. The Ever-Improving Story
   Write a better broadcast version of the following sentences (as in the first chapter, your instructor may want you to read the old version and your new version aloud in class, for everyone to hear the difference between them):

   • The plane exploded over Long Island, N.Y.
   • The police cornered the suspect at the end of an asphalt alley.
   • The stock market fell 13% today.
   • Both cars had been parked downtown and both drivers had been working.
   • The new 85,000 pound helicopter costs $6,032,425.
   • The new law isn't going to make a big difference in people's lives.
   • Jason L. Septeimeer, 28, was killed by a drunk driver tonight.
   • The terrorist said he wouldn't surrender his AK-47.
   • Today in Sacramento three legislators came down with food poisoning, and one of them claimed he felt ill for two hours before calling a hospital, and the others said they couldn't identify the cause.
   • The space agency NASA is cooperating with the FBI to reduce theft at its Fla. headquarters, which has passed the $1,000,000 mark.

3. The Rewritten Story
   Write a better broadcast version of the following stories:

   • Airport officials said a 737 slid off the runway in snowy conditions during the snowstorm that hit the eastern part of the city tonight. They stated that conditions on the runway were known to be slippery but that there hadn't been accidents before the 737 went into its skid. The repairs to the runway according to airport officials will come to more than $250,000.

- The Mayor has certainly never been convicted of theft, but questions still came up about his CV. The Mayor's critics especially Councilwoman Rebot, who was wearing a tan dress while she spoke, contend that the Mayor has probably hidden dark secrets from his past, and don't think he has revealed everything, and they fear the public will lose faith in gov't. *government* *The Mayor's critics*

4. The Restated Questions

   - What five words can you abbreviate in a broadcast script (you can answer with their abbreviations)? *Mr. Mrs. Ms. Dr. St.*
   - If a fire department spokesman says the damage estimate from a fire is "$3,968,200," how do you simplify it? *Almost four-million dollars*
   - Why do you hyphenate "F-B-I," "C-I-A," and the abbreviated names of other such agencies? *letters treated as words*
   - Why are contractions like "isn't," "wouldn't," "can't," and others dangerous in a broadcast script? *hearing confusion*

3

Being Perfectly Clear

What You'll Learn

The lesson of the last chapter was make your story easy to read. The lesson of this one is make it easy to understand. You'd think that would make this the longest chapter in the book. But if you follow all the lessons you learn here, you'll see why it can be the shortest. As you've already learned, your story will be easy if you stick to simple words, use language people can understand, and prepare a script that can be read smoothly, accurately, convincingly.

However, a few common qualities tend to get in the way in a lot of writing, and they are the themes of the three sections in this chapter: too much information, raising questions but not answering them, and generalizing. (*Everyone* generalizes. Okay, that's a joke, but if you didn't get it, you'd better read that section twice.)

What you'll learn in this chapter is the difference between too much information and just the right amount; why to avoid raising questions if you don't answer them too; and the irrevocable pitfalls of generalizations (there I go again!).

Oh, and one more thing. The title of the chapter is "Being Perfectly Clear." The best way to do that is to keep your sentences short. One sentence, one idea. Unlike the print media, listeners and viewers don't get to go back and read something again.

TMI (Too Much Information)

Generally I have taught my own broadcast newswriting courses in a computer lab equipped with Macintosh computers. As you probably know, Macs have a little icon at the bottom labeled "Trash." When correcting students' papers, I use the word a lot, to send a signal that the writer should have dragged a word or two into the trash. Sometimes it's because of a simple phrase like, "The man climbed the ladder in order to fix the rain gutter," and I strike out the words "in order" because they are unnecessary—meaning, they are "trash." But sometimes I use the word "trash" to say something else: TMI (Too Much Information).

For example, take a brief story about airlines' financial problems after the 2001 terrorist attacks on New York City and Washington. The chiefs of virtually all the U.S. airlines told Congress they needed a government bailout to survive. In a short story, that's all the public really needed to know. We didn't need to know every detail of the solution they proposed: part tax relief, part loan guarantees, part financial grants. That was TMI. If I were editing a script that gave all those details, I'd have thrown them out. TMI.

Sometimes it's not a long list of details, but just a single short detail, like someone's age. If you're covering a crime and the police officer tells you, "We have booked Greg Dobbs, age 42, on suspicion of armed robbery," does the public need or want to know the suspect's age (which in that example, by the way, is a lie)? Nope. TMI. In print, where there's a little more latitude, someone's age (and, as you'll read in a moment, someone's middle initial) can help the public more definitively identify the subject of a story. But in broadcasting, where being succinct is a necessary goal, they just get in the way. Yes, the age of a newsmaker can matter, as it did when I covered the story of an 11-year-old boy who had just enrolled at the University of California at Santa Cruz. In that case, his age *was* the story. And of course if you're writing about someone who has just died, the age is pertinent. But most of the time it just clutters the script.

Or what if a police officer you're talking to includes a suspect's middle initial, "We have booked Greg A. Dobbs on suspicion of armed robbery." Do you need that middle initial "A" in your script? Of course not. Sure, sometimes a middle initial is relevant, such as "President George W. Bush," to distinguish him from a previous president, his father. But most of the time, like someone's age, it's just clutter.

And sometimes the whole name is irrelevant. If a fire department spokesman gives you an estimate of property damage after a small store burns down, you don't have to write it this way:

> *Fire Department spokesman Walter Russell estimates property damage at more than two-million dollars.*

The sentence is about the size of the loss, not the name of the spokesman. Remove it, and see how much simpler the whole sentence is:

> *A Fire Department spokesman estimates property damage at more than two-million dollars.*

What's the Point?

If the public doesn't need to know it to understand the story, don't write it.

If It's a Question, Answer It

Don't raise questions you cannot answer. Sure, that seems like a strange thing to teach to budding broadcast journalists, but it doesn't suggest what you think it does. By all means, in the course of covering a story, ask and ask and ask until the answers come. But when writing a story, if you raise a question but don't answer it, you leave your audience wondering why, perhaps distracting them long enough that they lose the thread of the whole piece. Here's a simple example from a newspaper piece written shortly after the terrorist attacks against the United States on September 11, 2001:

> *Although every military base in the state is locked down, base officials say they aren't as vulnerable as civilian institutions.*

Huh? *Why* aren't they as vulnerable? The reporter raised a question but didn't answer it. The reader—that was me—stopped in his tracks. But at least the rest of the story wasn't going by on the printed page while I was trying to figure out that question. However, as you know by now, it's different in broadcasting. If people hear something that makes them stop and wonder, it means they're no longer hearing what follows, and they miss the rest of the story. (By the way, I got my answer from a competing paper. Terrorists are more likely to strike civilians than a place where professional opposition is likely.)

Raising questions but not answering them is a big issue. And it's easy to overlook, unless when you're proofreading, you think and think hard. In a paragraph midway into a feature story I wrote about the oldest postal carrier in the United States, I didn't.

> *Taylor got this job when the regular carrier on the route was drafted during the war. Since then he has worked on contract. This one's in force for four more years.*

Do you see what question I raised but didn't answer? This question: *what war?* World War II? World War I? Korea? Vietnam? In this case it wasn't a matter of missing the question; it was a matter of assuming there would be no question in anyone's mind, because Don Taylor was ninety-five years old at the time. I figured that anyone could figure it out. What I didn't realize was that no one would be "figuring" while they were listening. Thankfully, an editor caught the problem before we ran the story.

What's the Point?

It's easy to raise questions without answering them, whether you fail to think hard enough about your words or you assume the audience knows what you know. Keep that in mind when proofreading, so you can avoid losing your audience.

Generalizing Is Always Wrong

Let me present another example: this one comes from the usually excellent former NBC News correspondent Jim Avila. Covering massive fires dotting the map of the western United States in the summer of 2000, Avila began one report, "The West is on fire tonight." That must have come as quite a surprise to people sitting comfortably in their homes in Seattle, or heading for a mall in Denver, or driving through a car wash in Los Angeles. Were there flames just around the corner?

No, because "The West" was not on fire, not that night or any other. Avila's phrase was dramatic and, yes, it probably conveyed its point to some people quite nicely, but journalism is about fact, not fiction. Sometimes nifty literary tools must give way to straight factual reporting. How might it have been written differently? Here are just a few ideas:

There are fires tonight all over the West.
Throughout the West tonight, fires are burning.
The map of the entire West is dotted with fires.

The same point applies when you are asked to characterize the sentiment of a population. You often will hear something like, "Most people here say . . . ," but unless the reporter has actually interviewed everybody, or at least seen a reliable poll, it's just a guess. Maybe such a sweeping statement could be made about the population in a town of 50 people, but you'll hear the same kind of generalization about the people of New York. It's wrong. It's dishonest. Again, journalism is about facts, not guesswork.

What's more, I have challenged reporters on such generalizations, and what I've heard more than anything else is, "Well, I talked to 30 people at that intersection, and almost all of them felt the same way." Big deal. Does the population found at any one intersection—or bus stop, or bar—represent the demographics of the population as a whole? Not likely. Does the population found at the hour the reporter spent interviewing people represent the population found there at a different hour of the day or night? Not likely. If your assignment is to get the "pulse" of the public, the best you can do is talk to a few dozen people, then write it so the audience knows your limitations: "Of the 40 people we interviewed across from City Hall, 80-percent were against. . . ."

What's the Point?

One should never generalize. It's always wrong. (I hope you see the humor in that!)

Exercises to Hone Those Skills Even Sharper _____

1. The Never Ending Story
    Here it is again, the Never Ending Story; the lessons of the last two chapters have been applied. Your job now is to rewrite it again, applying the lessons of this chapter too—avoiding generalizations, eliminating too much information, and making sure no questions are raised but not answered. And good advice is always worth repeating: don't look at the next chapter until you've done this, because you'll learn more by doing than by peeking!

    In a place where a rear-ender traffic accident is usually the biggest event of the day there has been an event with an impact on everyone. Tonight the lives of three people have been claimed by a bomb, which set off a three-alarm fire that raised temperatures to almost two-hundred-degrees Fahrenheit at a clothing store at 36–45 Main Street, in the heart of Fort Stutter California, the police say. No group has taken credit for the blast, but forensics experts are combing the scene of the attack tonight and in case there is more danger there, a hazardous material team has dispatched to the scene. They are driving three separate emergency vehicles to get there. In order to explain why there was not a warning, the police chief of the city of Fort Stutter, Jazibeauz Perez, says there was definitely no sign that the—bomb was going to explode, then he said, "Everyone wishes to God we'd known this was going to transpire." The police department hasn't asked the FBI for help the chief says. The dead includes Jason J. Jones, 29, Sally S. Smyth, 24, and Greg G. Goldstein, who died at 22. None were employees at the bombed store. Two unidentified men are in critical condition, meaning they might die too. Everyone in Fort Stutter is scared now to go out on the street, and city officials say increased protection will cost the people of Fort Stutter a lot of money, six-point-one-million dollars. There is no date set for a decision about spending that amount of money, but the mayor cannot be back in town by Tuesday, which is not early enough for her critics. Whether it will really be helpful remains to be seen.

2. The Ever-Improving Story
   These are a few of the same sentences you should have made better in the last chapter. They're still not good enough. Change that.

   - Jason L. Septeimeer, 28, was killed tonight by a drunk driver.   *two of them*
   - Three legislators came down with food poisoning today in Sacramento and one of them said he felt ill for two hours before calling a hospital, and the others said they could not identify the cause.   *at its Florida h·q   more than one million dollar*
   - The space agency NASA is working with the F-B-I to reduce theft at its Florida head-quarters, which has passed the million dollar mark.

3. The Rewritten Story
   Again, improve on the improvements.

   - Airport officials said a seven-37 slid off the runway in snowy conditions tonight during the snowstorm that hit the eastern part of the city. They said conditions on the runway were known to be slippery but that there had not been accidents before the seven-37 went into its skid. The repairs to the runway, according to airport officials, will come to more than two-hundred-fifty-thousand-dollars.
   - The Mayor has certainly never been convicted of theft, but questions still came up about his C-V. The Mayor's critics, especially councilwoman Rebot, who was wearing a tan dress while she spoke, say the Mayor has probably hidden dark secrets from his past and do not think he has revealed everything, and they fear the public will lose faith in government.   *she fears*

4

The Right Way to Write It

Now we're getting away from the mechanics of writing a broadcast news story and into the idiosyncrasies. What does it mean when you're told that someone is in "fair condition" at the hospital, as opposed to "serious condition"? When do you attribute facts to someone else and when do you simply present them without attribution? How can you possibly count all the people participating in a huge public demonstration?

This chapter is sort of a "catch-all" for lessons that didn't logically fit into the chapters before it. It's about the kinds of things that can jeopardize your credibility, not to mention your respect, if you get them wrong. Unlike simple rules such as "don't abbreviate" and "don't use symbols," these aren't the kind you can memorize. No, these are the kind whose meaning and purpose you must learn, and almost make a part of you. They are about things that will come up often in your career as a journalist.

Eventually they will be second nature to you. Now though, just read them, think about them, and practice them in whatever you write. Your credibility, and your station's, are at stake.

Before you get started, look back to your own improved version of the "Never Ending Story." Here are the corrections you should have made:

In a place where a rear-ender traffic ~~accident's~~ **accident is** usually the biggest event of the day, ~~there's~~ **there has** been an event with an impact on everyone. Tonight the lives of three people have been claimed by a bomb, which set off a ~~3-alarm~~ **three-alarm** fire that raised temperatures to almost ~~200°~~ **200-degrees** Fahrenheit at a clothing store at 3645 Main Street, in the heart of ~~Ft.~~ **Fort** Stutter, ~~Calif.,~~ **California,** the police say. No group has taken credit for the blast, but forensics experts **tonight** are combing the scene of the attack. ~~tonight and in~~ **In** case ~~there's~~ **there is** more danger there, a hazardous material ~~team's~~ **team is** dispatched to the scene. They're driving three separate emergency vehicles to get there. ~~In order to~~ **To** explain why there ~~wasn't~~ **was not** a warning, the police chief of the city of ~~Ft.~~ **Fort** Stutter, Jazibeauz Perez (**JAZZ-uh-boo PEAR-ehz),** says there was definitely no sign that the bomb was going to explode, then he said, "Everyone wishes to God we'd known this was going to transpire." The police ~~dept.~~ **department** hasn't asked the ~~FBI~~ **F-B-I** for help, the chief says. The dead ~~includes~~ **include** Jason J. Jones, 29, Sally S. Smyth **(Smith)**, 24, and Greg G. Goldstein **(GOLD-steen),** who died at 22. None were employees at the bombed store. Two unidentified men are in critical condition, meaning they might die too. Everyone in ~~Ft.~~ **Fort** Stutter is scared now to go out on the street, and city officials say increased protection will cost the people of ~~Ft.~~ **Fort** Stutter a lot of money, ~~$6-million~~ **more than six million dollars.** There ~~isn't a~~ **is no** date set for a decision about spending that amount of money, but the mayor ~~can't~~ **cannot** be back in town by ~~Tues.~~ **Tuesday,** which ~~isn't~~ **is not** early enough for her critics. Whether ~~it'll~~ **it really will** ~~really~~ be helpful remains to be seen.

At the end of this chapter, you'll have another shot at fixing problems that won't seem like problems until you finish the chapter.

Leaving Expert Judgment to Others

We've all read it, or heard it: "The patient is in critical condition." Or "poor condition." Or whatever. When someone is taken to the hospital, whether due to a crime, an accident or an illness, you may be assigned to cover it because of the person's prominence or because of whatever got him there. You may have to write or speak these very words: "The patient is in _____ condition."

In rare circumstances you might be able to stay with the patient and hear what the doctors are saying about his condition. But usually you won't. Usually you'll have to depend on a spokesperson, someone whose job is to speak for the hospital, or for the patient (typical with entertainment, sports, and political celebrities).

What you'll probably be told is this: the patient is in critical, unstable, serious, poor, stable, fair, good, or excellent condition. Huh? What does "critical" mean versus "serious"? What's the difference between "stable" and "fair"?

Guess what: you don't have to know. This is one of those atypical cases—one of those "exceptions" to the rule of understanding everything you write—where you don't have to understand the patient's condition, you only have to describe it as it has been described to you. It's up to the doctors, or other medical experts there, to understand it and, through you, to convey it to your audience.

Why? Not because you can't possibly understand the difference between "stable" and "fair," but because you can't possibly know which one describes the person you've been sent to cover. You have to rely on what the spokesperson tells you.

Having said that, let me give you a rough idea what each of those terms means. To begin with, a couple of paragraphs earlier, I listed them roughly in order of their import from the worst to the best: critical, unstable, serious, poor, stable, fair, good, and excellent.

Now, only for your guidance, let me specifically define them. But bear two things in mind: the medical staff provides the "level of care" and you just report it without interpretation, and some of these terms are synonymous with, and only can be defined in relation to, others.

Critical	The patient is hovering between life and death.
Unstable	The patient is critical but if his or her vital signs can be stabilized, the condition will be upgraded to serious.
Serious	The patient has a life-challenging problem, but as long as medical staff can maintain the stability of the patient's vital signs, doctors do not expect the problem to be fatal.
Poor	The patient is very sick but his life is not threatened.
Stable	The patient's vital signs are under control and doctors have reason to believe they will be able to upgrade his condition to fair.
Fair	The patient can perform some functions for himself and is showing no indications of slipping into a worse condition.
Good	The patient is one step from the hospital's exit, and probably only needs additional resting or strength-building time before release.
Excellent	The patient is being observed but is showing no ill effects.

What's the Point?

As a journalist you should question everything. But in a handful of circumstances, you have to uncritically accept and apply the answer. One such case is attributing "responsibility" to terrorists for their acts, not "credit." Another is reporting a patient's condition just as it is reported to you, without embellishment, without elaboration.

Giving Credit Only Where Credit Is Due

Here's a lesson a lot of veteran journalists never have learned: if we don't want to glorify terrorists, we shouldn't write about them taking "credit" for their acts. Taking "credit" for something has a positive connotation. For instance, here's a defective headline from the *Rocky Mountain News* in Denver after a book was published about Oklahoma City federal building bomber Timothy McVeigh: "McVeigh takes lion's share of credit for bombing Murrah federal building." Or, in the spirit of equal time, here's an equally irresponsible headline from a story in the *News's* competitor, *The Denver Post,* after a radical environmental group said it had set some buildings afire at the Vail ski resort: "Earth Liberation Front takes credit."

No! By definition, terrorists do not deserve "credit." So whether you write newspaper headlines or broadcast scripts, remember this: terrorists themselves may consider the word "credit" to be credible, but if journalists buy into the word themselves, they provide an unintended but apparent endorsement of the act. Instead, terrorists "take responsibility." Or if someone says they did it but we cannot be sure (a lot of fanatics and just plain nut cases will say they did something terrible even if they didn't), we write that they "claim responsibility" for the terrorist action. Although in other contexts the word "responsibility" has a positive connotation (as "credit" does), in this context it merely means, "the people responsible." The lesson is, you *don't* want to attach a positive connotation to a negative act.

So when do you give credit? That brings me to attribution.

You Don't Always Have to Attribute Things

There are theories, and there are facts. There are accusations, and there are facts. There are assumptions, and there are facts. In each case, you as a journalist must distinguish between them. One way to do so is with "attribution."

What is attribution? It is the act of giving somebody credit or blame for something. It is the act of making it clear to your audience that you're merely reporting what somebody else has told you, rather than reporting something that you yourself have seen or irrefutably deduced. Here's a simple example of attribution:

> *The police spokeswoman says the ex-Marine was drunk when he pointed a gun at the bank teller, then during his getaway was injured in a four-car crash.*

The writer has "attributed" the description of the ex-Marine—that he was "drunk"—to the police spokeswoman. Why is it important to attribute the description? Because it might not be true. Maybe the ex-Marine was high on drugs rather than alcohol. Maybe he was afflicted with an illness that misleadingly gave him the appearance of drunkenness. Maybe the blood alcohol level in his blood was high but not high enough to qualify legally as "drunk." By attributing the "drunk" description to the police spokeswoman, you're making it clear that it is her description, not yours. Furthermore, you're partially protecting yourself (more in Chapter 20 under Libel) if eventually the ex-Marine proves that it's not true. And, you're being fair. A fair story attributes claims, charges and characterizations to their sources. So in the simplest sense, that's attribution, with a pretty good example of when it's necessary. But how necessary is attribution in this simpler example?

> *The police spokeswoman says the ex-Marine pointed a gun at the bank teller, then during his getaway was injured in a four-car crash.*

Well, while the bank teller herself probably will testify in court that the ex-Marine pointed a gun at her, the ex-Marine might testify that he was pointing it at the ceiling or at the floor. His lawyer then could make the case that the ex-Marine meant no harm to the teller, which could result in a lesser conviction or a lesser sentence. Or the ex-Marine might testify that he only had his hand in his pocket, but no gun. The point is, one of your responsibilities as a journalist is to avoid prejudicing a case. One safe way is to attribute things to your sources, rather than to state them yourself as facts. But attribution can go overboard too. Would you need attribution for the following?

> *The police spokeswoman says the ex-Marine was injured in a four-car crash.*

No, definitely not. If his injury in the crash is a fact, uncontroversial and indisputable, it can be stated as a fact, without attribution. Like this:

The ex-Marine was injured in a four-car crash.

Likewise, if you get a call from the police telling you that there is a bad accident blocking Main Street during the downtown rush hour, and you want to inform your audience right away, you don't have to write it this way:

Police say there is a bad accident blocking Main Street.

Why not? Because the accident is neither a theory, an accusation, or an assumption. It is a fact. Main Street is blocked. An accident caused it. Just say so, without attribution:

There is a bad accident blocking Main Street.

What's the Point?

If you don't know that it's true, attribute it. If you do know, or don't know firsthand but have absolutely no reason to doubt it, don't bother with attribution. It's unnecessary.

Print Journalists Don't Write the Way They Talk

How many times have you seen a sentence that ends like this in a newspaper or a magazine?

The suspect released his hostages and surrendered, police say.

Conceivably this is a story that is unfolding beyond your view, so you have to depend on police accounts of the event. Therefore the question here isn't about attribution. It's about writing the way you talk.

You probably wouldn't sit at the dinner table and tell your tablemates, "It's supposed to rain tomorrow, the weatherman says." Or you wouldn't say, "A helicopter crashed this afternoon at O'Hare Airport, Channel 4 reports." That's because you don't talk that way. No, you'd probably say:

I heard on Channel 4 that a helicopter crashed this afternoon at O'Hare.

What you want for a broadcast news story is that same sentence, modified to fulfill the needs of the newscast:

Channel 4 is reporting that a helicopter crashed this afternoon at O'Hare Airport.

Or in the case of the weather:

The weatherman says it's supposed to rain tomorrow.

Yet many broadcast writing students write news stories the way they've seen them written in newspapers and magazines, which I call "print style."

If you write like this because you've seen so much of this, then the lesson here is simple. Forget what you have seen. Print is a different medium with a different style than broadcasting. So if you're writing about the suspect releasing his hostages, write it this way:

Police say the suspect released his hostages and surrendered.

What's the Point?

I'll make this point as often as I can. Don't write the way you *read;* write the way you talk.

Crowds, Dead or Alive

The biggest crowd I ever saw was in Iran, during a revolution that ultimately overthrew the pro-Western leader, known as the Shah, and replaced him with a radical Islamic leader, known as Ayatollah Khomeini. The crowd was impossible for me to count. They were marching down the main street of the capital, Tehran, from a point beyond my field of view and to a point also beyond my view. What's more, the boulevard along which they marched was packed to the horizon, and wide enough to rival the widest avenues in the world.

So what could I do? In the chaos of the revolution, and since it was a third world country, no one reliable was offering any official estimates—and as you'll read in a moment, "official" estimates sometimes are the least reliable of all. (Actually, since an estimate is supposed to rely at least on evidence, occasionally what officials call an "estimate" actually is no more than a guess, which means mere conjecture, and sometimes that guess is shaped by the officials' political agenda.) Renting a helicopter to see everything from the air—which you might do in an American city—wouldn't work; airspace was closed to everything but military aircraft. Guesswork was out; you shouldn't guess at a crowd's size any more than you should guess at anything else.

Yet to reflect the volume of popular sentiment for the revolution, I wanted somehow to convey the enormity of the demonstration. I knew from experience estimating other crowds elsewhere that this was huge. I felt pretty sure that I could have said "half a million" and not been too high. But if I wasn't sure, I couldn't say it. Furthermore, if the crowd was twice that size, then "half a million" didn't come close to telling the story.

But I wasn't out of tools. Although I knew where the march started and where it ended and therefore knew how much I could *not* see, I also knew from the balcony where I stood what I *could* see. And that's what I worked with. How? By visually (actually, using my thumb and forefinger) cutting the crowd into segments. First I took in the whole scene in my field of view, which was maybe two miles long, and found the approximate halfway point. Then, by isolating just half my field of view (with my thumb and forefinger), I knew I was looking at about fifty percent of the crowd that I could see.

It seemed to go on forever.

Then I did the same thing again with that segment: I found its approximate halfway point and split it in half again. Now I had isolated just twenty-five percent of the crowd (that I could see). Then I didn't just split that part in half; I split it into fifths, so that my thumb and forefinger only framed about five percent of the visible part of the demonstration.

Sometimes that's small enough to make a roughly accurate count. If so, count the heads in the area you've segmented, and multiply by twenty (20 × 5% of a crowd = 100% of the crowd). If it's still not small enough, then split that segment into fifths again, so that essentially, you're isolating only about one percent of the crowd. Make your count, then multiply by one hundred (to come up with 100% of the crowd).

In the case of this colossal crowd in Tehran, I had to split my visual segments into even smaller parts, which became just fractions of one percent. But the process was the same, and I came up with a very rough figure of about 1.5 million people that I could see. Knowing the length of the route that was beyond my field of view both east and west, I could confidently write the following line, "Today's march, like others, stretches too many miles to be measured by the naked eye; millions is a fair estimate."

It's a lot of work for a single sentence in a story, but that's what journalism is about. Anyway, this was for television, so the pictures added a dimension that I didn't have to waste more words to describe.

Most of the time, you won't have millions to count. But you will have thousands, sometimes tens or hundreds of thousands. The trick is to find a high point—a window, a balcony, a hill, a rooftop, if not a helicopter—then use your fingers and do the math!

You may recall my admonition about "official" estimates. Here's what I mean. There was a big demonstration in Denver by people protesting gun control. The National Rifle Association, which supported the demonstration and arguably had an interest in inflating the figure, announced that more than twenty-five thousand gun rights supporters had taken part. The Denver Police Department, whose leaders favored gun control and therefore opposed the demonstration, arguably had an interest in deflating the figure and, sure enough, announced that the crowd didn't amount to more than ten thousand.

Who was right? By my own estimate from a window overlooking Civic Center Plaza where the protest took place, neither side. In fact, my independent and probably more scientific estimate came up with a figure close to halfway between the two advocates, about eighteen thousand. So that's what I said in my report. The two interested parties had *hoped* for a crowd the size they announced. I had *counted* and then made a more accurate estimate.

In a different kind of story, the other thing you need to know about counting people is that when there's a disaster like a hurricane or a plane crash, the count might keep changing. Maybe searchers find more bodies and the death toll rises. Maybe authorities discover the same name duplicated on two different lists and the death toll drops. That's part of the reason why the final official death toll from the terrorist attacks on September 11, 2001 ultimately was only about half the original estimates. This kind of thing happens all the time. The question is, how do you handle it? By letting your audience know. You'd like to give a precise number but you can't, so you make it clear that the number might change. Here are a few hypothetical examples.

A plane carrying ninety people has crashed and burned in a forest outside your city. The first body count to reach you is twenty-five, but common sense tells you that as more rescuers reach the scene, the count is likely to rise. So you write something like this:

At least 25 people have been killed in a plane crash.

Then, if it turns out that the rest of the people miraculously survived, you haven't misreported anything. But if the death toll does go up, you can clearly revise your next report:

80 bodies now have been found.

Give or take a body or two, official death tolls in plane crashes usually rise rather than fall as more reports come in.

The famed radio commentator Paul Harvey, dealing with the breaking news of a Chinese jetliner crashing into a mountain in South Korea when casualty counts still were fluctuating—in retrospect, one hundred-eighteen were killed but remarkably, thirty-nine survived—wrote it this way: "Some survived, most did not."

But how about natural disasters, where the devastation is generally more geographically widespread and where more agencies, not to mention civilians, are involved in search and rescue operations? It's not uncommon for initial death toll reports to be done this way:

200,000 people are dead in an earthquake in Turkey.

Typically this kind of round figure comes from a government official's initial impression, based on how many towns have reported devastation, combined with estimates of deaths from a few. But those estimates are almost never accurate, because they include people buried in rubble. It usually takes days—even weeks—for everyone to be dug out, and for survivors to report friends and family who are missing. So rather than writing a sentence like the one above, instead write a sentence which makes it clear that the death toll isn't yet official:

200,000 people are reported dead in an earthquake in Turkey.

Or:

Officials estimate that 200,000 people are dead in an earthquake in Turkey.

Here's How It Really Works

Let me give you real examples from three consecutive stories after an earthquake in one of the poorest countries on earth. It had toppled village after village in the central mountains of Yemen. Homes, primitively built of mud baked hard in the sun, collapsed on top of their occupants. Most of the dead were women, because in that part of the world, men socialize in the open air while women rarely stray from home. The proportion of women killed was especially high in this earthquake because it started just as they were home preparing the day's major meal. Sadder still, when the earthquake struck, many children were inside with their mothers.

It was impossible for anyone—foreign journalists, local journalists, government officials—to know how many people had been killed. It's probably fair to say that no one ever quite knew how many people inhabited these villages even before the earthquake.

Yet we had to try to characterize the scale of the earthquake's impact. Pictures helped, of course. From a Yemeni Army rescue helicopter on which we hitched a ride, we were able to shoot enough aerials—shots from the air—that any viewer would know that a lot of people must have died. It was obvious. But how many? Here's how we handled that question in the scripts.

- Story #1:

    They're not only finding more bodies here this morning—the official death toll continues to rise well beyond a thousand—but they're even finding more villages that were devastated by the earthquake and its three sharp aftershocks.

- Story #2:

    On the ground here today, searchers found still more bodies. The official death toll is past twelve hundred now, and enough people still are missing that authorities expect it to surpass two thousand.

- Story #3:

    (This one dealt with one particular village. Without giving a number I could not yet support, I still conveyed the scope of the tragedy there.)

    This village had about 600 inhabitants. About a quarter already have been dug out, and buried in these impromptu graves . . ."

One unforgettable example of the difficulty of coming up with good numbers hit Americans painfully close to home: those attacks on September 11, 2001. Terrorists hijacked four commercial airplanes, crashing two of them into the twin towers of New York's World Trade Center, another one into the Pentagon near Washington D.C., and the fourth—probably meant to destroy either the White House or the U.S. Capitol—into a field in Pennsylvania.

Officials from the two airlines whose planes were hijacked, American and United, knew precisely how many passengers and how many crew members died. But the military took days to figure out who was working in the part of the Pentagon that was hit, and who survived. What's more, there was no central clearinghouse for information from the World Trade Center in New York. Hundreds of companies had their offices and stores there. How many people had come to work? How many were out of town? How many visitors were in the building? How many delivery people? How many were eating in the spectacular restaurant at the top?

Nobody knew. Most of the corpses were burned or pulverized by the collapse of the skyscrapers. That's why the total death toll from the terrorist attacks wavered from week to week. At one point just a few days after September 11, it was put as high as twenty thousand. Once authorities started compiling lists, it dropped to about seven thousand. Eventually it was officially established below four thousand. But nobody knew for sure. In fact some news organizations, collating information from New York City's Medical Examiner, funeral homes, places of worship, courts and public agencies, death notices, employers, and families came up with figures even lower. Journalists had to qualify the number every time they reported it. It was "The latest death toll" or "The newest official death toll" or something similar.

Another story, just half a year later, also illustrates the need to qualify your numbers. Do you remember the commercial crematorium (or crematory, both words are correct) in Georgia where the owner wasn't bothering to burn the bodies entrusted to him? He said his oven was broken and he was having trouble getting it fixed. Instead of cremating the remains, he was stacking them in piles, stuffing them in sheds, dumping them in the woods, burying them helter skelter, and otherwise inappropriately and illegally disposing of his customers' beloved remains.

Originally, a few bones were discovered on the grounds of the crematorium. That led authorities on the chase. First they found more than a dozen bodies, then the number jumped to more than a hundred, then they added the grounds of the owner's nearby home to their search and the number reached almost two hundred, then just over two hundred, then close to three hundred and eventually well over three hundred—all in the space of about a week.

As a journalist, you could report the hard numbers, the death toll "to date." But it became obvious pretty fast that it would keep rising. So if at a certain point you only wrote something like, "Authorities have found one hundred eighty-six sets of human remains," it would be incomplete because it would *sound complete!* There are many ways to qualify it. Here are a few:

Authorities have found 186 sets of human remains, and they continue to search.
Authorities have found 186 sets of human remains, and they expect to find more.
Authorities have found 186 sets of human remains so far.

You might even tell *why* they don't think the number will stop at one hundred eighty-six:

> *Authorities have found 186 sets of human remains, but after consulting with local funeral parlors about the number of corpses sent in recent years to the crematorium, they expect to find more.*

What's the Point?

Whether you're reporting how many people marched in a protest or died in a plane crash, the principle is the same: find out as specifically as you can, and if you can't, it's better to say you don't know than to say you know when you don't. Additionally, when the number might change, make it clear to your audience.

Personalizing Complex Economics

A different kind of problem comes up with a different kind of number. An economic number.

Let's say you're writing a story about the latest national unemployment figures. The federal government's summary might just say something like, "Unemployment figures dropped this month to 4.5%." Is that good or bad? And relative to what? Your audience needs some kind of comparison to put the statistic into perspective. So when you write your story, compare it to one of two different figures: either last month's unemployment rate or the unemployment rate the same month last year:

> *Unemployment figures dropped this month to four-point-five percent, down from four-point-seven percent last month.*

Or:

> *Unemployment figures dropped this month to four-point-five percent, which is still worse than the four-point-two percent unemployment rate at this time a year ago.*

There's another way to present it too. Personalize it. Perhaps you still want to provide a comparison like the ones in the examples above. You can, and it's even better to add a context to which everyone can relate. For example:

> *Unemployment figures dropped this month to four-point-five percent. This is better than last month's four-point-seven percent rate, but it still means almost five million Americans are out of work.*

Or:

Unemployment figures dropped this month to four-point-five percent. This is better than last month's four-point-seven percent rate, but it still means one out of every 22 Americans is out of work.

An even drier kind of economic story you might have to write is the latest report on the Gross Domestic Product (GDP), which means the value of goods and services produced in the United States. It's a key figure on which many important economic projections are based. But for your audience, it's a figure in the trillions of dollars, almost impossible to comprehend. So you aren't really helping anyone understand it if you simply report, "The Gross Domestic Product has reached eleven-trillion dollars."

How can you personalize it? A couple of examples, which you can create by doing a bit of simple long division (dividing 11,000,000,000,000 by the United States population, which you can learn in an almanac is approaching 300,000,000 people. If you ask about the population on the search engine known as Ask Jeeves [www.ask.com], you'll learn that by the year 2050, the population of the United States is expected to reach *400* million.).

The Gross Domestic Product has reached eleven-trillion dollars. This comes to about 39-thousand dollars for every man, woman and child in the country.

Or:

The Gross Domestic Product reported by the Government today comes to about 39-thousand dollars for every man, woman and child in the country—a total of eleven-trillion dollars.

Notice, by the way, that I write that it comes to "*about* 39-thousand dollars." Why? Because most people, except a few fastidious accountants, don't need the precise figure down to the penny. Keep it simple. The rough per capita figure for the GDP—$39,000—is all your audience needs.

Of course if you work for a program that specializes in economic news, you may want to be more precise. This is particularly true when reporting stock market figures. If you're with a general interest news organization and the Dow Jones Industrial Average has gone up 49.2 points, you might want to simplify it by rounding it off, writing: *The Dow Jones Industrial Average went up today almost 50 points.*

On the other hand, if you report to an audience that wants more specifics, give 'em more!

When President George W. Bush presented his first federal budget to Congress, it was for more than $2 trillion. The number is just too huge to comprehend. So a writer for the Knight Ridder News Service decided to do a little feature putting "trillion" into perspective. Here are a few of the pictures he conjured up:

"You have not lived a trillion seconds. The country has not existed for a trillion seconds. Western civilization has not been around for a trillion seconds. One trillion seconds ago—31,688 years—Neanderthals stalked the plains of Europe."

"President Bush's budget request is for $2.128 trillion. Stacked in dollar bills, the pile would stretch nearly 144,419 miles. That's two-thirds of the distance to the moon, more than five laps around the Earth at the equator."

He helped us understand just how huge a trillion really is. Only half tongue-in-cheek, he also went on to write of government bureaucrats, "Not only can they comprehend it, they can spend it."

What's the Point?

The whole purpose of your job as a news writer is to convey information in a way the audience can understand. When working with big numbers it's especially important. Keep a calculator handy.

Take My Word for It

A hypothetical situation: you're in the newsroom when you hear that a bomb threat has been phoned into the local Wal–Mart. The store is being evacuated. One reporter immediately is dispatched to the store to cover the story firsthand; you're assigned to collect as much information as you can on the telephone.

Your first call? Wal–Mart, of course. And it's your lucky day, because the clerk who answers the phone is the one who took the call with the bomb threat. You ask, "What did the caller say?" The clerk answers, "All he said was, 'Get everyone out of there, a bomb's going to go off.'" You ask, "Were those his very words?" and the clerk says "Yes."

That's a dramatic quote. It's so dramatic that it deserves to be repeated on the air word for word. Why? Well, read the following sentences aloud and listen to the difference between a paraphrased summary and the quote itself:

Paraphrase:

The clerk says the caller told her to get everyone out of the store because a bomb was going to go off.

Actual quote:

The clerk says the caller told her, quote, "Get everyone out of there, a bomb's going to go off."

Paraphrase:

According to the clerk, the caller said that everyone should get out of there because a bomb was set to explode.

Actual quote:

According to the clerk, the caller said, and I quote, "Get everyone out of there, a bomb's going to go off."

Paraphrase:

The clerk says the caller told her that a bomb was going to go off, so everyone should get out of the store.

Actual quote:

The clerk says the caller's actual words were, "Get everyone out of there, a bomb's going to go off."

There's no question which version in each set of examples is the more dramatic. And more accurate. But now that that's clear, note that in the case of each "actual quote," there is a word or two just before it to make it absolutely clear to the audience that the words they're about to hear are the actual words of the man who phoned in the bomb threat. Why is that so important? Read the following sentence aloud where I *don't* make it clear, and ask yourself whether the audience would know for sure that it's an actual quote:

The clerk says the caller told her, "Get everyone out of there, a bomb's going to go off."

Have I set up the audience for the dramatic quote? No. Does the audience have any way of knowing that it is hearing the very words the caller used? No. Why not? Because the audience cannot see the script. The audience cannot see the quotation marks denoting the actual quote.

So the lesson is simple: when you're quoting someone, make it clear, crystal clear, that it's a quote. You've just seen three ways to do it:

- the caller told her, quote, "Get everyone out of there . . . "
- the caller said, and I quote, "Get everyone out of there . . . "
- the caller's actual words were, "Get everyone out of there . . . "

There are many more ways, and I won't try to show them all. But here are a few more examples:

- the caller said to her, in these very words, "Get everyone out of there . . . "
- the caller said, and this is a quote, "Get everyone out of there . . . "
- what the caller said, word for word was, "Get everyone out of there . . . "

By the way, while you should prepare the audience for an actual quote, in general practice you do *not* specifically have to tell the audience where the quote ends. In other words, do not write (or say) something like "end quote." Leave that to the anchorperson to achieve with voice inflection.

Speaking of voice inflection, sometimes the anchor's or reporter's voice inflection alone can clearly convey to an audience that the words they're hearing are someone else's actual words. For instance, one of my Emmy Awards is for one week's coverage of a terrible earthquake in the Appenine Mountains of southern Italy. It was a major story because it killed about two thousand people. But the single most dramatic piece I produced was about just one victim, a woman named Lisa. She had been buried for three days when searchers barely heard her make a noise, somewhere deep down in the rubble of a three story apartment building. Then, for six hours, stick by stick, stone by stone, rescuers dug to save her. If they broke the wrong stick or moved the wrong stone, the whole pile of rubble might have collapsed, burying Lisa even deeper, and them on top of her.

But despite the danger, one worker after another dug head-first, upside down in the hole, when at a certain point one of them pulled himself up and shouted, well, let me reprint that part of the script here, so you can see the quotation marks and realize that it would have been awkward to use "quote" or "word for word" or any other verbal signal. I did it strictly by raising both the timbre and tempo of my voice:

> *This rescue worker cut up his face but said, "I touched Lisa's hand, my blood doesn't matter."*

So yes, sometimes mere voice inflection works. But don't count on it. Unless a verbal signal would detract from the drama, better to be safe than sorry.

What's the Point?

If someone's words are worth quoting, then you want to be sure that the audience knows it's hearing those actual words, rather than a summary. So make it clear. Leave no doubt.

The Final Potpourri

When I type up a syllabus for my own students at the University of Colorado, I always make a point of telling them—as I told you at the very beginning of this book—that "syllabus" is the kind of word you never should use in a script. Likewise, "potpourri." Not everyone knows what it means and, what's more, it's not strictly an English language word.

But you probably understand it. A "potpourri" is a miscellaneous collection of some kind. This final section of the chapter is a collection of all the little items that don't neatly fit into the other sections in this chapter. They're pretty short, so I'll simply list them as bullet points.

- "It's" means only one thing: "it is." It isn't the possessive form of "it," as in, "The dog put its paws in the water." You may or may not understand why not, but make sure you understand this one thing. Unless you're contracting "It is," there is no apostrophe in "its."
- "None" is singular. So if you're writing about members of a jury that has just acquitted someone on trial, you don't write, "None were convinced of his guilt." That makes it plural. Instead write, "None was convinced of his guilt." Or if you want to tell me that not a single reader understands this sentence, don't write, "None under-

stand the sentence"; write, "None understands the sentence." An easy way to remember this is to think of "none" as "no one." You wouldn't write "No one understand the sentence," would you?

- If your city council or state legislature or congress is considering legislation, they are considering a "bill." When and if the mayor or the governor or the president signs it, then—and only then—it's a "law."
- Nothing "claims the life of 15 people." Not a hurricane, not an air crash, not a disease, not a war. That's because we'd never say it this way in conversation: "Gee, did ya hear, a hurricane *claimed the lives of* 15 people today down in Mississippi." No, the way we'd say it is, "A hurricane killed 15 people."
- When the police have picked up a man they believe committed a crime, he is only a "suspect." When can you accurately call him a "rapist," a "robber," a "murderer," or whatever? Only after he has been convicted in court. You can refer to him before the end of a trial as "the alleged robber" or "the suspected robber," but be very careful not to convict someone before a judge or jury does.
- No one "authors" a book. Someone "writes" it.

What's the Point?

It's easy to look silly if you don't think smart! And write smart too.

Exercises to Further Hone Your Writing Skills ⸻

1. The Never Ending Story
   Here it is again, the Never Ending Story. Rewrite it again by using what you have just learned. Don't make any other corrections. There's still more to come.

   > In a place where a rear-ender traffic accident is usually the biggest event of the day, there has been an event with an impact on everyone. Tonight the lives of three people have been claimed by a bomb, which set off a three-alarm fire that raised temperatures to almost 200-degrees at a clothing store in the heart of Fort Stutter, California, the police say. No group has taken credit for the blast, but forensics experts tonight are combing the scene of the attack. In case there is more danger there, a hazardous material team is dispatched to the scene. To explain why there was not a warning, the police chief of the city of Fort Stutter, Jazibeauz Perez (JAZZ-uh-boo PEAR-ehz), says there was definitely no sign that the bomb was going to explode, then he said, "Everyone wishes to God we'd known this was going to transpire." The police department hasn't asked the F-B-I for help, the chief says. The dead include Jason Jones, Sally Smyth (Smith), and Greg Goldstein (GOLD-steen). None were employees at the bombed store. Two unidentified men are in critical condition, meaning they might die too. Everyone in Fort Stutter is scared now to go out on the street, and city officials say increased protection will cost the people of Fort Stutter a lot of money, more than six million dollars. There is no date set for a decision about spending that amount of money, but the mayor cannot be back in town by Tuesday, which is not early enough for her critics. Whether it really will be helpful remains to be seen.

2. The Way to Quote a Quote
    Using a different setup word or words in each case, rewrite these sentences to make it perfectly clear to the audience that the words within the quotation marks are the actual words of the person being quoted, not just a paraphrased version:

    She has an word and I quote word for word

    - The fireman said "There have never been hotter flames in an apartment fire here."
    - The bank teller insists the man told her "All the money has to go into the bag or some people are gonna get shot."
    - A witness at the airport screamed "The plane was heading right for the control tower, and it seemed to be on fire."
    - The mayor was mad enough to say "There'll be no more concerts in the park, and that's final!"

3. Killing the "Pot" in "Pourri"
    Each of these sentences has a single mistake you have learned in this chapter to recognize. Correct it in each:

    - None of the students were in class. *was*
    - Both movie stars are in fair condition, ~~so they'll probably be released soon.~~ *are said to be*
    - The stadium is the biggest in it's state. *its*
    - The senator authored the bill herself. *wrote*
    - *Ercted* 18 new stop signs will be installed within a month the traffic department promises. *A traffic dept. spokesperson*
    - The march attracted somewhere between ten and twenty thousand protestors.
    - No one has taken credit for the bombing at the restaurant. *responsibility*
    - The thief will be put on trial next month. *tried*
    - Rescuers extricated *pulled* four people from the collapsed building.
    - Congress is considering a law *bill* that would allow guns in airplane cockpits.
    - The fire chief ~~says~~ the furnace exploded at exactly 8 o'clock.
    - The 120 workers at the factory will share the two-million-dollar reward. *(break it down*

4. Writing Right
    This paragraph is full of mistakes, the kinds of mistakes you should catch by now from the first few chapters of the book. It contains grammatical mistakes, style mistakes, and proofreading mistakes. Rewrite the paragraph so it has none.

    The fire in City Hall destroyed it's dome. As the wreckage fell to ~~the ground~~, a ~~group of~~ tourists had to run for their lives, witnesses said. None *was* were killed, but several had to be taken to the hospital, where doctors say two of them are in critical condition. So they could die, which would turn this into a murder investigation. The *It suspect* *alleged* arsonist already has been caught, but police are questioning him carefully because after his arrest, someone else called a local newspaper to claim *his plan* credit. Fire officials say it took four hours to put out the ~~last of the~~ flames. They also say *Five officials:* this might not have happened if the City Council had not passed the bill that makes it legal to buy *law* dynamite. *verbs plural?*

5

Saying It Twice

_____

One of the biggest differences between writing for print and writing for broadcast is in the use of sound—the sound of someone speaking, or simply the "natural sound" from a story, like rushing floodwaters, or noisy children, or machine gun fire. You have to choose the sound, then write a script that makes a transition smoothly into it, and just as smoothly out of it. I'll refer to the process subsequently in this chapter as simply "writing in" and "writing out." Print reporters don't have to worry about this. You do.

Making the best use of sound is one of the toughest things to do smoothly. Why? Because if, for instance, you have tape of someone speaking, you're stuck with what that person says in the sound bite. Unlike a print reporter who can begin quoting someone midway through a sentence that starts awkwardly, you have to write into the whole sound bite even if the top (beginning) of it is inarticulate, because it already has been recorded. You have to write out of it even if the end is meaningless.

But as tough as it is, it's important, because a broadcast story can be pretty monotonous without some sort of sound. I refer to this as "production value." This means it makes a story more interesting. It breaks up the narration of the reporter, adding a new dynamic, and grabbing our attention as viewers and listeners.

What's more, it gives you tools to tell your story that print reporters don't have. If it's from an interview or a news conference, a sound bite adds texture and information to the hard facts from the reporter. If it's "natural sound" (see The Terms of the Story next), it adds color, helping the listener or viewer feel almost like he is right there with you.

They say a picture is worth a thousand words. Good sound is too.

The Terms of the Story _____

NAT SOT "Natural Sound" (the abbreviation derives from "NATural Sound On Tape), like the rushing floodwaters, noisy children, or machine-gun fire.

Leadin A sentence either leading from an introduction into a report, or from narration into a sound bite.

SOT "Sound On Tape," usually this designates a spoken sound bite.

CG "Computer Generated Graphic," wording, typically at the bottom of the screen, that usually identifies the person or the place.

Reporter Package   A story covered by a reporter in the field and edited as a self-contained report, requiring only a brief introduction by the anchor.

Tag Line   The first line of narration after a sound bite, or the closing line in a story.

Verbatim   Word-for-word account of what someone says in an interview, a news conference, a speech or another setting in a story.

All right, at the end of the last chapter, you had another crack at the Never Ending Story. At this point, you should have made corrections like these:

In a place where a rear-ender traffic accident is usually the biggest event of the day, there has been an event with an impact on everyone. Tonight the ~~lives of~~ three people ~~have been claimed~~ have been killed by a bomb, which set off a three-alarm fire that raised temperatures to almost 200-degrees at a clothing store in the heart of Fort Stutter, California, the police say. No group has taken ~~credit~~ **responsibility** for the blast, but forensics experts tonight are combing the scene of the attack. In case there is more danger there, a hazardous material team is dispatched to the scene. To explain why there was not a warning, the police chief of the city of Fort Stutter, Jazibeauz Perez (JAZZ-uh-boo PEAR-ehz), says there was definitely no sign that the bomb was going to explode, then he said, **quote,** "Everyone wishes to God we'd known this was going to transpire." The **chief says the** police department hasn't asked the F-B-I for help, ~~the chief says.~~ The dead include Jason Jones, Sally Smyth (Smith), and Greg Goldstein (GOLD-steen). None ~~were employees~~ **was an employee** at the bombed store. Two unidentified men are in critical condition, meaning they might die too. Everyone in Fort Stutter is scared now to go ou t on the street, and city officials say increased protection will cost the people of Fort Stutter a lot of money, more than six million dollars, **which would come to about two-hundred dollars per citizen.** There is no date set for a decision about spending that amount of money, but the mayor cannot be back in town by Tuesday, which is not early enough for her critics. Whether it really will be helpful remains to be seen.

Is That a Fact?

If you're covering a terrible fire and you have interviewed the fire chief, what makes sense? To choose a sound bite where she tells you how many trucks and firefighters responded to the alarm? Or one where she reveals that the sight of the children who burned to death in the fire brought her to tears?

It's no contest. You, the journalist, can deliver the facts, like how many trucks and firefighters showed up. Frankly, you probably can deliver them more quickly and succinctly than the chief. There is no reason to waste precious air time by having the speaker say something the reporter can say as well or better.

But there's a huge difference between the reporter telling the audience that the fire chief was moved to tears, and the chief telling us herself. Hearing her is more dramatic and more direct. And it's something radio and TV can deliver well, because seeing her teary eyes or hearing her voice crack as she says it are qualities the written word cannot match.

Not every interview will offer you emotional sound bites. Not every one will give you a choice. Law enforcement officials, politicians, and business leaders in particular sometimes deliver "just the facts" and sometimes in a monotone. Then, you just have to choose the most interesting facts to use in your sound bites. Is it sometimes better to skip the sound bite and say it yourself? Well, you have to weigh the mundane quality of the sound bite against the otherwise unchanging narration. More often than not, I'd still go for the sound bite, unless it's downright horrible. It still has "production value." It still becomes an additional element for your story.

What's the Point?

The first lesson about sound bites is, choose wisely. When you can, take advantage of the emotional value of the speaker. Leave the dry reciting of information to your scripted narration.

Is That Gobbledygook?

You not only have to choose a sound bite for its emotional value (when you can), you also have to consider whether it will hold the audience's interest. I once had an incredible sound bite from a militia member in Northern Ireland, which would have sounded like this:

> *Aw, we don't care how many Prods (Protestants) die. They want to see us dead too. If we got to kill 'em all to get our way and get the f****** British out of our country, then that's what we'll do. It's a war, ya see, a f****** war, and people, they die in wars. If they wanna stop the dying, they gotta stop being here. They gotta get out. And if they don't get themselves out, we'll get 'em out.*

Pretty darned threatening. Pretty darned angry. Pretty darned dramatic. The trouble is, he didn't say it quite that way. No, it was more like this:

> *Aw, I gotta tell ya, um, um, we don't, well, care, how many Prods (Protestants), ya know, them that's on the other side, die. They want to, oh, see us, well, dead too. If we got to, ya know, kill 'em all to, aw, get our way and, aw, well, get the f****** British out of our, um, country, then, well, aw, that's what we'll do. It's, oh, a war, ya see, a f****** war, and, well, ya know, people, they die in wars. If they wanna, uh, stop the, ya know, dying, they gotta stop, ya know, being here. They gotta, well, get out. And if they don't, aw, get themselves out, we'll, um, get 'em out.*

This guy peppered a terrific sound bite with so many "ums," "ohs," "aws," "wells," "ya knows," and impertinent phrases that it was too darned cluttered to use. (Of course the vulgarities didn't help either, but they can be bleeped out if necessary.) No fault of his own, this guy never was trained to be a public speaker. It was my loss more than his. He not only broke up the drama with gobbledygook, but he dragged out his "ums" and "aws" so they were more like "uuuuuummmmm" and "aaaawwwww." Too long to use, and despite the fiery nature of his words, too boring.

Does this mean you cannot use a sound bite with these characteristics? Not at all. You just have to choose judiciously. For instance, let's say you have recorded this statement from a police detective:

> *Well, the fact of the matter is, we can't really, uh, I mean, we can't find the gun, which we need to nail our suspect, so even though we've got him behind bars right now, we're gonna have to let the guy go, which would really be unfortunate because, well, I guess the reasons are obvious if you consider all the possibilities, like he might, you know, maybe kill someone else, and he might, oh, who knows, he might get away from us before he faces justice. But believe you me, and I was telling my wife this very thing earlier this morning, or maybe it was yesterday, but the one thing for sure is, we're going to keep looking for that weapon and when we find it, you can bet your life we're going to arrest the guy again and put him away for life so he will never again roam the streets of Denver.*

What can you do with it when you're editing your story? Plenty. Obviously, you don't use the beginning. It's meaningless, what I call "trash." But if you want to use the *meat* of the first sentence—that they can't find the gun, so they have to let their suspect go—you begin using his voice immediately *after* the words, "I mean." Take a look, you'll see what *I* mean! As for the second meaty part of his statement—that they'll keep looking for the gun and hopefully find it and arrest the suspect again—no one cares that the detective had said the same thing to his wife, let alone when he said it to her. It's just more trash. No, to use him saying that sentence, you'd get into it beginning with the words, "We're going to keep looking . . ."

Of course sometimes, what works on paper doesn't always work on tape. Maybe he speaks too quickly to smoothly edit into his sentences where I'm suggesting it. But because there are commas there, I'm assuming there are pauses long enough to make my edits. If there are, then perhaps you can treat each part following a comma as the beginning of a new sentence.

It's a little harder to get out of a sentence in the middle. Take that first part of the detective's statement that begins, "we can't find the gun." It looks clean going in, but where do you get out? Ideally, after the words, ". . . let the guy go," because what follows becomes pretty useless to you. But can you get out there? Well, there's a comma, which suggests you can.

But there's another consideration: does the detective end where you want him to end with his voice on a "down" or on an "up"? What I'm asking is, does his voice inflect downward when he says "let the guy go" so that it sounds like it could be the end of a sentence? Or does it inflect upward, so it sounds like he has more to say? The former is a blessing. The latter is a barrier awkward enough that it may keep you from using that part as a sound bite.

What's the Point?

Let sound bites convey opinion, emotion, analysis, or perhaps eyewitness accounts. Just cut them cleanly, don't let them bore.

You've Got Your Bite, Now You Write

Okay, you are preparing your piece. After listening to what you recorded, you have chosen your sound bites. Now you have to write. To tell the story and maintain its flow, you need a sentence that "sets up" the sound bite. What does "sets up" mean? It means you prepare your audience for what the speaker is going to say. Simple? Not even close.

Why not? Because if you're careless, you might violate one of the rules of writing a setup:

1. Don't give away the content of the sound bite.
2. Don't say what the sound bite already says.
3. Say something that flows into the sound bite itself.
4. Establish the authority, credibility or identity of the speaker.
5. Don't just state the obvious.

Now let's look at an example of each. All but one come from my own scripts—my own mistakes.

1. Don't give away the content of the sound bite.

    I've done it more than once. Instead of piquing the audience's interest, I've burst the balloon before the speaker started speaking. In a story about a movement in Great Britain to legalize euthanasia (helping someone with an incurable illness to die), I had a sound bite in which an euthanasia advocate said:

    > *I don't think I would like to continue living longer than I want to do so. If left to nature, then you have no means of knowing. You may linger for a very long time and be very uncomfortable. And I see no point in it.*

    I should have written a simple leadin line like:

    > *One advocate says, she wants to die with dignity.*

    That would have set up the audience to hear her personal sentiment. But I didn't. Instead, I gave away the sound bite before anyone even heard it, by leading into it with:

    > *One advocate says, she doesn't know how long she'll live, or how painfully she'll die.*

    I gave it away. I wasted precious air time. And the audience's time.

2. Don't say what the sound bite already says.

    This can happen especially when you have only a sense of what the sound bite says, rather than the actual words on paper or on the computer screen in front of you (which shouldn't happen). For instance, in this story I reported from England's famous Wimbledon tennis tournament, I led into a sound bite with Martina Navratilova, the reigning champ at the time, this way:

> *Martina Navratilova, two-time Wimbledon woman's champ, said the*
> *pressure to win is greater this year than it has ever been before.*

That would be fine, until you see what she said in the sound bite:

> *The pressure is greater. Everyone expects you to win.*

By the time *she* said "The pressure is greater," *I* already had said it. The audience would be right to wonder, why did I include the sound bite at all? It would have been better if I had led into it with something like,

> *Martina Navratilova, two-time Wimbledon woman's champ, said this year is*
> *unlike any other year.*

Then she could have told us why, and the sound bite would have worked.

3. **Say something that flows into the sound bite itself.**

   You want your leadin sentence to flow almost seamlessly into the sound bite. Otherwise, the audience may need a moment to see the connection between the leadin and the sound bite. Once someone's mind goes on pause to search for that connection, she has stopped following the story itself. Good flow creates continuity, which means the audience absorbs it better.

   But like just almost everything else you're learning in this book, this is more easily said than done. I probably have written several thousand leadin sentences, and undoubtedly could have done better with many. Here, for example, is what I wrote leading into a sound bite with Mrs. Ziolkowski, the wife of the man who decades ago started the colossal sculpture of the Native American chief Crazy Horse. It is in South Dakota, not far from Mt. Rushmore.

   I think my excuse to the show's producer in New York was that I was rushing to make the deadline. Lousy excuse. Good writing doesn't take extra time, just extra thought.

   > **DOBBS:** *Based on a scale model of Crazy Horse on his stallion, this mountain has been whittled away for 42 years now. Its sculptor was the late Korczak Ziolkowski who wrote, "When legends die, dreams end."*
   > **SOT:** *Korczak always said time didn't matter, it didn't make any difference so long as we kept on working.*

   One thing had almost nothing to do with the other. In fact, it had *absolutely* nothing to do with the other. There was no flow. So anyone in the audience who actually thought about what I said, then about what Mrs. Ziolkowski said, could only scratch their heads. If I had made reference to the fact that the people still working on Crazy Horse today probably won't live to see it finished, Mrs. Ziolkowski's sound bite would have made much more sense.

4. **Establish the authority, credibility, or identity of the speaker.**

   Iowa is in the heartland. It also is one of the best educated states in the United States. So it's a pretty good place to go for articulate opinion from the heartland. We went to get a feel for what heartland Americans thought about sending surplus grain to the drought-stricken Soviet Union, even though the Soviets still were America's

Cold War enemy. I interviewed lots of citizens, some off camera and some on. Just look at some of the concise, articulate sound bites I collected:

> **SOT:** *We can be generous and help and it won't cost us a thing.* (From a seed company executive.)
> **SOT:** *We are not gonna get disarmament in the world with hungry people out there.* (From a big commercial farmer.)
> **SOT:** *If they're gonna solve their own problems, I think they need to do it on their own.* (From a small farmer.)
> **SOT:** *I think it's just a whole new arena for us to sell our products in. Question: Good business? Answer: Absolutely.* (From a man in the agricultural construction business.)
> **SOT:** *When I can properly take care of my own needs, then I can reach out and properly take care of other people.* (From a Des Moines homeless shelter director.)

Now look at how poorly I wrote into three of them, by failing to make clear that these people had a financial stake in the proposal to sell grain to the Soviets.

> **DOBBS:** *Many here are bullish on helping the Soviets.*
> **SOT:** *We can be generous and help and it won't cost us a thing.*
> **DOBBS:** *Garst says it's better to help them than to fight them.*
> **SOT:** *We are not gonna get disarmament in the world with hungry people out there.*
> **DOBBS:** *At Stetson Building Products, despite the negative national poll, there's a different point of view.*
> **SOT:** *I think it's just a whole new arena for us to sell our products in. Question: Good business? Answer: Absolutely.*

If someone has expertise, or standing, or bias on an issue, make it clear. I didn't.

5. Don't just state the obvious.

In radio, when you're writing your leadin, you have to tell us who's about to speak, because we can't see the speaker's face (it's radio, remember?) and unless it's the President of the United States, most of us probably won't recognize the voice. What this means is, whether it's a sound bite with a famous actress or athlete or your city's mayor, you must identify the speaker by name (and maybe title too) in your leadin *before* we hear the bite. However, sometimes you may not actually need the person's name, when the person's "authority" is more important. So leading into a sound bite with a witness to a shooting, you might simply write, "This woman was just three feet from the gunman."

In TV this isn't as important, because the CG can tell people visually who's speaking, so you don't have to in your script.

However, many television news leadin sentences also identify the upcoming speaker. In fact, many news directors require it, just to be sure it's clear.

Therefore when I say, "Don't just state the obvious," make sure there's a way for the audience to identify the speaker whose voice they're about to hear. But don't write a whole sentence *simply* identifying the speaker. An example? Let's assume

A control room technician can fill the screen with words you don't have to write. Courtesy of KCNC-TV.

you're leading into a sound bite with someone named Jennifer Smith. Ms. Smith witnessed an accident and says in her sound bite:

> *When the second car hit the guardrail, I thought it was going to go flying and come right through the window of my house. I thought my daughter and me were goners.*

Don't write an empty leadin like:

> *Jennifer Smith had this to say.*

That's just stating the obvious. Or even worse:

> *Jennifer Smith said,*

Give the audience information. Since Ms. Smith was witness to the accident, at the very least you could write for your leadin:

> *Jennifer Smith saw it happen.*

But since her sound bite is personal, you could make the leadin personal too.

> *Watching it happen, Jennifer Smith was scared.*

Or:

> *Jennifer Smith saw it happen, from the living room of her house.*

Of course as I've said before, there are exceptions to every rule. Although it is unimaginative, sometimes when your script already is running long and you want to save time, you can get away with simply stating the name of the person about to speak. So in the example with witness Jennifer Smith, you could lead into the sound bite with the shortest possible identification:

> *Jennifer Smith.*

Or maybe:

> *Witness Jennifer Smith.*

It's unimaginative, but it's economical too.

Sentences leading into a reporter's package must follow the same rules as leadins to sound bites. Pretend I'm a reporter with your station and I'm covering the accident Ms. Smith saw, and you are writing the introduction to be read by the anchor. You're focusing on the wrong thing—the reporter—if you write as your leadin:

Reporter Greg Dobbs was there.

Or even the commonly heard:

Greg Dobbs reports.

Or:

Here's Greg Dobbs.

Longer versions of this format are merely worse, such as:

Our reporter Greg Dobbs was there.

Or:

WXYX reporter Greg Dobbs is on the scene.

Or, as I've heard from time to time:

Here's WXYX reporter Greg Dobbs, who reports from the scene of the crash.

Yuck! All that stuff wastes time. If I'm standing there with a couple of totaled cars behind me, then *of course* I'm at the scene of the crash. More important, those sentences all make it sound like the report is about the reporter. It isn't. It's about the accident. So just like the lesson above, where you learned to *give the audience information,* include some information about the story when you lead into reporter packages.

A few hypothetical examples that could lead into the report?

Greg Dobbs reports that both drivers were tested for alcohol.

As Greg Dobbs reports, both drivers were tested for alcohol.

Both drivers were tested for alcohol, as Greg Dobbs reports.

WXYX's Greg Dobbs says one car came close to killing someone.

One car came close to killing someone, according to WXYX reporter Greg Dobbs.

What's the Point?

The words leading into a sound bite aren't really just an "introduction." They're part of the story. Think of them that way and you'll write good leadins.

Tag, You're It

Now that we've covered writing *into* a sound bite, let's look at how you write *out* of one. In fact, every time in this chapter that you read "sound bite," also think about applying the principle to the end of a whole reporter package, when you want to leave something for the anchor to say. That's often called the tag line. A lot of broadcast writers don't pay much attention to tag lines. Too bad. Their writing suffers. Yours can shine.

First of all, employ essentially the same principles you learned for leadins: don't repeat what the sound bite says, don't state the obvious, and sometimes, for clarity, verbally re-identify the speaker.

Additionally, you want to employ principles that enhance continuity, to make your tag line flow seamlessly from the sound bite. They are:

1. Play off the words at the end of the sound bite
2. Play off the idea of the sound bite
3. Find something else that wasn't in the sound bite
4. After the sound bite, give the contrary point of view.

A good tag line makes a story so much better that I'm going to give you several examples of each, again, from my own scripts. Luckily, I wrote these sentences right.

1. Play off the words at the end of the sound bite.

Playing off the speaker's words really means playing to the audience's ears. Using an actual word they just heard in the sound bite reinforces it, draws attention to it, and creates continuity with it. When you can, playing off a word or two is about the smoothest way to make your transition from sound bite to tag line. Here are several examples, just to make it clear.

One fun feature was about an American jockey named Steve Cauthen. He had fallen on hard times at home but jumpstarted his career in England. He became a champ. Midway through our story, we had a sound bite in which I asked a bookie named Gibbs whether he believed Steve Cauthen would become the winningest jockey in British history. His answer was:

SOT: *There's no doubt about that. In fact the betting's finished, yes.*

"The betting's finished." Surely one word from the sound bite of the bookie would work well in the tag line. It did:

DOBBS: *Now all that's left is the betting on Cauthen's chances next year, and the years after that.*

Another story from my limited world of sports was about the Sheep Dog Trials in Wales. A farmer must get his sheep dog to herd twenty sheep through a winding course and into a pen, using nothing but his natural whistle. I asked one contestant, "It's you giving the commands, right?" and he answered,

SOT: *Yea, but it's the dog that's taking them.*

Well, there were no words in this sound bite nearly as strong as the word "betting" in the Steve Cauthen story, but still, there might be a way to play off the words I had. There was:

DOBBS: *Taking those commands is hard work . . . nearly two miles to run.*

Another example shows up in a story about the first man to pilot a balloon alone from the United States to Europe. He not only made it across the Atlantic, but all the way to Italy. The only flaw in the whole adventure was that he was thrown out of his balloon on impact and broke a bone in his foot. When we got to him, I asked:

> **SOT:** (Question) *Although you've suffered an injury, no regrets? (Answer) Oh, of course not.*

This was easy. The tag line and closing line played off the word "injury" and became:

> **DOBBS:** *The injury after all, will soon be forgotten. The adventure won't.*

Finally, a nice use of the words from a sound bite in a Fourth of July feature from Paris about a little-known 151-foot high bronze replica of the Statue of Liberty. It was given to the French people by the American community in Paris, as thanks for the real statue, which had been made there. A former French ambassador to the United States told me that his own great grandfather had conceived of the original Statue of Liberty, then he ended with:

> **SOT:** *He said you can grow old, you can forget a lot of things in life, but you'll always remain in love with liberty.*

That one's a winner. You can go in a dozen directions with those closing words, "in love with liberty." Mine took me this way:

> **DOBBS:** *The love affair has not been broken. That love of liberty was celebrated today on both sides of the Atlantic.*

2. Play off the idea of the sound bite.

This is a bit tougher than playing off the sound bite's words, but not much. All you have to do is think a little harder. Another semi-sports feature that serves as an example was a story about the game of darts, which is so popular in Great Britain that it's televised. I had this exchange with an elderly woman watching a televised dart match in a pub.

> **SOT:** (Question) *What do you think TV does for darts? (Answer) Oh, it's made old people like me know what it's all about. It's made me know something I never knew in my life. (Question) So you like it? (Answer) Every part of it. TV is wonderful.*

"TV is wonderful." What a natural opening to the next part of the piece:

> **DOBBS:** *TV's not only wonderful, but for some sports fans here in Britain, it's also experimental.*

The story went on to tell how lawn bowling and "snooker," a kind of billiards, were about to be televised too.

Lest you forget that I worked for ABC *News,* not ABC *Sports,* here's an example from a breaking news story about a 747 that was hijacked from Kuwait to Iran. The hijackers had just been overtaken. A former president of Iran who now lived in exile told us he blamed Iran's radical government for the hijacking, ending his sound bite with,

> **SOT:** *Who are they to be judged by?*

For the tag line, I played off the word "judged," but more important, the tag line played off the idea of the sound bite by addressing his question:

> **DOBBS:** *Iran's Prime Minister has said that the hijackers will be judged by Iran. They will not be extradited.*

In a different version of the same story for another ABC show, we had a sound bite recorded before the hijacking ended with one of seven passengers who had been released, while the rest still were held hostage:

> **SOT:** *If you're religious or not religious, pray for the people on board, pray all night for them.*

Strong words, but I couldn't find a way to use them verbatim in the time I had left to end the story. But I could play off their meaning:

> **DOBBS:** *But no one had to wait that long. After asking the hijackers by radio to do nothing before midnight, Iranian security forces moved in . . .*

3. Find something else that wasn't in the sound bite.

Since you usually have more information about a story than you can use, this is a bonus. Simply look at all the facts you have, and decide which ones you definitely want to include. Then see which one flows most logically out of the sound bite.

Having covered the Soviet invasion of Afghanistan back in 1979, I was asked to do a "progress report" five years later. I interviewed a spokesman for the mujahedeen, the rebels then fighting the Soviets. He told me,

> **SOT:** *The Soviets have destroyed a lot, but they have not won the favor of the people, and because of that, I think they do not achieve their aim.*

At this point in the story, I had to turn a corner. I still wanted to make the following points.

- Westerners didn't have much chance of seeing Soviet soldiers in combat.
- Soviet citizens at home were not being shown Soviet soldiers in combat.
- Originally having sent draftees to Afghanistan, now the Soviets were sending professional assault troops.
- The Soviets originally sent about fifty thousand troops to Afghanistan but now had one hundred thousand soldiers there, which they were calling "a limited contingent."
- An estimated ten thousand Soviet soldiers already were dead
- The Soviets were providing food, fertilizer, and oil in exchange for the loyalty of some Afghanistani leaders.

Armed with those facts, I decided that the most logical thought to follow the mujahedeen spokesman's sound bite was the one about troop strength, because it helped to reinforce what the spokesman had just said about the Soviets' failure to "achieve their aim":

> **DOBBS:**   *Five years ago we watched as the Soviets rolled into Afghanistan, 50-thousand strong. Today, they have more than twice that number . . .*

This financial story about a European consortium whose rockets lifted communications satellites into space is another example of using something that isn't in the sound bite. It was attracting more business than the American space agency NASA. But the chairman of the company, called Ariane, told me they still had some technological hurdles to overcome.

> **SOT:**   *For us, technology is only a tool, not an end in itself.*

How he thought of technology didn't really matter. How he ran his business did. That's why I wrote this tag line out of the sound bite, which played a bit off his words but more importantly made a point he hadn't directly made himself:

> **DOBBS:**   *Ariane's boss says his goal is not to excel in technology, but in business.*

4. After the sound bite, give the contrary point of view.

This one's pretty obvious. If there is more than one side to a story, the sound bite provides one point of view; your tag line can provide the other. Here are a few quick examples, all coincidentally related to air travel and airplanes.

Back when passengers still were allowed to smoke in designated sections of airplanes, Congress was considering a bill to ban it, originally, just on flights of a certain duration. Our story had several consecutive sound bites with pilots, flight attendants, and even smokers who felt they could live with the ban. That told their side of the story. Then the tag line after the last sound bite gave the contrary view:

> **DOBBS:**   *The Air Transport Association, which represents the airlines, opposes the ban. It argues that with flight delays, the law might be hard to interpret, hard to enforce.*

A story about airport security had the Secretary of Transportation telling a committee of Congress:

> **SOT:**   *We need to have the best possible security systems on both the public side of the airport and what is called the back side of the airport, the part the airport passengers seldom see.*

At this point, it was time to use the tag line to tell what he wasn't telling:

> **DOBBS:**   *In hearings just last week, an investigator with the General Accounting Office cited problems in that "back side" of airports, like ID badges missing by the thousands, and unchallenged access for people with no ID badges at all.*

Finally, here's a story we did near Fallon, Nevada, where all the U.S. Navy's carrier pilots occasionally train to attack enemy targets. Ranchers in the remote desert east of Fallon complained about noise and vibrations. One of them said:

SOT: *The problem is, they cannot destroy the very people they have taken an oath and sworn to protect. And they have destroyed this valley and this people.*

The tag line, giving the contrary point of view:

DOBBS: *The Navy has responded to such complaints with restrictions to reduce the noise, like minimum distances and altitudes. But it says certain operations here are a necessary evil.*

This was followed by a sound bite with a Navy spokesman explaining that this valley was the only place where pilots could train in a realistic environment which emulated enemy terrain.

What's the Point?

Telling a story by yourself is difficult enough. In TV and radio it's tougher, because you alone don't dictate its direction. The sound bites play a role too. So you have to blend your narration lines and your sound bites into one seamless script. Leadins and tag lines must connect to the sound bites around them. Continuity is the key.

Exercises to Say It Twice _____

1. **The Never Ending Story**
   You deserve a break today. This is it. If you were covering the bomb blast at the heart of the Never Ending Story, no doubt you'd have some sound bites—with the police chief, with city officials, with frightened residents, maybe even with relatives of the victims (which is an unpleasant but necessary part of some news coverage).

   But you're not covering it, you're just correcting it. There are no changes to make as a result of this chapter. So enjoy your day off! The Never Ending Story will be back. That's why we call it that!

2. **Turning a Quote into a Sound Bite**
   Choose a newspaper story that includes at least three quotes. Most do. Then, rewrite it, but pretend those quotes are sound bites, meaning you actually have recorded these people's voices. Write good leadins and good tag lines, employing the lessons learned in this chapter. When you turn it in to your professor, include both your rewritten piece and the original, clipped from the newspaper. And make it easy for the professor—always a good piece of advice!—by highlighting or otherwise circling the quotes on the original.

3. **If It Ain't Broke, Don't Fix It**
   Find another newspaper article, just like you had to in Exercise 2, and do it again. Practice makes perfect.

4. **Recitation Makes Perfect Too**
   List the principles you should try to use when writing into and out of a sound bite.

6

The Story of the Story

What You'll Learn

Don't think of what you write as a news story. Think of it just as a story. Of course you have to think of yourself as a newsman or newswoman to collect your information and meet your deadline, but you also want to think of yourself as a story teller. This will help you develop a mental picture of your audience, and write for them with the same personal tone a parent uses to address a child when reading a bedtime story. You don't have to actually know who's in your audience; just know that when you're telling your story, someone's listening.

In this chapter, you'll see examples, good and bad. You'll learn how to find the real importance of the story, which may *not* be the most important "hard fact." And you'll learn the role that elements *other* than writing play—a strong start and a strong finish, the value of simplicity, and the impact of pictures, sound, and silence!

The Terms of the Story

Establishing Shot (Establisher)   The opening shot of a piece, setting the scene, showing where something takes place, like a building, a park, a news conference.
Wide Shot   The entire scene in front of the camera.
Closeup   Just one part of the entire scene, in closer detail.
Voiceover   In television (it doesn't apply in radio), video is illustrating the story on the screen, while the anchor's or reporter's voice is narrating, off camera.

Is That the Telephone Ringing?

Have you ever watched or heard a newscast in a bunker, or at least a room with thick, dark shades to block out the light and solid soundproofed walls to keep out the noise? Neither have I. Not often, anyway. Usually, wherever someone's watching television or listening to the radio, there is plenty of light—inviting other people or objects to attract your attention—and plenty of noise to distract you. It's too bad, but a fact of life. What this means to you as a broadcast writer is this: you can't do anything to reduce the external distractions when someone's trying to follow your newscast, but you can do a few things to hold their attention when those external distractions are the competition.

For one thing, you can keep your story simple. The less that people have to actively analyze what they see and hear in a newscast, the better. You want them to absorb it, not wonder about it. As you already have learned in this book, this means simple sentences, simple words.

It also means simple ideas. If you're telling a story, never lose sight of the core of the story. Don't get caught in complicated details. Those are best left to magazines and newspapers, where readers can read and reread something as many times as it takes to understand it. In other words, complexity has no home in broadcasting.

I didn't always understand this, so I didn't always practice it. Here's a script from a story I did on an offshore oil rig about government regulation of the oil industry. See if you can figure out where I went wrong. (By the way, right after the first piece of narration, you'll see the term "NAT SOT," which was defined in the last chapter. In this piece, it means I stop talking and "open" the script for a second or two, and the audience hears nothing but the sound of the oil rig.)

NARRATION

This particular offshore rig represents an investment in the area of 90-million-dollars. It cost the Shell Oil Company and its partners more than 40-million just to lease this site in the sea. Development of the gas deposits—everything you see here and more—roughly 50-million dollars. All this money spent here in the Gulf of Mexico before a single bit of gas here is produced and sold.

NAT SOT NOISE OF RIG

NARRATION

From this platform, they're drilling down some 19-thousand feet, which is part of what makes the process so costly. Many of the gas reserves near the surface, both on land and offshore, already have been developed. Now, the deeper they go, the harder it is, the longer it takes, the more it costs. And, once they reach their depth, they still can't be certain they'll find gas. The industry says there's now a shortage of interstate gas, because regulated prices are unrealistically low.

Is your head spinning yet? Mine is, and I'm the guy who wrote it! But let's keep going.

SOT GEORGE MITCHELL, MITCHELL ENERGY & DEVELOPMENT CORPORATION

The prospects are thinner than before and not as big, so if prospects are smaller, you must have a higher price to do this. And if we have to raise $30-billion instead *of the $10-billion we spent last year, you can see that the money has to come from somewhere to do it.*

NARRATION

But while the industry says we could have more gas if the price were deregulated, a proposal to do that lost last year in the U.S. House of Representatives. One deregulation critic tells why:

SOT REPRESENTATIVE JOHN DINGALL

Because the companies have made a poor case that deregulation will solve the problems, and a poor case as to protecting consumers, as to providing additional supplies or anything other than maximize company earning capacity to the detriment of the consuming public.

Still with us? Still following the thread of the story? That's amazing if you are, because there doesn't seem to be one! Here's the rest.

NARRATION

The Federal Power Commission estimates right now that this year's shortages will exceed last year's by about 25-percent. And while homeowners have the highest priority, stores, factories, even schools have been cut short. The industry says supply is related to price. The question is, do we have to pay more to get more? Greg Dobbs, ABC News in the Louisiana Gulf.

That story is hard to follow for a couple of reasons:

1. It begins with so many facts and figures that it is easy to get lost.

Just look again at the first three sentences:

This particular offshore rig represents an investment in the area of 90-million-dollars. It cost the Shell Oil Company and its partners more than 40-million just to lease this site in the sea. Development of the gas deposits—everything you see here and more—roughly 50-million dollars.

There is a dollar figure in every sentence. Maybe at times this kind of thing is necessary, but not in this story. The key figure that does belong here is "90-million-dollars." The audience doesn't need to know the breakdown ($40-million for the lease, $50-million to develop the deposits).

So how should I have written it to make the key point but not overwhelm the audience? A few possibilities:

This particular Shell Oil offshore rig represents an investment—for the lease and the equipment to drill—of about 90-million-dollars

Or:

> *Shell Oil sank about 90-million-dollars into this offshore rig, for the lease and the equipment to drill.*

Or:

> *Between the lease and the equipment to drill, Shell Oil invested about 90-million-dollars in this offshore rig.*

2. It is more like an education than a story.

It tells (and shows) the audience what it cost Shell to drill, then how they drill, then what they do or don't find. And that is all before the first sound bite! What I failed to do was tell them a story. Here's the real story.

> *Offshore drilling is increasingly costly and because of that, oil companies want to get rid of regulation and raise their prices. Meantime, there's an oil shortage, which already has made oil prices go up. If the industry has its way, will those prices rise even higher?*

Granted, it's an economic story, not an emotional story, but still, it's a story. I didn't think that through when I wrote it. You should. Learn from my mistakes.

And my achievements. This next story goes back a ways, but it sticks in my mind as a good job of storytelling. It's about an execution—the first execution in the United States after a moratorium of almost a decade. The man who would die, a double murderer named Gary Gilmore, sat before a firing squad in an abandoned cannery at the Utah State Prison in January, 1977.

Just read the piece and picture the story. Interestingly, we couldn't even show the key scenes in the story itself. Cameras at executions some day might be allowed, but in 1977 (as today), we had to rely on the descriptions of witnesses and the illustrations of a sketch artist, based on what those witnesses said. Fortunately, we had excellent video of almost everything else described in the script.

You may need a bit of background to understand a few references in the story. For one thing, Gary Gilmore wanted to die. He had spent more than half his 36 years behind bars, and knew the endless misery he'd face awaiting his natural death in prison. Therefore, Gilmore told the civil rights groups that were trying to save his life and extend the death penalty moratorium to quit. For another thing, thanks to a girlfriend who visited him on Death Row, Gilmore was able to obtain sleeping pills twice, and tried to kill himself in his cell. Both times he was discovered, and saved. And lastly, the American Civil Liberties Union was the prime force behind appeals to prevent Gilmore's execution, and was well known by the acronym "A.C.L.U."

As you'll see, there are no verbatims for the sound bites. Quite simply, they have been lost. The story's fairly long for a half-hour newscast, but it was a big story because of its significance: the freeze on capital punishment in America was ending. Remember, read it and try to picture what we showed.

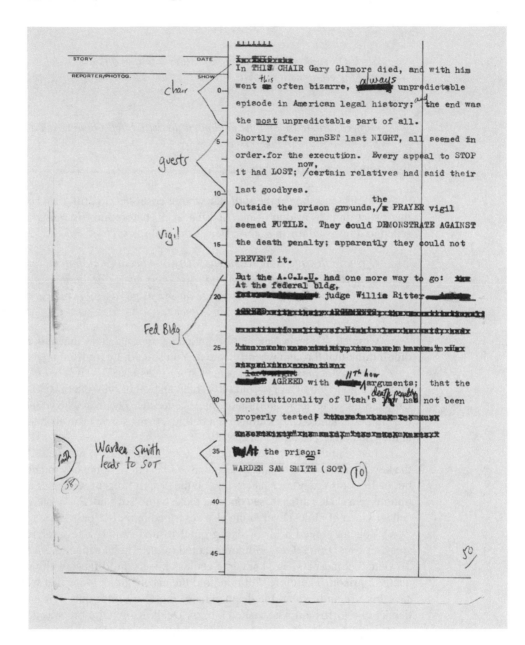

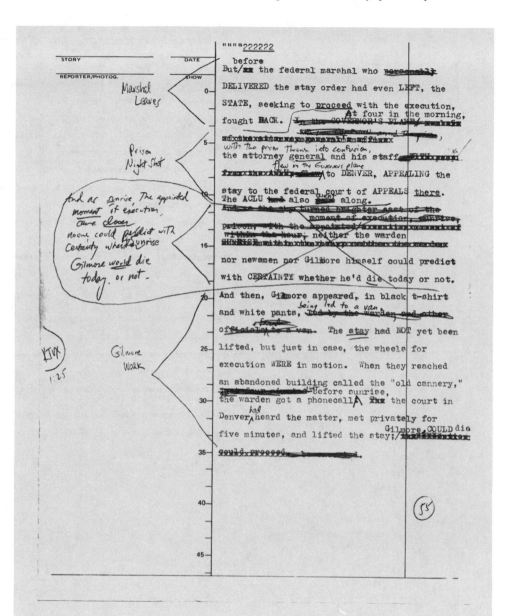

```
""""""??????
          before
But/xx the federal marshal who personally
DELIVERED the stay order had even LEFT, the
STATE, seeking to proceed with the execution,
                          At four in the morning,
fought BACK. In the GOVERNOR'S PLANE, seeking
xxjxxkxxxkkkxxxxxyxxxxxxxxkxmxxxxfxxxxx
with the prison thrown into confusion,
the attorney general and his staff within
                     flew in the Governor's plane
fromxthexkxxkkyxkkaxxxto DENVER, APPEALING the
                            went
stay to the federal court of APPEALS there.
The ACLU had also went along.
Andxxxxhexxkxyxturnedxkaughterxxxxtxxxthe
              moment of execution, couldxx
prisonyxwithxthexappointedxexecutionxxxxxxxx
withinxxthexhourx, neither the warden
xxxExxxxxkkxxxnxxxxxkxxxxxxxxxkkxxxxxkaxwarden
nor newsmen nor Gilmore himself could predict
with CERTAINTY whether he'd die today or not.

And then, Gilmore appeared, in black t-shirt
                   being led to a van
and white pants, led by the warden and other
       few
officialsxtoxaxvan.  The stay had NOT yet been
lifted, but just in case, the wheels for
execution WERE in motion.  When they reached
an abandoned building called the "old cannery,"
xxxxfxxxxxxxxxxxBefore sunrise,
the warden got a phonecall.  The the court in
         had
Denver, heard the matter, met privately for
                              Gilmore, COULD die
five minutes, and lifted the stay; xxxxxxxxxxxx
xxxxxxxxxxxxx xxxxxxxxxxx.
```

Handwritten annotations on the left:

Marshal
Leaves

0

Prison
Night Shot

5

And as sunrise, The appointed
moment if execution,
came closer
noone could predict with
certainty whether sunrise
Gilmore would die
today or not.

10

15

20

Gilmore
Walk

KTVX
1:25

25

30

35

40

45

(55)

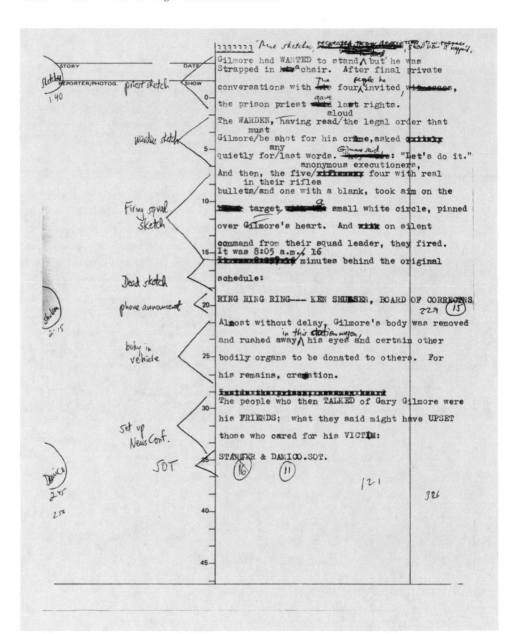

Gilmore had WANTED to stand but he was
Strapped in a chair. After final private
conversations with the four invited people he
the prison priest gave last rights.
The WARDEN, having read aloud the legal order that
Gilmore must be shot for his crime, asked
quietly for any last words. Gilmore said: "Let's do it."
And then, the five anonymous executioners,
four with real bullets in their rifles
and one with a blank, took aim on the
target, a small white circle, pinned
over Gilmore's heart. And on silent
command from their squad leader, they fired.
It was 8:05 a.m., 16
minutes behind the original
schedule:

RING RING RING--- KEN SHULSEN, BOARD OF CORRECTNS

Almost without delay, Gilmore's body was removed
and rushed away in this station wagon, his eyes and certain other
bodily organs to be donated to others. For
his remains, cremation.

The people who then TALKED of Gary Gilmore were
his FRIENDS; what they said might have UPSET
those who cared for his VICTIM:

STANGER & DAMICO.SOT.

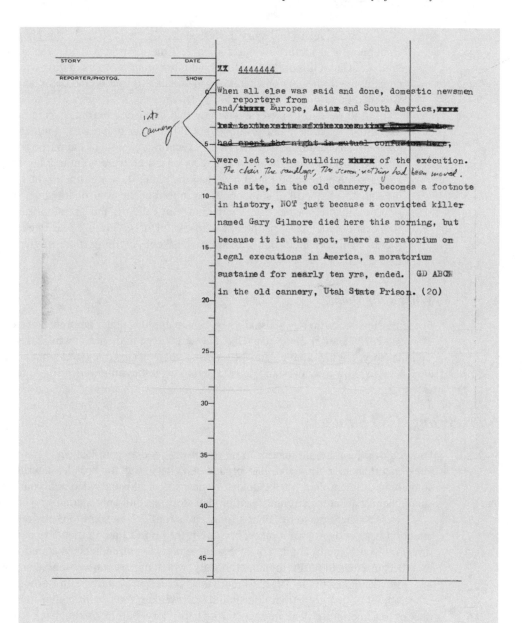

XX 4444444

into
Cannery

When all else was said and done, domestic newsmen
reporters from
and/ꭗꭗꭗꭗ Europe, Asiaꭗ and South America, ꭗꭗꭗꭗ
ꭗꭗꭗꭗꭗꭗꭗꭗꭗꭗꭗꭗꭗꭗꭗꭗꭗꭗꭗꭗꭗ ~~had spent the night in mutual confusion here,~~
were led to the building ꭗꭗꭗ of the execution.
The chair, The sandbags, The screen; nothing had been moved.
This site, in the old cannery, becomes a footnote
in history, NOT just because a convicted killer
named Gary Gilmore died here this morning, but
because it is the spot, where a moratorium on
legal executions in America, a moratorium
sustained for nearly ten yrs, ended.   GD ABCN
in the old cannery, Utah State Prison. (20)

You can see in that story the lessons you've read so far in this chapter. We had something of a picture of our audience: Americans who had been following the drama of Gary Gilmore's case for about three months, now wanting to know as they came home from work and sat down to dinner if it finally had come to an end. That was their question; we tried to answer it.

And we had to cover everything that happened before, during, and after the execution, yet keep the idea simple. I could have written reams of material about the eleventh hour arguments to delay the execution, explained the purpose of four bullets and a blank (it was to allow an executioner—all were volunteer law enforcement officers—to believe he might have had the blank if, some time in the future, he regrets that he helped kill somebody), even told of the controversy over the distribution of Gilmore's ashes after cremation. But I didn't. The simple idea of the story was that despite some people's exhaustive efforts, Gilmore was executed and the moratorium on capital punishment was broken. Anything more might have been a distraction.

What's the Point?

For television and radio news, usually you cannot duplicate the comprehensive offerings of *The New York Times* or *Time* magazine. If you try, your audience can miss the main point. Tell the story, not the details. How? By asking yourself this question: what does the audience *need* to know to understand, as opposed to what they might *also* find interesting?

Start Strong, End Strong

Did you ever hear the old maxim "You're only as good as your last act"? It's true, for athletes, entertainers, politicians, *and* broadcast writers. But for broadcast writers it means something different than for the others. It means your closing video and your closing line should be just about the strongest part of your story, second only, perhaps, to how you start.

Here's what I mean by "start strong, end strong." You want to grab your audience's attention right at the top of a piece, because if they don't tune in mentally at the top, they probably won't tune in at all. You also want to revive your audience's attention at the bottom, because then they'll remember the story, which means you've done your job.

Incidentally, not all broadcast journalists agree, particularly with starting strong. The other school of thought is that you should start weaker, then *build,* either to a closing climax or to some sort of peak midway through the story, before sinking back to dullsville at the end. My bias is, this can lead to uninteresting establishing shots of buildings, highways, or people walking along sidewalks. Does that advance anyone's understanding of a story? Is it going to grab anyone's attention?

On a few occasions, yes, if for example it's a story about, say, termites infesting an historic building. You might want to visually establish the building in a wide shot at the top of the piece before going to closeups of the termites that are slowly eating it! That might get the audience's attention. And of course when you're writing a script for an anchorman's voiceover rather than for a reporter's package, there's less opportunity to "build to a climax" and it might make more sense to begin with shots that establish the whole scene. But still, the most effective stories on TV are those that start strong.

The same lesson applies to the first words you write. For one thing, ideally they will be dictated by your opening shot (rather than the other way around), which is why it's important to choose something interesting, even dramatic if possible. For another, they will catch the audience's ears while your video catches their eyes. Interesting is interesting, dull is dull. Know the difference, and think about it every time you start and end a story. There will be more about choosing your lead and choosing your close in the chapters cleverly entitled "Choosing Your Lead" and "Choosing Your Close" (Chapters 8 and 9).

Here are a few examples. First I'll give you the leads as I wrote and narrated them, then, "what might have been."

There was an epidemic of arson in a lumber mill town in eastern Washington. Two churches, an elementary school . . . six fires altogether. Finally the police caught a man, who confessed. The opening line was:

> *For the first time in two-and-a-half months, these children today can breathe a little easier.*

I chose to begin with the little kids of Omak, Washington. Why? Because cute kids are a natural draw. Cute kids in danger, even more. That's why this worked better than something more conventional like:

> *Police have caught a 23-year-old local man, who has confessed to the fires that have plagued this town for two-and-a-half months.*

A Kuwaiti Airlines 747 was hijacked and eventually sat for days at the airport in Algiers in North Africa, idled by a standoff between the hijackers and negotiators for the Algerian government. Midway through the crisis, the hijackers demanded new negotiators: journalists. So the story started this way:

> **DOBBS:**   *A hijacker spoke on the cockpit radio.*

> **HIJACKER SOT:**   *We need one Algerian journalist and two foreign journalists . . .*

For Americans who had been following the story, the hijackers were a mysterious group to which we couldn't put a face. Opening the story this way didn't give them a face but it did give them a voice. This would fascinate the audience, a lot better than a more predictable lead like:

> *The hijackers of the Kuwaiti 747, frustrated by their standoff with Algerian negotiators, today demanded that journalists enter the aircraft to negotiate with them.*

Forest fires were spreading out of control in the Sierra Nevada mountains of northern California. They threatened homes near the towns of Grass Valley and Nevada City. The lead sentence was:

> *This fire has more than tripled in size, just since last night.*

What I figured was, this incredible and scary statistic would be enough to get you to put aside your book and look. The dramatic video at that point would hold you for the duration of the story. Better to reach out and grab the audience than to use the old tried-and-true,

More than 15-thousand acres have burned now, and 30 homes have been destroyed.

This final example was a medical feature story about a new advance in X-ray technology, which gave doctors a real-time view of a trauma patient's blood flow. Pretty dry stuff, and fairly complicated, unless you lead with pictures and words that make the story feel more like an episode of the long running TV drama, *ER:*

The trick in the case of trauma has always been to trim time, to diagnose and save the patient, when his body is trying hard to die.

Having camped out for a while in the emergency room of the University of New Mexico Hospital, we had footage of several trauma patients close to death. When one became a candidate for this new technology, we had our lead. That's so much better than the kind of lead you might find in a medical journal but shouldn't hear on television:

Researchers have invented a new kind of X-Ray machine that . . .

It's easier to come up with a dynamite open than with a dynamite close. From the standpoint of video, this is because if you have something compelling, you're not going to want to save it for the end. That's why often we try to close with what we call a "beauty shot"—the proverbial sunset, the train disappearing down the tracks, the flag flapping in the wind. It's a little tough to end a story about a city council hearing this way, but when you can, try to come up with a shot that wraps up the story in one nice little bow. Or, since you're only as good as your last act, a shot people will remember.

As for your script, you want to leave people with some sense of what the whole story means, or where the story is going, or with a simple summary; you'll read more about how to figure this out in Chapter 9. But for now, I just want to tell you about the single strongest closing lines I ever heard. It was many years ago after a fire started in the kitchen of a nightclub in Covington, Kentucky, just across the Ohio River from Cincinnati. By the time several hundred customers smelled smoke, it was too late for an orderly evacuation, and they rushed to the three double-door exits. The trouble was, the doors opened *inward.* By the time the first people at each set of doors tried to pull them open, the crush behind them was too strong. The doors might as well have been chained shut. More than a hundred people died, some from burns, some from smoke inhalation.

What we learned was local fire authorities already had warned this business and others that all fire exit doors should open outward, not inward. But city officials, wary of imposing major expenses on local business owners, hadn't made it the law. So the owners of the nightclub hadn't made the change. Therefore it seemed that the owners, the fire authorities, and city officials all had shirked their responsibility.

I was there doing a sidebar story specifically about fire regulations, but ABC News's anchorman at the time, the late Frank Reynolds, had flown in to report the story of the fire itself. And after telling of its toll, its cause, and the many people who could have prevented it, he ended his report with four unforgettable words:

So simple. So sad.

What's the Point?

I don't think there's a better summary for this section than a couple of lines from the early part, "interesting is interesting, dull is dull." If you want to hold your audience from top to bottom, know the difference, and think about it—be strong, be interesting—every time you start and end a story.

The Sounds of Silence

Some of the best moments in radio or television news come when the reporter or anchorperson stops talking. Really! Not because it's such a relief to have an end to the yakking, but because if the reporter or anchor stops talking, it's probably because there's other sound that's more effective. Maybe a conventional sound bite, but even better, maybe NAT SOT. So "silence" doesn't really mean silence; it just means the reporter goes silent long enough for other sound to fit in.

If you are covering a story about a fire in an apartment building, and you have sound (and picture for TV) of a woman standing on a balcony holding her baby and screaming with terror, "Help us, help us, we're gonna die," you wouldn't just run non-stop narration, would you? No, you'd "open the piece for natural sound." That woman isn't just part of the story, she *is* the story. Sure, you have to report how many fire trucks were there and what caused the fire and how many were killed or injured, but what you can do so much better than a print reporter is convey the emotion of the moment—in this case, the woman's fear, and perhaps the firefighters' desperation to rescue her. It's all in the sound of her voice.

The best use of natural sound in my experience was in the story you read about the earthquake in Italy back in Chapter 4. Do you remember? Days after the quake, a woman named Lisa was rescued from under the rubble, after all others who were missing from the town were given up for dead.

What you read in that chapter was that "for six hours, stick by stick, stone by stone, rescuers dug to save her. If they broke the wrong stick or moved the wrong stone, the whole pile of rubble might have collapsed, burying Lisa even deeper, and them on top of her."

Well, it's even better to let the audience see it and hear it, so that's what we did all the way through the story, allowing the NAT SOT sections to run several seconds long, at least. Pictures and sound would chill the viewers; my words would just fill in the holes. The script, by the way, was scribbled on a notepad while speeding in a helicopter back to Naples, where we'd edit.

As you read the script, reproduced below, you can race through the words but try to imagine what you're seeing and hearing in the pauses; this is the heart of the story.

NAT SOT WEAK MOANING

DOBBS: *Somewhere down there is a woman named Lisa. Her cries were heard by rescuers as they were digging out bodies this morning from the ruins of Laviano.*

NAT SOT SHOVELS IN RUBBLE

Stick by stick, stone by stone, they dug to save her. Move the wrong stone though and their own precarious position could collapse, burying them, as well as Lisa, down below.

NAT SOT TWO HANDS SLOWLY, GINGERLY BREAKING A SINGLE TWIG

DOBBS: *This rescue worker cut up his face but said, "I touched Lisa's hand, my blood doesn't matter." And soon, they could touch Lisa's face. 64 hours she had been buried, in the dark, in the dust . . .*

NAT SOT WORKER CLEARING BIGGER HOLE WITH HIS HANDS

DOBBS: *. . . her older sister dead on top of her. All of her family is dead now, but Lisa, today, has been saved.*

NAT SOT PULLING LISA FROM HOLE

DOBBS: *Laviano though cannot be saved. One man told me today, "Laviano doesn't exist any more." 15-hundred lived here Sunday. When the survivors gathered together after the disaster, they counted only three-hundred. Still, for the survivors and the rescue workers from elsewhere in Italy, there is a lot of gruesome work to do. Most of those presumed dead, after three days, have yet to be removed from the rubble. The smell of death here has yet to go away.*

NAT SOT MORE SHOVELS

DOBBS: *As corpses are dug out—and as quickly as they are removed, more are discovered—they are carried to what was Laviano's public square.*

NAT SOT WOMAN CRYING OVER OPEN COFFIN

DOBBS: *If possible they are identified, then sealed away . . . as they died.*

NAT SOT HANDS CLOSE COFFIN

DOBBS ON CAMERA: *For Laviano's survivors, there is only a past here now. No future. In all these remote devastated valleys in southern Italy, there is no money to rebuild, nobody to even comfort the survivors, as all those left are suffering equally.*

NAT SOT WOMAN CRYING

DOBBS: *The village is destroyed. Most people are dead. Lisa? Lucky. Maybe. Greg Dobbs, ABC News, Laviano, Italy.*

What's the Point?

One way to put it is, let your story breathe. Another way is, when you have good NAT SOT, shut up! You're in broadcasting, not print. Use the tools you have. That's how you'll maximize the impact.

Exercises to Test Your Judgment

1. At the Heart of Good Writing
    You have covered a tour your mayor has taken of an inner city slum housing project, part of her campaign to convince the city council to spend another $50-million for clean, modern, low cost housing. Here are the notes you have made:

    - Crime rate in slum housing is three times the rest of the city
    - Mayor asked council for extra $50 million for new low cost housing
    - Average residents' income below poverty level
    - Current housing built in 1960s
    - Local high school has highest dropout rate in city
    - Some council members want extra money spent instead on more police
    - Cockroaches outnumber inhabitants in slum housing
    - Slum housing has highest population density in entire state
    - Children afraid to play in slum housing courtyards
    - New housing would be modeled after successful projects in Cleveland
    - Mayor made promise during campaign to destroy old slum housing

    And you have the following video:

    - Long shot of slum housing project
    - Cockroaches gathered on resident's kitchen counter
    - Mayor looking up at biggest existing slum building
    - Teenagers hanging out on street corner
    - Parking lot full of old rusty cars
    - File footage of the mayor speaking during her election campaign
    - Mayor hugging 4-year-old who lives in slum housing
    - Still photos of successful Cleveland project
    - Closeups of broken windows, graffiti
    - Mayor chips away at deteriorating paint with hand
    - Mayor shakes hands with adult residents

    The exercise is to write a television report about the mayor's tour. Don't worry about format (we'll cover that later), sound bites or anything else. The point here is to start strong and end strong—to choose a lead and a close for your story, in words and picture, that will appeal to the audience. A lead and a close that will capture the heart of the story (and of the audience), as only TV and radio can do.

The practice of effectively marrying words to pictures will come up in Chapter 14, "Letting It All Hang Out." But with a strong top and a strong bottom as your goal, include a notation about the shot with which you'd open, and the shot with which you'd close. The purpose here is to start to "think picture." Make the whole piece forty-five seconds long.

2. The Never Ending Story

Here it is again, the Never Ending Story. Rewriting it this time requires more than a good grasp of the mechanics of writing. This time, it's about judgment: finding the core of the story, figuring out what your audience wants and needs to know, and starting and ending strong.

> In a place where a rear-ender traffic accident is usually the biggest event of the day, there has been an event with an impact on everyone. Tonight the lives of three people have been claimed by a bomb, which set off a three-alarm fire that raised temperatures to almost 200-degrees at a clothing in the heart of Fort Stutter, California, the police say. No group has taken credit for the blast, but forensics experts tonight are combing the scene of the attack. In case there is more danger there, a hazardous material team is dispatched to the scene. To explain why there was not a warning, the police chief of the city of Fort Stutter, Jazibeauz Perez (JAZZ-uh-boo PEAR-ehz), says there was definitely no sign that the bomb was going to explode, then he said, "Everyone wishes to God we'd known this was going to transpire." The police department hasn't asked the F-B-I for help, the chief says. The dead include Jason Jones, Sally Smyth (Smith), and Greg Goldstein (GOLD-steen). None were employees at the bombed store. Two unidentified men are in critical condition, meaning they might die too. Everyone in Fort Stutter is scared now to go out on the street, and city officials say increased protection will cost the people of Fort Stutter a lot of money, more than six million dollars. There is no date set for a decision about spending that amount of money, but the mayor cannot be back in town by Tuesday, which is not early enough for her critics. Whether it really will be helpful remains to be seen.

II

But Before You Write . . .

7

Organizing Your Facts, Organizing Your Story

What You'll Learn _____

Maybe you're one of those people who, when talking on the telephone, works from a casually compiled list of points. Why? Because you don't want to forget something significant. If you're not like that, chances are that you've been on the phone with someone who is. I do it all the time, when the call is important in my work. Better safe than sorry!

When you're writing a news story, it's equally critical that you ensure against forgetting important information. How? The same way, by organizing your notes right before you begin to write. If you don't, then you can't proceed to the central step: selecting a logical sequence to tell the story. Furthermore, if you don't get organized, and you depend instead strictly on your memory, well . . . oh my, I forget what I wanted to tell you. Sure, I'm only kidding here, but if you've ever thought of something later that you wish you had said earlier, you should pay close attention to the tips you'll get in this chapter.

Organized notes are like a blueprint, or a road map. They help you get where you want to go. Organized notes mean an organized story. They'll not only help you remember every point you want to make, but they'll also help you choose a lead and choose a close (some sort of conclusion). Furthermore, they'll help you communicate your most important information in a sensible sequence. And maybe most important, reviewing everything you've learned in an organized way—which you're able to do simply by creating the notes, let alone rereading them—will help you make some of the toughest decisions journalists in any medium have to make: what to exclude from your story.

This chapter is about organizing yourself so you can organize your work. It's about the processes that will help ensure that a broadcast story has a strong beginning, an illustrative and logical middle, and a meaningful end.

The Terms of the Story _____

Wirecopy   Stories you have printed out or brought up on your computer screen from wire services like The Associated Press and Reuters.

Standup Close   The reporter appearing on camera at the end of the story.

Bridge   A portion of the story that appears somewhere in the middle of the piece rather than at the beginning or the end—a bridge between the beginning and the end.

Giving New Meaning to "Running to the Bathroom"

Sometimes you don't want to intimidate your interviewee by taking notes, so you store everything in your head until the interview ends, then rush into a bathroom to write it all down! By the time you finish personally covering a story in the field (or by telephone from the newsroom), you may have a half dozen or more sources of information: wirecopy, newspaper reports, telephone interview notes, printouts from the Internet, verbatim texts of nice sound bites from recorded interviews, memories of people you've heard and scenes you've seen. You might have observations you've scribbled on the backs of restaurant receipts, on pages you've torn from airline magazines, or even on toilet paper. It's better, of course, if you always have a pocket-size notepad at the ready, but people who are that organized probably gravitate to careers in empirical fields like math and science, not journalism.

   Take a look at the script below, from a two-part story on a rape epidemic in San Antonio, Texas. Rape itself is newsworthy, but what really attracted our attention was that the victims were young girls, not grown women, and the rapists apparently were just young boys.

   As you read through the script, consider this: it reflects articles culled from San Antonio newspapers, statistics sent from federal offices, telephone conversations with officials in several city, state and federal agencies, off-camera face-to-face conversations with more government officials as well as rape victims, on-camera interviews with victims, relatives, counselors, and even more officials. We rode overnight with the police and we entered the scene of the crime: vacant apartments in a rape-ridden housing project. And it all came down to this script; read it aloud and you'll better absorb it for the lessons that follow. As you read, ask yourself how *you* would have kept all the sources of information organized.

Children Raped and Raping

NARRATION

For years now, although home to hundreds of kids, this has been one of San Antonio's most dangerous low income housing projects. Host to drugs, prostitution, violence. Now, another blight: youngsters, preteens apparently called "The Sexy Boys," sexually assaulting young girls.

SOT CYNTHIA MCCARTY/SCHOOL COUNSELOR

I have heard nightmare stories. And I have held children on my lap and cried with them, because it hurts so bad to hear the stories that they have told.

NARRATION

The stories say, girls have been lured—usually by boys they know—into vacant apartments in the project. Disrepair in places like this provides not just a safe haven for sexual assault, but part of its cause.

SOT JUDGE TOM RICKHOFF/SAN ANTONIO JUVENILE COURT

It tells you the image it projects to society. And if it tells people it's a slovenly place and there's glass all over the place, what do you think it says to all the children that show up there? It tells them that's how life should be.

NARRATION

Police reports suggest that for the boys, raping younger girls is a new kind of ganglike rite of initiation. At the nearby elementary school, confirmation: many more reports this year than last year. Nationwide, adolescents now account for 30-percent of rape arrests!

SOT TERRY PRINCE/VICTIM'S MOTHER

It broke my heart. . . . .

NARRATION

Terry Prince is the mother of one 10-year-old victim.

MORE SOT TERRY PRINCE

They molested a lot of the girls. They fondled. They threatened them. They did a lot. They scared 'em.

NARRATION

The consensus of experts is, victims of sexual abuse—girls and boys—stand at high risk of turning into abusers themselves. It becomes a vicious cycle. But across the country, youngsters caught up in it are not just written off. There are creative efforts to break this cycle of sexual assault.

NAT SOT AT COUNSELING SESSION

Are the boys still messing with you baby?. . . . .

NARRATION

That is the question from the counselor at the elementary school where some twenty young girls recently have been assaulted by young boys in their neighborhood.

NAT SOT COUNSELOR

Is it your fault? (Girls) No! (Counselor) Noooooo!

NARRATION

She role-plays with the victims.

NAT SOT AT COUNSELING SESSION

(Counselor) What did you do when they started messing with you?
(Girl) I went and told you.
(Counselor) Very good. How did you get away from those boys?
(Girl) I ran.
(Counselor) You ran? You did the right thing!

NARRATION

Elsewhere, experts from the local rape crisis center visit schools not to counsel, but to educate.

SOT GRACE DAVIS AT HIGH SCHOOL

What I want to know from you is, what is your definition of rape?

(continued)

Children Raped and Raping Continued

NARRATION

Students learn that rape doesn't have to be intercourse to be illegal, and harmful.

MORE SOT GRACE DAVIS

If he touches your breast, does that make a big difference? Has anyone been hurt? Well, some people might say no, but if inside it makes you feel bad, then there's something wrong with that.

SOT SHERRI SUNAZ/ALAMA AREA RAPE CRISIS CENTER

I think a lot of adults want to look at it as playing doctor or a normal part of development. Children sexually assaulting other children is not a normal part of development.

NARRATION

Another group called "Avance," working in the poorest parts of town, teaches parenting to combat one cause of adolescent rape: parental neglect.

NAT SOT FROM AVANCE CLASS

The children here are in great need of love, attention . . .

NARRATION

Mothers learn here to nurture their children.

SOT VIRGINIA GARCIA/STUDENT-PARENT

It's different now. It's not a power struggle. It's communication, and in a way it gets us ready for society.

DOBBS ON CAMERA

None of these approaches is considered a cure. Not for the abuser, or the abused. But the theory is, if shown other ways to deal with frustration and abuse, people might make better choices. And the cycle of sexual assault may be broken. Greg Dobbs, ABC News, San Antonio.

To do this story, my team and I learned and saw and videotaped a lot more than we could possibly squeeze into the roughly four-minute hole our piece would fill in *Good Morning America*. Yet we had to learn and shoot everything pertinent, because the only way to make sure you get all the information you need to cover your story right is to treat it, time permitting, as if it is going to be an hour-long documentary.

Was every piece of information given to us in a logical sequence? Not at all. Was everyone we talked to clear and concise? Not even close. Was each fact we picked up in our research central to the story we wanted to tell? Not by a longshot. Was every scene full of color and action, and every sound bite compelling? Only in our dreams.

What's the Point?

The point is, we had to make cuts. We had to decide what information we didn't need, and what video and audio we couldn't use. Read on.

Figuring Out What to Keep, What to Cut

The easiest way to figure out what to cut is by being organized. For this rape story, the first thing to do after shooting and viewing our tapes was to pull together all those notes on the disparate scraps of paper I described earlier in the chapter, and transfer them to my computer.

Once I started, there was no immediate need to put them down in any kind of prioritized order. Thanks to the "cut and paste" function in my word processing program, that would come later. No, it was just a matter of getting them down in black and white: the names and titles of people I had interviewed; a verbatim account of the on-camera standup close that I did at the housing project; verbatims of all the sound bites (SOT and NAT SOT) that I liked when I viewed the video tapes; facts about the program called "Avance" from the National Adolescent Perpetrator Network, the Baylor University Adolescent Sex Offender Program, and the National Coalition Against Sexual Assault; relevant federal government and municipal crime and poverty statistics; plus interesting comments from people with whom I spoke and observations about people about whom I read. And of course, words and phrases I had jotted down while working the story in San Antonio, thinking they might be useful in the piece. "Another blight" was one of them, "vicious cycle" was another.

In short, you start out with dozens of disconnected observations and impressions but end up with a few pages of neat notes. Then you cut and paste them into logical categories. Also, you isolate the verbatims of all your probable sound bites, not only to make it easy to find the ones you want to use, but also to read through them as you're writing to glean script information from what an interviewee told you. You don't have to actually show someone in your piece to make use of what he knows.

Once you've done all that, the fun begins.

What's fun? First, choosing your lead. Since you'll learn in depth in the next chapter how to choose the best leads, I won't go into it now, except to say that once you've reduced all your work to a few well organized pages of print, usually the lead will jump out at you as the obvious choice. For this rape story, one of the notes said, "Rigsby Apartments: drugs, violence, prostitution tolerated. No evictions." Another simply said, "The Sexy Boys." Put them together and it sets up the whole story. Bingo.

Then, choosing your close. Obviously in the case of this story in San Antonio, I locked down the close in the field by doing it on-camera at the scene (more about that in Chapter 15). But if the on-camera portion of a story is designed to play as a bridge, then you should choose your voiceover close the same way you chose your lead: by reading through your notes and seeing what works best—what will you say that tells the audience what the story means, or how someone is solving it, or where it's going from here? (In the San Antonio story, I opted for the "solution": prevention and education programs.) You should have learned enough about your story by the time you're writing it to make the choice obvious.

Next are those tough decisions I mentioned earlier. All those conversations, all that reading, all those interviews, three days in San Antonio . . . it couldn't all fit into a few precious minutes of air time. So I went through the organized notes and started striking. "700

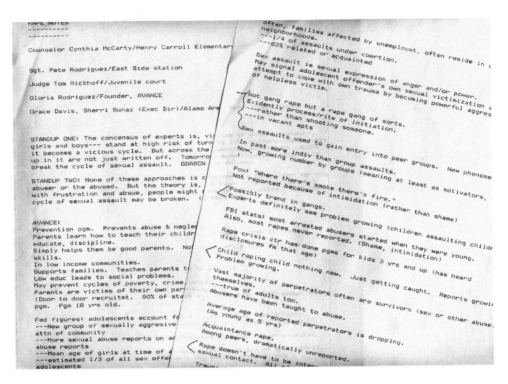

The first couple of pages of organized notes.

prevention programs nationally"; interesting, but less important than a brief description of just two or three. Perpetrators "as young as 5 years"; shocking, but not necessary to communicate this horrible trend. "83% related or acquainted"; that of course became the line, "Girls have been lured—usually by boys they know . . ." Most of my notes never made it into the script. But if I hadn't gone through the process, I wouldn't have known with conviction what to eventually include.

Finally, filling in the middle. This definitely is not as easy as it will sound here, but if you know how you're going to begin your piece, and you know how it's going to end, then it's just a matter of going through those well organized notes you've created and building a logical path from "point A" to "point Z."

Remember, it's all about telling a story. Simple? No. Better than any other way? Absolutely. That's how I chose the first sound bite in the rape story, for instance. After naming "The Sexy Boys" near the end of the first part of the script, it made sense to have the school counselor set the tone about "nightmare stories." As the cliché goes, the story then wrote itself.

What's the Point?

If you don't organize your notes and look through them before sitting down to write, you stand the chance of choosing a lead or a close based on something that stands out in your mind at the moment but isn't necessarily the best choice. You also stand the chance of building a disjointed piece because you are working without blueprints.

What to Note After the Notes

Working from well organized notes is only the framework for what you write. Think of those notes in fact as a picture frame; you still have to paint in the picture—the lead, the close, the sound bites, the natural sound, the emotions, the explanations, and everything else that belongs on the canvas. This is the most important part.

So let me carry you through the process of prioritizing your notes, not from most important to least important, but in the logical manner that the task of writing and editing a story requires: from the beginning of the story to the end. For an example, I'll use an event in Moscow way back when the Iron Curtain still hung darkly over eastern Europe, and today's Russia was merely the core of the Communist superpower, the Soviet Union. The Soviet leader, Mikhail Gorbachev, had just traveled to Geneva, Switzerland, to meet the American President, Ronald Reagan. This first meeting of these two men was a milestone that ultimately led to the fall of the Soviet Empire and the end of the Cold War.

I won't bother showing you the notes I excluded from the story; by the time I wrote my short piece for ABC's *World News Tonight* (allotted just a minute and ten seconds on what was a very busy day), that part of the process had passed. But here are the notes from which I ended up working, in the order they were written in my notepad. You may not understand my shorthand, but it'll be clear when you read the final script. The assignment for the story was pretty straightforward—report on how the summit is playing in Moscow.

- RR never on TV, always war monger in Sov press
- RR normally in bad light
- Forn Ministry: "No promises." No one knows how will end
- Sov Forn Ministry anti-Amer rhetoric ctr
- Gorb 2nd ever spontaneous n.c., both seen
- Never done in USSR
- Summit substance thin, photo ops, get to know
- US admin didn't want create expectations
- RR speech uncut, undelayed
- Gorb wife: not invisible but 1st time alone on TV

As for sound bites, thanks to the momentous nature of the event, we were allowed by our "minders"—the Soviet government officials who accompanied us almost everywhere we went with a camera—to stand in Moscow's colorful *Arbat* neighborhood, near the center of the capital, where we most likely would find Russians who speak English. We would ask them what they thought about what they had seen of the summit. From the answers we got from citizens on camera, I isolated the following:

- "I think President Reagan is a very wonderful actor."
- (Question) "Do you like him any more than maybe you did before?" (Answer) "I would like to like him more."
- "He is a very charming person."

And from two officials we were allowed to interview, I isolated these sound bites:

- "We do not expect these concrete agreements from this meeting. We expect Gorbachev and Reagan to meet, and that is enough. Only you Americans expect everything to happen tomorrow." (from a worker at the Soviet Foreign Ministry)
- (Question) "Are you disappointed that it looks like there will be no agreements between the U.S. and the Soviet Union to reduce the threat of nuclear arms, or to find ways to reduce the tension between the two superpowers?" (Answer) "No, Mr. Gorbachev did not go to Geneva to fight President Reagan about our differences. He went there to meet President Reagan. That alone is good for both countries." (from the editor of the Communist Party newspaper)

After excluding what I knew we could not use in the story, the ten bullet points and the five sound bites I've already listed were all that was left. Everything would come from those ingredients.

The first order of business was to find the lead. Well, the winner happened to be the first bullet point—"RR never on TV, always war monger in Sov press." What this meant was, Ronald Reagan often had been discussed harshly on Soviet Television (and in Soviet newspapers) where the government completely controlled content. Never before had his picture been shown.

I'd been in Moscow enough in the past to recognize this remarkable shift; by letting its people see that the American president was just a human being who put his pants on one leg at a time like the rest of us, the world's most propagandistic media never again could portray Reagan as they had for so long, a bloodthirsty war-mongering devil incarnate. I imagine many Soviet citizens truly were surprised to see that the leader of the free world didn't have horns! All I had to do was summarize that in a single sentence.

What's more, it had to be merged with the fourth bullet point: "Sov Forn Ministry anti-Amer rhetoric ctr," because the fact that I had watched Reagan on a television set in the Soviet Foreign Ministry, which had always inspired the communist country's anti-American propaganda machine, made the whole thing even more remarkable.

Finally, if the story was going to characterize the unprecedented way Soviet television covered the summit for its viewers, I had to underscore Reagan's appearance with the ninth bullet point: "RR speech uncut, undelayed."

Thus, the opening sentence, the story's "lead":

NARRATION

This was a strange sight today here at the Soviet Foreign Ministry, where anti-American rhetoric sometimes crests—this morning's speech by the President of the United States, uncut, and aired without delay.

Of course this lead was dictated by something else too: the picture (more about the role of video in determining your lead in Chapter 8). If the most remarkable thing about this day in Moscow was the appearance of an American president on Soviet television, then that's how the story should start visually. Happily, the best video and the key information coincided.

Since I had been given less than a minute-and-a-quarter for the piece to air, and since I knew I wanted to use several sound bites so the audience could hear the thoughts of real Soviet citizens and not just this reporter's impression of their thoughts, it was already time to use sound (those seconds tick away awfully fast). And since the assignment was to report on how the summit played in Moscow, the first sound in the story should be common citizens, not public officials. So we used those three "man-on-the-street" interviews I had already isolated. It was just a matter of putting them in the most seamless order possible.

Thus, the story's logical progression:

NARRATION

This was a strange sight today here at the Soviet Foreign Ministry, where anti-American rhetoric sometimes crests—this morning's speech by the President of the United States, uncut, and aired without delay. Peoples' impressions?

> ***SOT MAN-ON-THE-STREET #1:***   *He is a very charming person.*
> ***SOT MAN-ON-THE-STREET #2:***   *I think President Reagan is a very wonderful actor.*
> ***SOT MAN-ON-THE-STREET #3:***   *(Question) "Do you like him any more than maybe you did before?" (Answer) "I would like to like him more."*

Second only to seeing the President of the United States on their televisions for the first time was the specter of seeing their own leader, Chairman Gorbachev, answering questions from potentially aggressive foreign reporters whose jobs and well-being didn't depend on him ("Gorb 2nd ever spontaneous n.c., both seen" and "Never done in USSR"). It was logical to construct the piece in the same order:

NARRATION

Just seeing President Reagan without harsh rhetoric is one novelty for Soviets from the summit. Another was seeing their own leader, for only the second time ever, in a spontaneous news conference . . . which he has still never held here in his own country.

Finally, since we had that final bullet point about Mrs. Gorbachev—"Gorb wife: not invisible but 1st time alone on TV"—as well as video of her with Mrs. Reagan in Geneva voiced over by a Soviet anchorman, I got in one line about the Soviet leader's wife, using NAT SOT of the anchorman to separate it from the line about her husband:

NAT SOT SOV ANNOUNCER

NARRATION

And there has been the novelty of the Soviet first lady . . . for the first time ever, featured in her own right.

So far, so good. Short though it is, the story is covering all the bases I needed to cover, and moving logically from one point to another. But remember, the assignment was to tell our viewers how the summit was playing in Moscow. So the story had to shift from wonderment to wondering. Since this first Reagan–Gorbachev meeting was producing little more than a personal relationship ("Summit substance thin, photo ops, get to know"), did Soviets care? That was the point I had decided to end with in my close. To do it, I used two techniques: one more sound bite basically answering the question, this time with a government official, and a close that incorporated the heart of another sound bite:

NARRATION

And there has been the novelty of the Soviet first lady . . . for the first time ever, featured in her own right. But as for substance from the summit, were Soviets disappointed?

SOT NEWSPAPER EDITOR

No, Mr. Gorbachev did not go to Geneva to fight President Reagan about our differences. He went there to meet President Reagan. That alone is good for both countries.

NARRATION

So, what do the Soviet people think of the summit? One man at the foreign ministry said he was disappointed, but not surprised at the lack of major concrete agreements. "Only you Americans" he told me, "expect everything to happen tomorrow!" Greg Dobbs, ABC News, Moscow.

What's the Point?

There's more than one way to construct most any broadcast news story. But whatever way you choose, it should be smooth and logical. The best way to achieve that is to organize your notes—facts, impressions, verbatims of sound bites—and have everything in front of you when you write.

Exercises to Hone Your Organizing Skills _____

1. Just the Facts
   Choose a story from today's newspaper—any story. Then, after reading through it:
   - List all the germane facts, each as a separate item. If you're doing this together as a class, call them out and let someone list them up on the whiteboard or blackboard.
   - Choose the best one(s) to use in your lead.
   - Figure out which one(s) to use as your close.
   - Look for the items that aren't central to the story you want to tell, and cross them out.
   - Prioritize what's left, not from most to least important, but from the beginning to the end of the story.
   - Write it, or if you please, rewrite it. See if you can make it appropriate for broadcast and perhaps even more compelling than the newspaper writer wrote it.

2. An Exercise to Organize
   Here is a randomly ordered list of facts, sound bite verbatims, and other items that might end up in your notes after covering a fatal fire. Go through the process you need to organize these notes. Then, write the story for television. Make it one minute, fifteen seconds.

   - 4 dead
   - woman & 3 year old dead
   - baby 1 year 3 months old
   - 16 apartments in bldg
   - 4 apartments gutted
   - other residents afraid of either malfunction in bldg. Or arson
   - sunny day
   - sot (five seconds): "I wanted to climb up there and get her down myself." (spectator: Jim Gill)
   - dead woman is babysitter
   - arson team investigating
   - dead man in 50s
   - traffic diverted for fire equipment
   - nat sot (three seconds): "help us help us" (woman on balcony with baby)
   - nat sot (two seconds): sirens
   - 13 taken to hospital
   - 4 critical, 7 fair, 2 released
   - sot (nine seconds): "We're investigating all possible causes, and won't comment on what set off the blaze until we know." (fire chief)
   - furnace repaired for gas leak last week
   - top floor destroyed
   - second unexplained fire in same neighborhood in a month
   - fire hoses like spaghetti
   - 4th & Market Streets
   - fire trucks responded immediately
   - anniversary party in one apt.
   - anniversary couple unhurt
   - nat sot (four seconds): spectator crying
   - sot (ten seconds): "I was scared, terribly scared that with all that smoke in the air, that it would set off my asthma." (spectator: Nancy Low)

- 3 hours to put out fire
- hook and ladder fully extended for top balcony
- City Councilwoman on scene wants investigation
- sot (twelve seconds): (crying) "I was screaming for help up there, but I didn't think they could save us. I thought my baby and me were going to die." (woman from balcony)
- low water pressure from hydrants
- adjacent clothing store evacuated
- one of firemen on first fire ever
- 4 hospitals: City Memorial, Mt. Zion, Crescent Community, St. Joseph
- ambulances carry injured to hospitals

8

Choosing Your Lead

What You'll Learn

Remember that maxim used back in Chapter 6, "You're only as good as your last act"? It's true in Hollywood and in politics too. A hundred triumphs can be wiped out if your last act falls flat. Well, at risk of putting you in the same category as actors and politicians, journalists also have to heed the maxim, because the second most important part of a report, or of a whole newscast, is the last part—the last sentence, the last story.

Note what I just wrote: the end is "the *second* most important part." What's first? The beginning, or as it's known in broadcasting, the ***lead***. If you're producing a newscast and one story in your rundown (the list of stories in a newscast) is an apartment house fire that killed four children, but you lead your newscast with a story about the city council debating what color to paint the curbs in front of City Hall, you have "buried" the lead. Who cares? The audience, which probably will change the channel before your fire story—which should be your lead story—even begins.

The same is true when you're planning a single story. If, again, it's about a fatal apartment house fire but you begin your report with the number of fire trucks that responded, you have buried your lead. You haven't told your audience what they really need to know, and you probably haven't kept their attention. Lose your audience a few times and eventually you'll lose the ratings war. After that, your job.

In this chapter, you'll learn how to choose your lead to maximize your story's impact on the audience. A by-product is that you will capture the attention of your audience from the very beginning and their minds won't wander. Isn't that the point? Partly, yes!

(We'll deal with choosing the lead story when you're producing an entire newscast, and constructing an intelligent, cohesive, dynamic rundown, in Chapter 17.)

The Terms of the Story

Rundown   The list of stories to run in a newscast, arranged in a logical sequence and timed to fit precisely into the length of the program.

Burial in My Darkest Hour

This chapter's message begins with a lesson I learned the hard way—the hardest I'd ever learned. All because I buried the lead.

I was in San Francisco covering a story when the pager went off, telling me to call ABC in New York. Their orders? Get to ABC's San Francisco station—KGO-TV—as quickly as possible. ABC News was about to break into network programming for a Special Report, which I would anchor from KGO's studio. The story? Mr. and Mrs. Randolph Hearst, newspaper magnates who lived in a wealthy suburb south of the city, had gotten a note from their daughter, Patty.

Now a bit of background: Patty Hearst was heiress to the company her father ran and her grandfather had founded: the Hearst newspaper chain, which eventually also included TV and radio stations. One night, she was kidnapped from her student apartment near the University of California at Berkeley. The group that took her called itself the S.L.A. (Symbionese Liberation Army) and rather than demanding a cash ransom, it ordered the Hearsts to spend upwards of $400 million to feed poor people in California.

At some point while she was held hostage, Patty Hearst evidently succumbed to what is known as the Stockholm Syndrome; the captive begins to sympathize with her captors. Eventually she behaved like a full-fledged member of the S.L.A., and was even photographed participating in the robbery of a San Francisco bank.

Okay, back to "Burial in My Darkest Hour." After weeks of silence from both the S.L.A. and Patty, news organizations got word that she finally had sent her parents some kind of note. What's more, the parents agreed to appear before the media on the front steps of their home to talk about it. ABC would have a live camera near the Hearsts' front steps and me in the studio.

The appointed moment came, and the voice of an announcer from network studios in New York intoned over a Special Report graphic, "We interrupt this program to bring you a special report from ABC News. In San Francisco, here's correspondent Greg Dobbs."

I started out something like this:

> *Nine weeks ago, Patty Hearst, heiress to the Hearst newspaper fortune, was kidnapped from her apartment near the University of California at Berkeley. The group that took her? The Symbionese Liberation Army. No one had heard of this group before the kidnapping; everyone knows about it now.*

And on, and on, and on I went, telling and retelling the history of the story, leading up to the forthcoming event that had us on the air now. I told of the episodes of feeding the poor people, negotiations for more food, Patty Hearst's apparent conversion from student to militant (known from a series of "communiques" issued by the S.L.A., some with Patty's voice). What I *didn't* tell was the actual reason we had interrupted regular programming: that after weeks without a word from their daughter, Patty's parents had gotten a note and soon would come out of their house to talk about it.

I can't tell you how many viewers switched stations, but since I was recounting history that everyone already knew, the numbers must have been massive. And more would have switched away if the *president* of ABC News hadn't suddenly yelled through my earpiece, "Tell the f****** story!!!" (I later learned that he was watching from his home, and called the control room and snapped something like, "Patch me through to Dobbs. I wanna talk to him, NOW.")

Let me tell you, when your boss, the person who approves your paychecks and can order your dismissal, shouts a command like that, it gets your attention! What he was saying was, Tell the audience why they're watching. Tell 'em the Hearsts got a note. Tell 'em we're waiting for the Hearsts to come outside and talk about it. Tell 'em the *news!*

Good point. I had told them everything but the news. I had backed into the story. I had buried the lead.

Only a moment after my boss's loving missive, my brain clicked into gear and I got to the critical news. Thankfully, just moments after that, the Hearsts appeared and my you-know-what was saved. So was my job. It was a painful but permanent lesson about not burying the lead. But still, it was my Darkest Hour.

What's the Point?

It's news. So tell it. First. Don't bury the lead!

How to Recognize the Lead If It Doesn't Recognize You

In some stories the lead is obvious: four dead in a fire; the Hearsts finally hear from Patty. In cases like that, you don't have to think very hard to figure out how to start your story; it kind of jumps out at you as the inevitable choice.

But in other cases—most cases, in my experience—you do have to think about it and you do have to make a choice. So here are the three questions you must ask:

1. What's the most *important* thing about this story?
2. What's the most *interesting* thing about this story?
3. What's the most *immediate* thing (the most recent development) about this story?

If you ask *and answer* those questions, choosing your lead will be a slam dunk.

Pretend you're in my sorry shoes for the Hearst story in San Francisco. I won't list all the facts here, but here are a few. Read through them and ask yourself, which is the most important, *and/or* the most interesting, *and/or* the most immediate?

- Hearst kidnapped February
- Taken from student apartment near Cal (nickname for U.C. Berkeley)
- Parents William and Catherine
- Food giveaways for Calif poor
- SLA demand $400-m, Hearsts counter $2-m.
- Stockholm Syndrome—from notes & tapes
- Parents get note today
- Contents unknown—parents to talk on front steps

Is there any question about your lead? This one's easy, because the fact that Patty finally sent her parents a note became, in the context of the whole story, the most important *and* interesting *and* immediate development! (If I had thought about it there at the anchor desk in San Francisco, I might have come to the same conclusion and saved myself some embarrassment and angst.)

It's not always so easy though, because in some stories, one fact might be the most important but another is the most interesting, and some third element might be the most immediate. The most immediate fact is especially useful as a lead when you're rehashing the same story over and over again, which is most common with radio newscasts that have to change every hour. Otherwise, when you've get three choices, it's a judgment call. Take into account not just the three questions, but try to figure out which one most likely will capture the attention of your audience.

So look at the questions again:

1. What's the most *important* thing about this story?
2. What's the most *interesting* thing about this story?
3. What's the most *immediate* thing (the most recent development) about this story?

What's the Point?

Make sure that whatever you choose for your lead is the most important, most interesting, and/or most immediate element of the story.

Choosing One Lead From among More Than One

As I said in the last section, sometimes you don't have a single element that fulfills all the requirements of a good lead. That's when you have to pick and choose. That's what this section is about.

While based in ABC's Denver bureau in the 1990s, we had what was then the Mother Of All Blizzards: 22 inches of snow fell in parts of Colorado. It was the snowiest January day ever. *World News Tonight* wanted a story (probably to make the show's producers feel good about living in New York). The "twenty-two inches in a single day" angle seemed like a pretty obvious lead, but there were a few other elements to think about:

*   Forecasters had predicted between one and three inches, *not* 22
*   Interstate 70 was closed from Denver to the Kansas border
*   Visibility for motorists reportedly was less than a car length
*   Denver's airport, which always boasted "We never close," did, which put 30,000 travellers in a holding pattern
*   Most schools closed, or never even opened
*   The storm finally was moving out, to the northeast

In this case, what was most important to some people was less important to others. If you were heading for Colorado by road, you wanted to know about the roads. If you were heading there by air, you wanted to know about the airport. If you were a student in a Colorado school, you probably didn't care; you were skiing, sledding, or throwing snowballs.

Therefore, I didn't think I could choose my lead based on what was "most important." Rather, I decided to go with "most interesting." While some people might think that twenty-two inches in twenty-four hours is awfully interesting, I thought the most interesting thing was that the forecasters, having predicted just one to three inches, had gotten it so wrong. That's where the judgment call comes in. So here's how I decided to start:

NARRATION

Forecasters predicted one-to-three inches of snow. Turned out to be an inch-or-more an hour when the blizzard reached its peak.

Remember, to convey the depth of the snow, I had pictures to help me. Pictures of snow up to the high fenders of a truck, or up to someone's waist. The opening line—the lead—didn't contradict what viewers were seeing, it reinforced the wonder of it!

Now here's a different kind of example from a different kind of story, done for *Good Morning America.* It was based on a phenomenon, pegged to an event. Namely, the nation's major brewers preparing to tell the United States Surgeon General that their print ads and broadcast commercial campaigns to discourage drunk driving deserved credit for lower drunk driving casualties among the nation's young. The lead:

NARRATION

Accidents involving alcohol still are the leading cause of death and disability for young people. But in the last ten years, the number of such accidents has dropped. The nation's brewers will tell the Surgeon General today, they deserve some credit.

SOT ANHEUSER-BUSCH SPOKESWOMAN

We're members of society ourselves. We have children, we're parents, we drive on the nation's highways too, and we don't want drunk drivers out there.

The dilemma was, do I begin the way I did, saying that drunk driving accidents still are the leading cause of death and disability for the young? Arguably, that was the most important single fact in the story. Or do I begin by saying that the number of drunk driving accidents hurting or killing young people has dropped? Or that the nation's brewers wanted credit for reducing drunk driving accidents involving young people? (Some people who don't like the brewing industry would find that pretty interesting!)

Another judgment call. And perhaps the judgment was partly editorial in nature. On the one hand, drunk driving accidents with young people had been reduced. On the other hand, they hadn't been eliminated. As critics of the brewing industry had charged while I researched the story, the brewers—using catchy phrases like "know when to say when" but never directly referring to "drunk driving"—hadn't gone nearly far enough.

So the decision was, the ongoing accident rate was the most important element in the story. It said, "this is a problem, it hasn't gone away." Then the story would describe how the problem wasn't as bad as it used to be, and get to what the brewers wanted: credit for the improvement.

Could it have been written differently? Of course. Here's one way:

NARRATION

The nation's brewers will tell the Surgeon General today that because of their commercial campaign, they deserve some credit for the lower rate of accidents involving young people and alcohol.

Here's another:

NARRATION

Accidents involving young people and alcohol haven't gone away, but there are fewer now than ten years ago. The nation's brewers will tell the Surgeon General today, they deserve some credit.

Each example is different. Even insofar as the opening video, the first and third examples would start with video of a relevant dramatic accident, but the middle example would start with a beer industry commercial. However, all three versions have a common thread. All three begin with something that someone could credibly call the most important fact. Who's right? It doesn't matter, as long as you can support your decision.

What's the Point?

There are three objective questions you can ask when choosing your lead. But sometimes the answers are subjective. As long as you are honest to the process, there is no wrong answer.

The Exception to Every Rule

You knew it was coming, didn't you? The exception to the rule is that while it's true that you should figure out your lead based on the three questions about the most important, interesting, and/or immediate fact, it's also true that sometimes your best video won't be any of the three.

If, for example, you cover a horrible fire in an apartment house where four people have died, but your camera and microphone have captured an irresistibly dramatic scene of a woman holding an infant up on a third-floor balcony with flames lapping at their backs and she is screaming "help me, help me, my baby, my baby" (and eventually the woman and baby are rescued alive), what're you going to show first? A fire truck rushing to the fire? A fireman connecting a hose? NO! Start with your best stuff. Start with the woman holding her baby, screaming for their lives. It's for television. That's your lead! I guarantee you, use an opening like that and the audience won't get up and leave in the middle of the story.

But what about the most important *fact,* that four people are dead? You can get to it soon enough (you must). So here's a reasonable opening for the story.

NARRATION

This woman and her baby survived, but four people died today when . . ."

Simple enough, eh? We began with the best picture, but after only half-a-dozen words, we told the most important fact—the lead. You always can return to that dramatic video later in the piece if there is more to show. For the beginning of the story, we have whetted the audience's appetite. Okay, now two more examples of writing a lead, based on the picture:

In a story about a fund raising campaign for the American Indian College Fund, the most *important* fact was that the Fund had based its future on the campaign. The most *interesting* fact was that there are more than two dozen colleges now established on Indian reservations. The most *immediate* was that these colleges had just achieved a graduation (and post-graduation employment) rate of almost 90 percent.

But we began with a shot of Little Big Horn College in Crow Agency, Montana, showing a classroom with plywood floors and cinderblock walls. The shot said to the audience, "this isn't like any college you've ever seen." And I said essentially the same thing in the lead sentences of the script:

NARRATION

With cinderblock walls and plywood floors, Little Big Horn College isn't Harvard. Its founders have a different kind of dream.

Another example is a feature story about the oldest postal carrier in the country. He was Don Taylor, ninety-five years old, operating out of Lusk, Wyoming. Conventional wisdom says you should start by showing the man—after all, he was *ninety-five!* But what struck me was that he not only was the nation's oldest postal carrier, he also delivered the mail in what had to be pretty much the most difficult conditions in the country. So we opened the piece with video of a desolate, windswept, hardscrabble Wyoming plain, with a lone ranch house way off in the distance, and wrote the leading line:

NARRATION

Postal routes don't get a whole lot more rural than this.

In the very next line, I explained that Don Taylor drove sixty-six miles every day, mostly on dirt roads, to deliver mail to twenty-nine Wyoming families. And of course, that neither rain, nor snow, nor heat, nor gloom of night had ever stopped him. Nor age!

One last thing. Sometimes audio dictates your lead, not video. In radio of course, audio is the *only* element other than information. But in television, you might use a shot of an airplane taking off because the sound of the jet engines is powerful, and relevant to the subject of the story. Or in the case of the piece about the brewers and their broadcast commercial campaign, you might choose the most revealing spoken line from a commercial, and start with it.

What's the Point?

If it's for television, video trumps all. If the video makes sense along with the lead fact of the story, great. If it doesn't, use it anyway. Just make sure you get to the real lead as soon as you can.

After You've Picked It, You Have to Write It

Choosing a good lead is one thing. Writing it is another. The most important principle is that when writing the first sentence of a story, you should bend over backwards to apply the rules about simplicity that you've already learned here. Then bend over backwards again! If your lead sentence is too long, too complex, too packed with information, you might confuse your audience and lose them for the story's duration. For instance, from my own collection of lousy leads:

NARRATION

For the last 30 years there has been an almost ceaseless flow of lava from Kilauea, one of the world's most active volcanoes, here on the big island of Hawaii, and for the last 15 years, defying the laws of nature, some of Kilauea's lava has flowed right back.

Yuk! In this story about people illegally taking lava rock home with them and then, after bad luck befell them, returning it because of local superstitions, I could have made the opening much better by taking one single step: dividing it into two sentences instead of one:

For the last 30 years there has been an almost ceaseless flow of lava from Kilauea, one of the world's most active volcanoes. For the last 15 years, defying the laws of nature, some of Kilauea's lava has flowed right back.

In the following feature about the ongoing construction of the Crazy Horse Memorial in South Dakota (it will be bigger than Mt. Rushmore), I did even worse:

NARRATION

Here in the Black Hills not 20 miles from Mt. Rushmore, another mountain is being carved, not to memorialize the heroes of democracy but to show, in the words of a Sioux chief, that "the red man had great heroes too."

I didn't need the Black Hills reference, not in the lead sentence. And I didn't have to contrast the purpose of Crazy Horse with the purpose of Mt. Rushmore, at least not in the lead sentence.

Look at how much better, shorter, and sharper, it would have been if I had thought it through more carefully:

Not 20 miles from Mt. Rushmore, another mountain is being carved to show, in the worlds of a Sioux chief, that "the red man had great heroes too."

And now, having sorted through old scripts, here's the worst-constructed lead I could find. Why so bad? Because it seems like I'm trying to tell the whole story—setting the scene, explaining the purpose—in a single run-on sentence.

NARRATION

Here in the high country of Colorado, amidst sparkling streams and thousands of species of plants, an experiment has been set up on a sloping meadow with infrared heaters hanging overhead, simulating the greenhouse effect.

Take a look at that one. This time, *you* figure out how you can make it simpler, shorter, and better!

What's the Point?

Take it easy. *Make* it easy. Don't try to squeeze too much into your lead. If you have details— figures, times, names and so forth—see if you can find a place to put them deeper into the script. Remember, for the audience it only goes by once. Don't let it be cluttered or confusing.

Another Exception: Soft as You Go

Although for the purpose of illustrating the main points of this chapter there have been exceptions (such as the "Greenhouse" example a few paragraphs back), fundamentally I've written here about "hard" leads. But sometimes a "soft" lead makes more sense. Not for a hard news story but for a soft story, a feature story. This is when you can slowly lure your audience into the piece, perhaps leading with a scene setter, or with an individual whose story is a microcosm of the bigger picture.

One example is a story about a financial shortfall at our nation's National Park Service. We chose to tell the story from Utah's spectacular Lake Powell, because there weren't enough rangers, paramedics, litter collectors, or lifeguards there.

But I didn't want to start by writing something mundane like, "There aren't enough rangers, paramedics, litter collectors, or lifeguards here at Lake Powell." (And don't forget, sometimes the "setup" for the story is handled in the anchorperson's introduction.) Nor did I want to start with the big picture, something like, "budgets at the National Park Service have not kept up with visitation." It was true, but there was nothing in it to lure the audience. So bearing in mind the beautiful video we had shot, I chose a soft lead:

NARRATION

Lake Powell is one of America's most scenic sites run by the National Park Service. Being within a day's drive of 25-million people, it also is one of the most successful.

Another example is a story about an elementary school that welcomed senior citizens as classroom volunteers, giving them a rebate on their property taxes in return. Again, I could have started with something basic like, "Schools in the Denver suburb of Littleton Colorado are using the skills of senior citizens in their classrooms, and giving them a tax break in return." But that just didn't sound very interesting. Likewise, a line like, "Littleton Colorado helps senior citizens save money by getting involved in their schools." True, but not personal enough for the story. So I wrote the lead this way:

Wall Street Journal lead.

NARRATION

Dorothy DeJong, 64 years old and retired, has time on her hands. She never has found volunteer work fulfilling. That's not a problem any more.

From there we went to a piece of NAT SOT in which Mrs. DeJong walked into a classroom saying to a little girl, "Well hi, how are ya Jessica, good to see you . . ." It was warm and touching, and set up the rest of the story perfectly.

As you should understand by now, your lead is designed to capture the audience, and the purpose of the soft lead is to capture that audience when none of those classic "hard lead" elements—most important, most interesting, most immediate—is quite enough. It would be fruitless to try to describe the variety of soft leads available on many stories; there are as many possibilities as there are stories. Suffice to say that if you make it your goal to start your story with the most compelling words, the most compelling thought, the most compelling video, you've done it right.

What's the Point?

A soft lead is rarely appropriate for a hard news story. Even some soft stories are better off without it. But sometimes, if pictures and sound lend themselves, it works, which means it helps get the audience involved in the story, the characters, and the subject.

And on the Second Day . . .

What do you do when you're reporting the same story more than once? Maybe it's on a later newscast the same day, maybe it's on a newscast the following day (or even for days after that). The answer is, you write a "second day" lead.

What this means is, you tell the same story a different way. Here's where the "most immediate" fact can be helpful. Even if there's no major new development in the story, a minor development helps give you a fresh lead. Maybe it's a new charge against a recently arrested suspect. Maybe it's a new death toll in a plane crash.

But when you don't even have a recent development, you sometimes have to rewrite the same story. One of the best examples is coverage in Anchorage, Alaska of the trial of Joseph Hazelwood, the captain of the supertanker *Exxon Valdez.* It had run aground in Alaska's Prince William Sound, spilling tens of thousands of barrels of crude oil and spoiling hundreds of miles of coastline and countless birds and fish. Hazelwood was characterized as a drunken skipper and charged with criminal mischief.

When the verdict came down, acquitting Hazelwood of the serious charge and convicting him only for a mild misdemeanor, it was a major story. The verdict broke just before air time for *World News Tonight,* so I had to hustle and write a piece for them, then several pieces for the ongoing newscasts of ABC Radio, then prepare a piece for *Nightline* and, after that, one for *Good Morning America.* All based on the same verdict, the same information, the same facts.

How to do it? By taking all my information and choosing a different lead for each piece. Each ultimately would contain all the same facts, but in a different order. Maybe the best way to demonstrate this is simply to give you the opening for each of the newscasts.

Remember, whether television or radio, each piece was preceded by an anchorperson's intro, so I didn't have to begin with the basics.

(World News Tonight)

NARRATION

After eight weeks of trial by jury and exactly a year now of trial by public opinion, Joseph Hazelwood finally won a decision.

SOT JUDGE KARL JOHNSTONE

We the jury find the defendant Joseph Hazelwood not guilty of criminal mischief . . .

(ABC Radio #1)

An alternate from the jury, a woman who heard every argument, every word of testimony, says she would have acquitted Joseph Hazelwood. She says the prosecution failed to prove that on the night of the spill, Hazelwood was drunk.

(ABC Radio #2)

Technically Hazelwood was judged guilty of a crime: the negligent discharge of oil. But that's a misdemeanor, and with a maximum penalty of 90 days in jail and a thousand-dollar fine, it's the mildest misdemeanor with which he was charged.

(ABC Radio #3)

The jury, while it deliberated for only ten-and-a-half hours, didn't reach its decision easily. On each of the four charges against Hazelwood, the jury had to vote more than once before reaching unanimity.

(Nightline)

The state's case against Captain Hazelwood centered on his absence from the bridge when the ship, on a delicate detour to avoid icebergs, ran aground.

(Good Morning America)

Note how we used the same sound we had used in the *World News Tonight* piece the night before, but even higher in the story.

SOT JUDGE KARL JOHNSTONE

We the jury find the defendant Joseph Hazelwood not guilty of criminal mischief . . .

NARRATION

Not guilty in fact of any charge except the mildest misdemeanor: "negligent discharge of oil."

What's the Point?

Whether it's because you have a lot of newscasts to cover, or because news is slow and you have to keep a story alive just to fill air time (yes, it happens), you have to be inventive. Don't assume every member of each new audience hasn't heard it before. Assume they have. So you must keep it interesting, keep it fresh.

Exercises to Put Your Lead in the Lead _____

1. **Secondhand Rose**
   Choose the headline story from today's newspaper. Whatever it is, write four different leads for the same story, as if you're working at a radio station with newscasts every half hour. You want your four consecutive stories to each sound fresh.

2. **Hard and Soft**
   From the same newspaper, clip out three "hard" news stories, and three "soft" stories. Label each as "hard" or "soft" and turn them in to your instructor, demonstrating that you recognize the difference.

3. **Drama as Your Best Lead**
   Now, find a story in the paper which, pretending you have covered it for television, has a dramatic, breathtaking, or colorful element in it that begs to be the lead, even though it isn't necessarily the most important, interesting or immediate fact. Now, write it up the way you would for television, making reference to that irresistible opening element but quickly making your transition to the real lead of the story.

4. **Most Important, Most Interesting, Most Immediate**
   Here is the same randomly ordered list of facts and other items about a fatal fire (except the sound bite verbatims and NAT SOT) that you worked with in the last chapter. Pare it down to just three—the most important, the most interesting, and the most immediate.

(handwritten margin notes: important - the dead / interesting - 2nd unexplained fire / immediate - cause)

- 4 dead
- woman & 3 year old dead
- baby 1 year 3 months old
- 16 apartments in bldg
- 4 apartments gutted
- other residents afraid of either malfunction in bldg. Or arson
- sunny day
- dead woman is babysitter
- arson team investigating
- dead man in 50s
- traffic diverted for fire equipment
- 13 taken to hospital
- 4 critical, 7 fair, 2 released
- furnace repaired for gas leak last week
- top floor destroyed
- second unexplained fire in same neighborhood in a month

- fire hoses like spaghetti
- 4th & Market Streets
- fire trucks responded immediately
- anniversary party in one apt.
- anniversary couple unhurt
- 3 hours to put out fire
- hook and ladder fully extended for top balcony
- City Councilwoman on scene wants investigation
- low water pressure from hydrants
- adjacent clothing store evacuated
- one of firemen on first fire ever
- 4 hospitals: City Memorial, Mt. Zion, Crescent Community, St. Joseph
- ambulances carry injured to hospitals

9

Choosing Your Close

At the beginning of the last chapter, the very first lesson was "You're only as good as your last act." But the other part of the lesson was that in broadcast writing, your last act—your close—actually is "the *second* most important part" of a story, second behind the lead.

Okay, you can live with that. "Second most important" is a bigger deal than "least" important. So let's talk about it. How do you choose your close? When do you choose your close? Why do you choose a close?

The last question is the easiest to answer. You choose a close to wrap up a story. To bring closure for the viewer, at least until the next newscast. Obviously some stories are destined to go on, and on, and on. There will be new information, new developments. But since we're talking here about daily or even hourly newscasts, you need to let the audience know where things stand *now,* rather than leaving them hanging.

This means you want to tell people either what a story means, or where it's going from here. Or, you want to simply tie it up in a nice little knot.

Simplicity

I had to give little thought to this section, entitled "Simplicity," because it's not necessary to construct complexities to teach you about simplicity.

How does this relate to your close? Simple. It should be simple. Why? Because if you've done your job right, then by the time you close out your story, you've already communicated the background, the information, the emotion. All that's left is to end it.

More often than not, you'll find that the easiest kind of close, especially on a story that's not likely to become a series, is to tie it up in a bow. I didn't have to think very hard either to come up with what I consider the best close of this kind (or any kind) ever spoken on television. Unfortunately, it wasn't mine, it was anchorman Frank Reynolds'. I told you about this in Chapter 6. He and I together covered a fatal fire.

As you might recall, the fire was at a nightclub in Covington, Kentucky, just across the Ohio River from Cincinnati. It started in the kitchen, and a busboy came calmly onto the stage, took the microphone, and in his fairly thick foreign accent coolly told the audience of several hundred that there was a fire in the kitchen, so they should stand up, not panic, and walk toward the three double-door exits from the room.

The problem was, there was a comedian doing his act on stage when the busboy took the mike. For reasons we never could determine—because almost no one survived, and those who did were badly hurt—the audience thought the busboy was part of the act, so all anyone did was laugh, until smoke started seeping in.

Then, everyone stampeded, pressing against the doors like a herd of cattle on the run. But what they found was, the doors didn't open outwards, they opened inwards. The people in front couldn't pull the doors open because hundreds more people, thousands of pounds in panic, were pressed up against them.

Some died of smoke inhalation, others from burns. But all who died ended up in three bulging piles of soot. Not because someone had chained the exit doors shut to keep unpaid intruders out—which I've seen at a few other fatal fires—but simply because whoever designed the nightclub, and whoever inspected and improved it, and whoever ran it at the time of the catastrophe, didn't think. They didn't think about the purpose of the exit doors. They didn't think about how they'd work in a fire.

Which brings me back to Frank Reynolds. I had done my piece in the broadcast about the fire itself, then Frank reported about the lessons that should be learned. He ended by talking about the doors, and all the people who could have rectified their design and prevented this tragedy. And then he closed his piece with the four words I mentioned in Chapter 6, simple words that said it all: "So simple. So sad."

A simple close. A perfect close.

What's the Point?

Sometimes, you don't need predictions to close your story, just conclusions. Simple ones. Precisely what the audience would be thinking if they knew what you know.

How to Find Your Close When the Story Is Still Open

You may remember (you certainly should) that in the last chapter, you learned that there are three things you look for with your lead: the most important, the most interesting, and/or the most immediate part of a story. Well, there are similar standards for choosing your close, to which I alluded earlier in this chapter:

1. What does the story mean?.
2. Where is the story going from here?
3. Tie it up in a nice little knot.

The close you just read from the nightclub fire is the best possible example of tying up a story in a nice little knot. It leaves you sad, yes, but not hanging out there wondering. Of course the following day we did stories about fire inspections and regulations in the area, and the day after that, our main story was that right across the river, the Cincinnati City Council—having learned a valuable lesson even though the fire wasn't in Cincinnati itself—changed its fire ordinance to require all fire exit doors in public places to open outward.

But what do you do when your story can't be tied up so simply? What do you do when it's too early to summarize, because the story still is developing before your eyes? The answer is you go for one of the other of two good elements in a close: what does this story mean, or where is it going from here?

What Does the Story Mean?

Let me start this section with a story. It's pretty funny as long as you're not me, or any of the other seven correspondents appearing on *World News Tonight* one fall evening.

Our executive producer, an accomplished journalist named Av Westin, was tired of hearing correspondents close stories by saying nothing useful. It was the fault of all of us who sometimes made the mistake of writing virtually everything there was to write in the voiceover portion of a story, then doing on-camera standup closes (in those days, almost all the on-camera pieces were closes) without anything significant left to say. It happened all the time.

So one day, Westin sent a message to every correspondent who worked for ABC News. It went something like this:

"I have become more and more aware that when you do your standup closes, you have nothing left to say. As a result, what you say is meaningless, sometimes even inane. From now on, I want every close to tell us, 'What this means is . . .' This will force you to save something important for the end."

Well, maybe you have anticipated what happened. Yes, of the eight of us with pieces on the air that night, *every one of us* began our standups with, "What this means is . . ." I did mine from Budapest, Hungary, where the U.S. Secretary of State had just returned a treasured gold crown to the Hungarians. American soldiers had taken it at the end of World War II and the U.S. government had held onto it, pending certification that Hungary respected human rights. My close read in part, "What this means is, a major source of friction between the U.S. and Hungary has been removed . . ."

Have you figured out what happened next? Yep. Westin fired off another message, again to all correspondents. Its tone was along the lines of, "No No No you stupid jerks, I didn't mean you all should actually *say the words,* 'What this means is . . .' I only meant, put some meaning into your standups. Tell the audience why the story was important!" Sometimes you have to learn the hard way.

But not always. Here are summaries of a range of stories, followed in each case by the close. Each does a decent job of explaining, "What this means is . . ."

First, the Gary Gilmore execution in Utah, about which you read in Chapter 6. I did my standup close a few hours after Gilmore died, standing in front of the sturdy wooden chair to which he was strapped when he was shot. The whole story up to this point was about the dramatic day and its outcome; the close was about the bigger picture:

> *This site, in the old cannery, becomes a footnote in history, not just because a convicted killer named Gary Gilmore died here this morning, but because it is the spot where a moratorium on legal executions in America, a moratorium sustained for nearly ten years, ended.*

In a story about a court-imposed busing plan to achieve public school racial integration in Louisville, I reported on a campaign by anti-busing forces to have a federal court

Learning the hard way.
Courtesy of Greg Dobbs.

rule that the plan was unconstitutional. Concluding that racial segregation in the city had been accidental rather than the result of anyone's deliberate actions, the court decided in their favor. Here's the close:

> *Today's decision means to some here that segregation will be tolerated as long as it's an accident. And it means to many that sweeping remedies for segregation are now old-fashioned—that the cure must fit the specific case.*

Here's something from a feature about some interesting research at the University of Michigan into drownings. Namely, that in some bodies found floating in very cold water, the heartbeat slows down dramatically and these victims sometimes can be healthily resuscitated. This defied all conventional wisdom. As you'll see, the close doesn't just explain what it meant; it also explains what it didn't mean.

> *The study done here does not mean that the seven to eight thousand yearly drownings in this country can all be prevented. But it does mean that some people, with the right conditions and provided that their rescuers know what to do, can have life after drowning.*

Before British Airways and Air France retired their fleets of supersonic passenger jets, the supersonic Concorde flew only from London and Paris to the American east coast. It didn't cross our country. Why not? Because there was a consensus in the United States that it would cause sonic booms, and destroy every antique china collection beneath its flight path! For a while, that meant it couldn't even land at coastal airports, until the day came when New York City decided to give it a try. My close that day—reflecting the popularity of anti-French attitudes long before the Iraq War—explained the ultimate potential meaning of the whole arrangement.

> *Today, the French will land 90 seconds ahead of the British which, considering many attitudes in New York, may be more harmful than helpful to French public relations.*

Finally, a piece about pancakes—pancakes that racing waiters have to carry 415 yards in a skillet, flipping their flapjacks three times while they're running. It's a traditional race between waiters in the U.S. and waiters in England, and the Yankees won! Which means what?

The English may still have a stiffer upper lip. But Americans apparently have a faster flip.

Do not try this at home.

What's the Point?

If it means something, tell us. Your close is a good place to do it.

Where Does the Story Go from Here?

If it's a crime story but no suspect is in custody, you might want to end by telling us what the police are doing to catch one. If a suspect is in custody, you might want to tell us what charges and penalties he faces. Those are easy examples of how to end certain kinds of stories with a "here's what's next" kind of close. But it's not always so easy. Sometimes you have to glean the "next development" from sources, from subjects you've interviewed, even from your own instinctive knowledge of the story.

The point is to help the audience by pointing a finger in the direction where they ought to be looking. To tell them, in other words, what to expect next.

Here's a range of examples once again, beginning with an easy one from that Kentucky nightclub fire, in a story when I returned there about two weeks later.

The investigative team had been looking not just into the reasons why people couldn't get out, but also into the reasons the fire started, then spread so quickly in the first place. But their report, which said the fire had been burning in a concealed space for a while before breaking out, left more questions. Could anyone be held to blame? Was the building more flammable than the law allowed? This led to the close:

Sometime this summer, when investigators complete their interviews, we should know whether local fire officials, state fire officials, the supperclub's owners or anyone else, will be held criminally responsible.

Now back to the Gary Gilmore execution. Twice during the saga before he died, he overdosed on drugs apparently smuggled in to him by his girlfriend. Twice he was hospitalized, forcing postponement of his execution date, and compelling the state Board of Pardons to set a new one. So one day, he appeared before them, appealing to be allowed to die. It was easy to write a straightforward close about his appearance before the board, and what to expect next:

They're expected to uphold Gilmore's death sentence, and unless the U.S. Supreme Court then steps in, the execution will take place here, probably less than a week from now.

When Jimmy Carter was president, he decided to give the Panama Canal, and all the facilities the U.S. had built there, to Panama, ahead of a schedule mandated in a treaty. He sent his chief negotiator out to Vail, Colorado, to explain the deal to former President Gerald Ford and hopefully win his endorsement. Ford gave it. I covered the meeting in Vail, and while the story's close acknowledged that Carter had accomplished his purpose, it also acknowledged a rocky future for his plan.

> *The success of this personal visit, winning President Ford's support, does not necessarily mean that all other prominent Republicans will fall into line. Many have long-held beliefs that control of the Panama Canal should never be given away.*

In Chicago, an El train—a commuter train on tracks elevated above the city's downtown loop—rear-ended another during rush hour. Four cars fell more than 20 feet into a key downtown intersection. Many passengers were killed or injured. A day later, we did a follow-up story about the investigation into why it happened (they blamed the motorman of the rear train). The close reflected where the story already had gone, and what was coming up next:

> *By this morning, workmen were removing the last of the wreckage. All trains again are running. The intersection at this hour is clear. Many people remain hospitalized. The first funerals are tomorrow.*

One winter, a sixty-mile stretch of the mighty Mississippi River froze. Barge cargo north and south of the ice came to a halt. How to close a story like this? Easy. Tell what local officials think might happen next:

> *Officials fear that all this ice will thaw, then freeze again and jam the river further south. Or that it will cause local flooding as it melts away.*

Another kind of flood now, in Appalachian Kentucky. Rivers had risen, then fallen, leaving a residue of sticky smelly mud over streets and sidewalks, church pews and store shelves. And inside everyone's homes.

But in the story's last sound bite, a woman in a town called Pinesville said things weren't so bad, because God had spared her life. I took a bit of liberty with the close I wrote to come out of her sound bite, but it seemed right for the circumstance:

> *With that kind of attitude, the stricken towns of eastern Kentucky can be expected to rebuild.*

The U.S. Environmental Protection Agency went to war with the country's biggest steelmaker, U.S. Steel. The issue: about thirteen tons of pollutants being poured every day into Lake Michigan. Ultimately, with the backing of the White House, the EPA imposed a huge penalty on U.S. Steel, and the company cried "uncle," agreeing to spend tens of millions of dollars to reduce pollution. After talking with government contacts, my close about "what's next" was easy:

> *The federal government intends to press harder now to bring others into compliance with the law.*

The huge medical insurance company, Blue Shield, announced that unless it had a doctor's justification in writing, it would stop paying for twenty-eight medical procedures which it had previously funded, no questions asked. The close told policy holders exactly what to expect:

> *According to Blue Shield, policy prices won't drop; they just won't rise as fast any more.*

The school district in Las Vegas, Nevada, was just like all others: kids weren't eating cafeteria food. So, long before it was fashionable, the district decided to disguise healthy food as *fast* food. No high-fat pork in the hotdogs, no ice cream in the milkshakes, and wheatgerm in every slice of pizza! And it worked, leading to a close that projected the consequence of this experiment to districts elsewhere in America:

> *Instead of complaints here, school lunches win plaudits. There is sufficient nutrition, there is minimum waste. The message to other school districts: jet-age kids won't eat horse and buggy meals.*

Finally, two stories about sports. One was about a high school basketball player, a guard, who was never allowed to take a shot. Why not? Because according to league rules, guards couldn't shoot. Oh by the way, it was a league for *girls*. So she took her grievance to the United States Supreme Court. It hadn't yet decided the case when we did our story, but my close reflected the possibilities if she won:

> *So, Vicki Cape hopes to score points with the Supreme Court. If she does, then girls everywhere, if they can't play with the boys, at least will have the chance to play like them.*

The other sports story was straightforward coverage of the Wimbledon Tennis Tournament, in which I identified the semi-final men's singles winners, then closed simply:

> *That final showdown is scheduled for Sunday.*

What's the Point?

If you want to close a story, *close* it! Don't just throw in a fact you hadn't used earlier. Close it by pointing to the next likely development.

The Point of the Point

At the top of this chapter, you read that you'd learn how to choose your close, and when. I hope it occurred to you that you'd already learned *when* in Chapter 7. If you're on overload, let me briefly repeat it here.

Once you've reviewed all the information you need, from conversations, from notes, from Internet research, from newspaper archives and from all the video or audio you've collected, you should put everything down on paper. Not in any prioritized order, just note it as you come to it.

Then, as perhaps you recall from Chapter 8, do what the title says and choose your lead: the most important, and/or interesting, and/or immediate piece of information. And next, choose your close. That's *when,* and now, here's *how.* Look at all those facts you've put on paper, and ask yourself if any imparts either the meaning of the story, or the future of the story, or a neat summary of the story. That's your close.

Exercises to Put an End to All This _____

1. Thirdhand Rose
   Choose the headline story from today's newspaper. If you still have whatever you chose for a similar exercise in the last chapter, you can use it. In any event, write four different closes for the story, as if you're working at a station with hourly newscasts and you have to run this particular piece of news with a fresh close every hour.

2. A Different Part of the Same Story
   Here is the same randomly ordered list of facts and other items about a fatal fire (without the sound bite verbatims and NAT SOT) that you've now worked with twice before. Find and make a list of the elements that indicate: a summary of what happened, what the story means, and where the story's going.

   - 4 dead
   - woman & 3 year old dead
   - baby 1 year 3 months old
   - 16 apartments in bldg
   - 4 apartments gutted
   - other residents afraid of either malfunction in bldg. Or arson
   - sunny day
   - dead woman is babysitter
   - arson team investigating
   - dead man in 50s
   - traffic diverted for fire equipment
   - 13 taken to hospital
   - 4 critical, 7 fair, 2 released
   - furnace repaired for gas leak last week
   - top floor destroyed
   - second unexplained fire in same neighborhood in a month
   - fire hoses like spaghetti
   - 4th & Market Streets
   - fire trucks responded immediately
   - anniversary party in one apt.
   - anniversary couple unhurt
   - 3 hours to put out fire
   - hook and ladder fully extended for top balcony
   - City Councilwoman on scene wants investigation
   - low water pressure from hydrants
   - adjacent clothing store evacuated
   - one of firemen on first fire ever
   - 4 hospitals: City Memorial, Mt. Zion, Crescent Community, St. Joseph
   - ambulances carry injured to hospitals

3. Finding Fault
   Watch as many TV newscasts as it takes to hear closes on three stories that don't say much of anything. Take notes as stories run, because for this assignment, you will explain what the story is about, explain why the close was vacuous, and tell what the reporter should and could have said instead.

III

And After You Write

10

Proof Positive of Proofreading

What You'll Learn

When you're writing your piece, you're probably reviewing and revising it piecemeal as you go along. Even if you're not, you need to review it thoroughly when you think you're finished. Why? Because while you *think* you're finished, you're probably not. Why not? Because you have to ask yourself several questions about what you have written. Until you do, you cannot be sure of the answers. This is one of the most critical parts of the whole job. It's called proofreading.

What You Are Looking For

There are certain writing errors that are obvious—the kinds of mechanical flaws you have learned to avoid or correct in earlier chapters in this book. I shall list them below as brief bullet points, although if they don't make sense to you, you should reread the relevant sections of those earlier chapters. The main point is, you really don't want these traps to turn up in the final version of your story!

If you have time, you should proofread once for each of the potential problems listed below. If you don't have time, you should do it anyway, by shaving minutes from some other part of the process. Proofreading is indispensable.

For example, proofread this sentence:

Proofread carefully to see if you any words out.

Finding Mistakes Before They Find You

What follows is a long list of mistakes you might make in a script. "Might make?" Absolutely. Everyone does at one time or another, and maybe the most important lesson in this whole book is, *your spell check tool won't catch mistakes like these!*

- You must proofread your script for flaws like bad grammar, the wrong tense, an inconsistent tense, and singular pronouns coupled with plural nouns and vice versa. Make sure you haven't improperly pluralized a word such as "none."
- You want to look for complex words to simplify, and for unnecessary or judgmental words and irrelevant facts to eliminate.
- You want to check that you haven't inappropriately started or ended sentences with time references like "today," "yesterday," "tomorrow."
- You should do one more search of your sentences to find places where passive verbs can be replaced with active ones, or where one long sentence full of dependent clauses can be turned into two shorter ones without them.
- You want to make sure you haven't accidentally let potentially confusing conversational contractions like "couldn't" and "isn't" slip in, and that you haven't written a line in the unconversational style of print news.
- You have to use words that make it clear to the audience that when you're quoting someone in the narration, it's really a "quote." (This can be done with voice intonation too.)
- You should make sure that when a questionable or controversial fact should be attributed to a source, it is. But also that when attribution is unnecessary, you don't waste time giving it.
- You also should make sure that when a person's name or a place name might be pronounced more than one way, you have written as a phonetic pronouncer.
- You must get rid of commas that might make the newsreader pause when she shouldn't, and you must insert them in places where the newsreader ought to pause but won't because there is no comma.
- These days, for the hearing-challenged and for non-English-speaking natives and others, scripts often are converted electronically into computer generated words on the bottom of the television screen. Words like "their" when you mean "there," or "too" when you mean "to" (I could write a whole book on these anomalies in our language) may not sound wrong when spoken, but they look downright stupid when seen. So check your spelling.
- And check for typographical errors (typos).

It's a lot to think about, isn't it?! Yes, but don't let that make you lazy. If you don't think about each and every one of these potential traps, you're inevitably going to miss some, and someone's going to be embarrassed, possibly on the air. Whether it's you or someone else, if it's your mistake, it'll come back to haunt you (especially if the one who's embarrassed on the air is your boss!).

Mistakes that would have been caught if you had proofread the script are one of my huge pet peeves. (Another is in restaurants when they serve your glass of water with a lemon wedge in it. If I want lemonade, I'll order lemonade!) If unproofread mistakes are my pet peeve, they're others' too, others for whom you might be working.

Pros Who Didn't Proofread

Here are a few real examples of lines from pieces that ended up on a wire service without having been proofread—certainly not with any conscious thought. I've saved these for years, waiting for the opportunity to make use of them. This is it!

Of course a wire service isn't a broadcast outlet, but its output can end up in front of a news anchorperson electronically word for word, or at some smaller stations where they still "rip and read" (which means they don't rewrite a thing). Put yourself in the shoes of that anchorperson and think about how you'd get through these smoothly. The fact is, you probably couldn't! They are presented precisely as they appeared.

From United Press International, when Richard Nixon was President of the United States:

"President Nixon says his wife Pat, who celebrates her 19th birthday Tuesday . . . "

Also from United Press International. Not a funny story, but sloppy.

"A teen-ager was charged with destruction of public property Wednesday fors tearing up a blanket in the city jail and using iz to try to hang himself."

With all due respect to the Church of Jesus Christ of Latter-day Saints (also known as the Mormon church) . . .

"Three young Moron missionaries were rescued early Tuesday . . ."

This one is more of an advisory than a news story, but it's still an example of telling a different story than the writer meant to tell.

"Police were fathering at the church and nearby."

If you can't take dirty words, skip this one. If you can, it'll give you a good laugh, unless you're the one reading it "word for word" on the air. It's from Chicago's storied City News Service.

"The federal government this afternoon filed two shits in federal district court charging a real estate corporation . . ."

My all-time favorite, also from Chicago's City News Service.

"A Gage Park high school student, Antoinette Perfecto, 14, was eaten by a group of teenage boys on a CTA bus yesterday as he rode home from school."

Don't you just bet those writers wished they had proofread a little more carefully, or even just consciously?

Being Noisy

What's the most efficient way to proofread a script and search for all these potential pit-falls? The answer's simple: proofread it **ALOUD**. And I don't mean by mumbling or whis-pering. Why?

1. If you have written the script for television or radio, then it is meant to be heard, not seen. How are you going to know how it sounds if you don't hear it? That seems ob-vious enough, but we've learned to read printed words on a page (or on a computer screen) silently; it's what we do with every other printed page we see. Learn to over-come that behavior. Proofread a broadcast script **ALOUD!**

2. If during the writing process you have missed one or more flaws, you're simply more likely to catch them with your ears than with your eyes. I say this from experience. Take a little test here and read this popular phrase **silently**:

I

love

Paris in

in the springtime

Find anything wrong? Good for you if you did. If you didn't, read it again. And again. And again. If you still haven't found it (and many don't), then instead of read-ing it silently, read it aloud. Plenty of people catch the mistake the first time, but plenty more don't. If *you* didn't, think about how much more obvious it would have been if you had read it aloud. Trust me!

3. Reading aloud is the only way you're going to catch words that combine to create un-intended meanings. Reading silently, a phrase like "that dam project" probably sounds okay. Now read the same phrase aloud. Get the point?

4. Reading aloud is definitely the only way to catch tongue twisters; the eye certainly won't catch them. For a couple of years a long time ago I was national radio com-mentator Paul Harvey's editor. He didn't read a single word on his broadcasts that he hadn't read aloud several times first, to make sure there was nothing that could tie up his tongue in knots.

5. How are you going to time your piece if you don't read it aloud? When a show pro-ducer or news director tells you to bring in your story at a specific length, say, a minute and forty seconds, he is going to be mighty unhappy if it comes in too long (what's the producer going to cut?), or even too short (what does the producer have to fill the hole?). Notwithstanding computer programs some newsrooms have to mea-sure the length of a script and convert it to the preprogrammed reading pace of an an-chorperson, there is no way you can accurately time a piece if you read it silently, or even in a whisper or a mumble. Your pace for that kind of read is different, probably too fast.

Want to test this? Get a stopwatch and read the paragraph you just finished three ways: silently in your head, mumbling the way you might verbally scan a per-sonal letter, and aloud. I'm convinced that you'll be convinced!

Is It a Bother to Proofread aloud?

Some students are reluctant to proofread aloud because they think it's rude, that they'll bother the people around them. Let me dissuade you of that. Journalists in broadcasting and print alike have to learn to shut out the distractions, especially at deadline time. What this means is, if you're in a newsroom proofreading aloud, you shouldn't be bothering your colleagues because they should have learned to ignore you. Anyway, they ought to be doing the same thing themselves. On the bright side, imagine the cacophony (another word you should never, never, never, use on the air)!

No Excuse Is a Good Excuse

As a journalism teacher, I've heard a few excuses for poor or nonexistent proofreading:

- I was in too big a hurry.
- I knew someone else would fix it.
- But I *did* proofread it!

Uh-uh. Excuses like that simply demonstrate that you're careless, or lazy, or sloppy. The fact is, because of the high probability of mistakes, there is no excuse for considering a script finished without having thoroughly proofread it, ideally several times.

One thing that contributes to this problem—the failure to proofread because it doesn't seem important—is email. For reasons I find difficult to fathom, most of us treat email as if no one on the receiving end cares whether it is neat or not, clear or not, articulate or not, proofread or not. Maybe it's because of the impermanent nature of email, maybe it's something else, but whatever it is, *don't* treat a news story the way you probably treat email. It's neither impermanent nor unimportant.

Son of Pros Who Didn't Proofread

The earlier box about poorly proofread wire service stories dealt with simple typographical errors. Here are just two more examples of poorly proofread stories, but in these it's more a matter of mauling the meaning, or the message itself.

This one conjures up a vision that I suspect is not quite accurate. What was in bed with the mother, the note or the body?

"Police found a note near the girl's body, which was in bed with her mother in her home in this southeastern Pennsylvania community."

This last one comes from an almost disastrous personal experience. While working as Paul Harvey's editor at ABC Radio News, my job while he was live on the air was to watch the wire services for late breaking stories or developments. I'd quickly rewrite them in his style if there was time, but sometimes it was so important—or so late in the show—that I'd simply run the wire service printout straight into the studio and place it right in front of him.

(continued)

Son of Pros Who Didn't Proofread   **Continued**

Such was almost the case with the following Associated Press story about a plagued American flight to the moon. It broke just minutes before the broadcast was to end. It was so poorly written that anyone reading it momentarily would be convinced the nation had a catastrophe on its hands. It was so alarming, I came within seconds of running this bulletin into the studio without even finishing the first sentence, which began this way:

"The stricken Apollo 13 spaceship is slightly off course and its astronauts will miss the earth by 60 miles and soar off into a distant fatal orbit. . . ."

As it turned out, the story went on to explain that this was just a possibility *if* a steering course correction could not be made. But do you think the writer might have noticed how misleadingly convoluted the presentation was if he had proofread it? Especially if he had proofread it aloud?

Whoops, More Reasons to Proofread Aloud

The reasons to proofread aloud that I've already discussed in this chapter won't necessarily help you answer the following "big picture" questions. Does it flow? Is the story as straightforward as possible? Did I write the way I talk? Do I actually understand what I have written?

Without much elaboration, I now want to list the questions separately and distinctly, so you'll think of them that way and proofread your scripts with each of them in mind. They're as important as or maybe even more important than all the other details for which you must proofread.

1. Does it flow?

    Read your narration and your sound bite verbatims aloud and you're much more likely to find (and fix) the rough spots, like an introduction to a sound bite that says something like, "she says she is really upset," followed by the sound bite itself where a woman begins, "I'm really upset!"

2. Is the story as straightforward as possible?

    Think about that wire service story about the troubled moon shot, Apollo 13. It would have been much more straightforward if the writer had done it this way:

    "If its astronauts cannot successfully make a steering course correction tonight, the stricken Apollo 13 spaceship will stay slightly off course and miss the earth by 60 miles and soar off into a distant fatal orbit. . . . "

3. Did I write the way I talk?

    This applies to words as well as sentences. If you see a crash, do you tell your family at dinner, "Two automobiles this morning collided at the corner of 6th and Main?" No. If you don't explain it that way at dinner, don't explain it that way on the air.

4. Do I actually understand what I have written? Will the audience? If you don't, the audience certainly won't. Even if you do, make sure you're not conveying information you understand only because you're grounded in the subject (remember "hazmat"?). If that's why you understand it, maybe the audience still won't!

This applies to "background" information in your stories too. When I worked overseas, in the days before satellite phones, I often shared phone calls to the United States from particularly remote places with colleagues—not colleagues from other networks I was trying to beat, but colleagues from major newspapers or magazines with whom I had teamed up. I'd reach ABC News in New York, I'd finish my business, then I'd ask the ABC switchboard operator to connect the call to my partner's U.S. office. On alternate days it worked in reverse.

Often, my phone call partner was a reporter from the *New York Times*. Since usually we were standing together, I'd hear his whole end of the conversation. If we were covering an ongoing story for days on end, he had to include essentially the same paragraph of "background" information day after day. For instance, once we were together covering the hijacking of a Kuwaiti Airlines 747 to Algiers, which I mentioned earlier in the book. Each of the sixteen days while it stood on the ground, there was a new development. But each day, both of us had to repeat in our stories the same basic information: the jumbo jet was hijacked on a Sunday, the hijackers had made certain demands, there were a few dozen people on board, including members of the Kuwaiti royal family. The *Times* reporter already knew it, I knew it, and most of our audiences probably knew it. But did everyone? No. Some might have been reading or hearing the story for the first time. They wouldn't understand it if they weren't given that "background" information.

5. Finally, something to which I referred earlier in this chapter, but something you *must* ask to stay in the good graces of whoever produces the show: Is the piece the right length?

The show rundown is fluid (you'll learn the basics of creating rundowns in Chapter 17), but its length is cast in stone. If it's a half hour TV news show, with seven minutes of commercials and three minutes of weather and four minutes of sports and a minute of hellos and goodbyes by the anchorpeople, that's half the time right there. What does that leave for news? Fifteen minutes. Translate that to seconds and it's almost scary: just nine hundred seconds to play with.

That's why, as I wrote earlier, the broadcast producer is going to be upset if your piece comes in too far from the length you were assigned, which is why you don't want it to. Sure, those computer programs work in some cases, but there's nothing to measure a story's length like reading it against a stopwatch, aloud.

How to Almost Undo a Productive Career in Less Than Three Minutes

When I was based in London, there was a frivolous feature story I always had wanted to do about cricket, that arcane sport played throughout the old British empire, with terms like "century" and "sticky wicket" and games that go on for days.

I'd always wanted to do it, but the executive producer of *World News Tonight* in New York hadn't. So when I called him super early one morning because circumstances were right

(continued)

How to Almost Undo a Productive Career in Less Than Three Minutes   Continued

and news was slow, he finally approved my request to do the piece for that night's show. But he closed with a chilling admonition, "It better be good."

Oh, it was good all right! But because I didn't insist on proofreading, it was *too much* of a good thing.

What happened was, it rained. Not odd for London, but calamitous for our coverage. Instead of having a leisurely afternoon at a cricket match, then four or five hours to write and cut and craft the piece before feeding it via satellite to New York, we got back to our office not two hours before show time and had to "crash," which means hurry, rush, panic.

The executive producer had allotted two minutes and fifteen seconds at the end of his rundown. In the spirit of "leave 'em laughing," he would close the show with my feature about cricket.

After hastily scrolling through the video we had shot and noting the scenes and sound bites I liked, I started writing, while the producer and tape editor started editing. I'd finish a section of the script and record it on the spot so the producer and tape editor could cut it to pictures. Despite the shortened schedule, we were on a roll; the piece was going to be not just good, but great!

The only trouble was, we were getting closer and closer to show time. So close that the executive producer started calling from New York more and more frequently and feverishly to ask if we were going to make it. Although we were still editing, I was sure we would make it, and assured him of it.

Well, we missed the window for our satellite feed time, which was fifteen minutes before the network broadcast would begin in New York. What we were left to do was feed it via satellite "live" into the show, meaning the control room director in New York would shout "roll" through an intercom and a technician in London would start the piece, and that's how Americans would see it. On the fly. Hey, we'd done it a zillion times before!

How did it go? Let me show you the first couple of pages of the script, before I give you an answer.

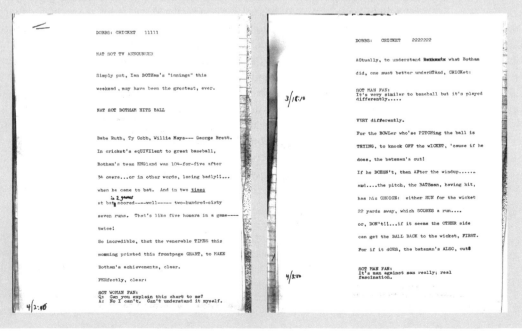

Frivolous as hoped for, fun as promised. And a full half minute too long. It wouldn't have mattered nearly as much if we weren't running it—and watching and timing it for the first time—live on the air. Look back for a moment to the point in the script where I asked the female fan, *"Do you understand everything about cricket?"* In the script she answered *"No, but my husband brings me, so I have to come, don't I?"*

The audience never heard that part of the script, let alone the satirical "tea towel" (that's British for "dish towel," by the way) explanation of cricket that followed. Since the piece ran too long, and it ran right at the end of the show, my irate executive producer had to order his control room crew to dump out right in the middle of the word "*husband*," so that anchorman Peter Jennings would have just a few seconds to quickly say goodnight.

It was ugly, it was embarrassing, and it could have cost me my job. Yet it all could have been avoided, if only I had managed my time better and carved out at least three more minutes while we were still editing, to proofread, with a stopwatch, aloud!

What's the Point?

The point is what it was near the beginning of this chapter: proofreading, for so many reasons, is indispensable. Without it mistakes are likely to end up on the air, and in the very worst case scenario, your piece might end up too long for the show. Without it, at best, a script is likely to be rougher and more incomplete than it has to be.

Exercises to Hone Your Proofreading Skills _____

1. The Never Ending Story Finally Ends

   Did you ever see *Back To The Future*? That's where we're going now. The first section of this book started with a horribly written piece, the Never Ending Story. After each subsequent chapter in that opening section, you made corrections based on what you had learned.

   Now it's time for one more shot at it. Proofread this first original version, the raw version, with all the original mistakes. Find them. Correct them. Rewrite them. Produce a piece you'd be proud to broadcast. That will be the end of the Never Ending Story.

   In a place where a rear-ender traffic mishap's usually the most consequential event of the day, there has been a huge occurrence with a terrible impact on each and everyone. Tonight the lives of three persons were tragically claimed by a bomb, which set off a 3-alarm blaze that raised temperatures to almost 200° Fahrenheit at a garment store at 3645 Main Street, in the heart of Ft. Sutter, Calif., the police said. No group took credit for the horrific blast, but forensics experts are combing the scene of the senseless attack on them tonight. And in case there's more danger there, a hazmat team's dispatched to the scene. In order to explain why there wasn't an admonition, the police chief of the city of Ft. Sutter, Jazibou Perez, claims there was no indication that the explosive device was going to detonate, then he said, "Everyone wishes to God we had known this was going to transpire." The police dept. asked the FBI for help, the chief said. The deceased includes John J. Jones, 29, Sally S. Smith, 24, and Greg G. Grog, who died at 22. Everyone in Ft. Sutter is absolutely petrified now to go out on the street, and city officials admit increased protection will cost the population of Ft. Sutter a lot of wampum, $6-million. There isn't a date set for a decision about expending that aggregate of money, but the mayor won't be back in the community until Tues. Whether such an expenditure'll really be beneficial remains to be observed.

2. Testing Your Eyes
    You had a chance in the beginning of this chapter to read a sentence in which one key word was missing. Here are more. Test your eyes when you read them and see whether you instantly spot the missing links. Some are entire words, while others are just parts of words. If you don't find them, test your voice instead and read aloud. Then, you're sure to catch them.

    • She was enrolled in the county jail and ordered transform into her prison apparel.
    • Three vehicles were involved in the crash, but no was grievously incapacitated.
    • The tornado tore through trailer park, claiming the lives six children and hurting four juveniles.
    • The president address congress and announced his plan to append three quarters of billion dollars to the Defense Department budget.
    • The skiers were seen getting submerged by the avalanche, but none found by search faction.

3. Testing Your Mind
    Spotting a missing word might be easier than spotting the wrong word. Read these same sentences, with the missing words now filled in, and fix the incorrect words.

    • She was enrolled in the county jail and ordered to transform into her prison apparel.
    • Three vehicles were involved in the crash, but no one was grievously incapacitated.
    • The tornado tore through the trailer park, claiming the lives of six children and hurting four juveniles.
    • The president addressed congress and announced his plan to append three quarters of a billion dollars to the Defense Department budget.
    • The skiers were observed getting submerged by the avalanche, but none was found by the search faction.

4. Testing Your Education
    Here now, all kinds of problems for you to find in these broadcast sentences through proofreading! One last time, don't forget: "proofreading" means proofreading aloud.

    • Today the hospital announced that it's emergency room, long rated as the worst in the entire county, wouldn't terminate operations in order to reevaluate its methods.
    • The mayor's spokesman said the mayor will be departing whether or not she became the target of there probe.
    • Three horribly loud explosions ripped through city hall, but the terrorist was seen by no one, the police chief commented.
    • The gun rights demonstration was attended by a quarter million people many of whom were shouting in support of the bill because they claimed they were victims of crime themselves, and city hall plaza was absolutely filled, by the large crowd this afternoon.
    • Last night the plane tragically crashed into the runway at exactly 10 o'clock, the airport claims, and all 130 persons on board was killed according to the airport fire chief.
    • The councilwoman remarked, that there isn't a good reason for so many citizens to be frightened when a police car races fast though there neighborhood.
    • She confessed that none of her dogs were on leashes, and that she received to many complaints to ignore.
    • The victim claimed he is not part of the gang, but that he was endeavoring to stop is from robbing the vault.
    • The man just ran into the ornate lobby and shouted that he wanted everyone, to "get on the floor, he's got a bomb."

11

The Correct Corrections

There are few things more embarrassing to a broadcaster on the air than coming to a typo on a script, and finding his tongue toed up in knights. Oops, sorry, I mean, *tied* up in *knots*. (Lucky that I caught that!)

You wouldn't expect it to happen if someone has carefully proofread the script, as you were taught to do in the last chapter. But it does, for several reasons. Sometimes it's because, well, someone (you) hasn't proofread well enough. And sometimes it's because someone (you *again*) has carelessly corrected it in ways only a Martian could understand.

It's easy enough to make these mistakes. But it's not acceptable. Here's the good news though: it's easy to avoid them. In the last chapter, you learned how *and why* to proofread. In this chapter, you'll learn how and why to make proper corrections if proofreading, somehow, has failed.

Bringing Out the Worst

I've written a story. Oh, it's fictional, but it's good. *Very* good. As you'll see, it's about a fatal plane crash. Among others, the airplane was carrying singing sensation Rock Starr. Along with the other passengers, Starr was on a humanitarian mission from the United States to Russia. I could tell you more, but you'll read it all in the story, which I have written *flawlessly*. Well, almost flawlessly. If you look hard, you might find a few flaws I missed.

I've put it in a box, and left plenty of space between the lines, because I want you to correct whatever careless mistakes or poor writing you find. Don't rewrite the story on a new sheet of paper; make your changes and corrections on the script in the box. If you don't think you're going to sell this book to someone else when you're through with it, go ahead and make the corrections right here on the page. If you don't want to do that, photocopy the box and work from the copy you make. But whatever you do, do NOT read beyond the box. Not yet.

Today sinker Rock Starr died at 28, and 11 people, 6 males and 5 females, were also killed too today when a US Airforce C5A transport carrying the singing sensation and the others tragically crashed today in NY's Long Island Sound. The plane, based at Lake Champlain Ill., had been flying at 43,000 ft. at the time, carrying the volunteer workers and supplies to an air base in Leningrad where a dam building project is underway with US help. Analysts conclude that altitude is a dangerous one is a dangerous one to fly at. The spokesman for the AF, Chris Goldstein, estimates that the loss to the govt from this mishap is estimated at $29,037,292. "We pride ourselves for our air skills, and we're flat-out shocked by the crash," the Air Force Chief of Staff told reporters at the Pentagon.

Okay, did you make any changes? I sure hope so, because the piece as originally written wouldn't pass muster in a fourth grade writing class. Luckily for you, previous chapters in this book have armed you to find just about all the flaws that I missed.

The first ones probably were obvious, for instance, absurdly repetitive language:

- The word "*today*" shows up three times in the first sentence. It should appear only once, and certainly not at the very top of the story. That's another rule you should remember.
- In the phrase, "*. . . 11 people. . . were also killed too today. . .*" we don't need "*also*" and "*too*" in the same sentence.
- "*Analysts conclude that altitude is a dangerous one is a dangerous one to fly at.*" If you didn't catch the repetition here, you need to re-read the last chapter on proofreading aloud! (Do you remember now?) And by the way, do we really want that sentence to end with a preposition?
- Here's another repetition that's not quite as easy to catch, but you should have caught it anyway: "*The spokesman for the AF, Chris Goldstein, estimates that the loss to the govt is estimated at $2,037,292.*" He "*estimates*" that the loss is "*estimated at. . .*" Ugly!

You've also learned a lot of things in previous chapters that should have helped you catch and correct the following:

- If you're going to break down the gender of passengers at all, ". . . *6 males and 5 females*" should be ". . . 6 men and 5 women." But that's not all. As you know by now, we spell out numbers from 1 to 11. So it ought to read, ". . . six men and five women."

- While we're at it, you should have corrected "*11 people*" to read, "eleven people." But here too, there's more. According to the story, Rock Starr died, and "*11 people. . . were also killed.*" But unless his music was even worse than I think, Starr himself was human, so it's "eleven *other* people." It required clarification.

- Speaking of spelling out numbers, you should never leave a long numerical figure like "*$29,037,292.*" How to correct it to make it readable on the air? "29-million-37-thousand-two-hundred-92-dollars." (Notice that I change the dollar-sign symbol to the word "dollars" too.) But wait. Do we really need the loss, right down to the dollar? Of course not. You can round it off to "about 29-million-dollars." And while we're on a roll, "*43,000 ft.*" should have been "43-thousand ft."

- But of course, "*ft.*" is an abbreviation that shouldn't appear in a script. So it should be, "43-thousand feet." Likewise, "*Ill.*" should be "Illinois," "*NY*" should be "New York," "*gov't.*" should be "government" and "*AF*" should be "Air Force."

- There are a couple of names that require pronouncers. Does everyone know how to pronounce Lake "*Champlain?*" Probably not. And how about the name of the Air Force spokesman, Chris Goldstein? Does it sound like "Goldsteen" or "Goldstine?"

- Remember "*6 males and 5 females?*" Maybe you don't need that kind of detail at all. What's important is how many people died, not a breakdown of their genders. That may be Too Much Information (TMI)!

- Since we're talking now about TMI, how about the name of the Air Force spokesman? Whether it's pronounced "GOLD-steen" or "GOLD-stine," we really don't need it at all. He's a spokesman; his name doesn't matter.

- There may be a few other cases of TMI, such as where the plane was based, what the people were going to help build in Russia. But facts like that might be important to some members of the audience, so whether they're important enough to keep is subjective.

- A cousin of TMI is "trash." When the sentence in the story reads (after removing the repetition pointed out earlier), ". . . *analysts conclude that altitude is a dangerous one to fly at,*" did you think, "I should kill the words 'to fly at' because they add nothing?" You should have. "Analysts conclude that is a dangerous altitude" is enough.

- Did you change "*Analysts conclude. . .*" to "Analysts say. . ."? Should have! Write the way you talk.

- Likewise, if you wouldn't use "mishap" in normal conversation, don't use it in a script. So the "*mishap*" was a "crash." (And be careful about something else. It was not necessarily an accident. We don't know why the plane went down.)

- The plane "*tragically crashed,*" according to the original. Maybe even according to everyone you might have spoken to about the crash. But don't get in the habit of using judgmental words, even when the judgment probably is universal. Kill the adverb. Anyway, everyone knows a plane crash is tragic, and doesn't need you to explain it.

- If someone doesn't know what a C5A is, then she might misread it on the air. Remember why? Because it's actually read as three words. That's why "FBI" should be "F-B-I" on a script. Likewise, the "C5A" should be hyphenated on the script to read, "C-5-A."
- In the last line of the original story, there are two mistakes you should have caught:
    1. If you choose to use it, then you have to make clear to the audience that these are the very words of the Air Force chief of staff—this alone probably makes it worth using.
    2. The quote, followed by the reference to who said it, is old-fashioned print style. We don't talk that way, so we don't write that way for broadcast. Therefore, if you choose to use it, the way to change that sentence would be along the lines of, "The Air Force chief of staff says, and I quote, 'We pride ourselves for our air skills, and we're flat-out shocked by the crash.'" And this leads to yet another point: in the original, he "*said*," but because it's recent and the gist of his statement hasn't changed, you can make it "says."

Finally, without the benefit of what you're about to learn in this chapter—which will help you turn this molehill into a mountain—you should have caught a few other flaws deliberately built into the story:

- You don't want the anchorperson to sound like he is swearing. . . . so you don't want little traps like ". . . *where a dam building project is underway with U.S. help.*" If you want to mention the project at all, you should correct it to read something like, ". . . where the U.S. is helping to build a dam."
- "*Leningrad*" isn't Leningrad any more. It is "St. Petersburg." The name was changed after the Soviet Union, founded by Lenin, fell. You don't know that from this book, but you ought to know it from your class in geography.
- Oh, and maybe at the very top of the story, you noticed the typo "*sinker.*" Knowing that Rock Starr was a "singing sensation," you should have corrected it to read, "singer." If you're still on the computer, the correction is simple to make. If you're working from a page you've already printed out, there's a right way and a wrong way to make even a simple correction like that. By the end of this chapter, you'll know how.

Okay, that pretty much covers it. Although you probably found many of these flaws and made corrections, chances are you didn't find them all. So here's another box, with the same story in its original bad form. Correct it again, knowing now of all the flaws built into it. Why do it all again? Because this chapter isn't just about finding the flaws; it's about how to make corrections in a universally readable way. What this means is, when you have finished the chapter and, near the end, made these corrections a third time, you'll be surprised at how much easier they are to follow.

Today sinker Rock Starr died at 28, and 11 people, 6 males and 5 females, were also killed too today when a US Airforce C5A transport carrying the singing sensation and the others tragically crashed today in NY's Long Island Sound. The plane, based at Lake Champlain Ill., had been flying at 43,000 ft. at the time, carrying the volunteer workers and supplies to an air base in Leningrad where a dam building project is underway with US help. Analysts conclude that altitude is a dangerous one is a dangerous one to fly at. The spokesman for the AF, Chris Goldstein, estimates that the loss to the govt from this mishap is estimated at $29,037,292. "We pride ourselves for our air skills, and we're flat-out shocked by the crash," the Air Force Chief of Staff told reporters at the Pentagon.

Good. Now just one more exercise to complete this section. Pretend you're an anchorperson. Read what you've just corrected as if you're on the air. If anything makes you stumble—*anything*—then you need to correct your corrections. That's what you'll learn to do in the rest of this chapter.

What's the Point?

Writing a story by the rules is one thing. Having a readable copy on the air is another. Most of the time, corrections will be made in the computer. But you might be working with a printed copy and correcting it at the last minute, or handing your corrected copy to someone else to put back—properly corrected—into the computer. It must be clean and comprehensible to whoever gets it.

Just Follow the Roadmap

A script is like a roadmap. Sometimes, as you just read, it's going to get all marked up. But if everyone uses the same lines, the same signs, the same symbols, it shouldn't be a problem. Everyone will be able to read everyone else's script.

I can't guarantee that every producer in every newsroom will agree with the universal appeal of the formats you're about to learn. Some, in fact, may have been educated in and adhere to another organization's rules of style. If so, then needless to say, do it the way they do it there. But by and large, the rules you'll read here will serve you well.

Since I covered most of what you need to know already in earlier chapters, we're down to just the mechanics of corrections, the proper format. There are just a few rules to learn. They ought to become second-nature to you, because if you haven't learned them well before a script goes into the studio, it may be too late.

The whole purpose of the exercise is this: the script must be clear and clean enough to read on the air, even if the person reading it hasn't seen it before! What this means is, whether your manual markings are in someone else's hands to enter in the computer or to read from a printed page at the last minute on the air, they should be easy for anyone to figure out.

- All ~~alterations~~ *changes* go above the line, not ~~beneath~~ *below* it.

- Use clearly drawn ~~markings~~ *brackets* and include the ~~exclamations!~~ *punctuation!*

- If it's an addition, put it in either like *this* or, equally acceptable, *like* this.

- When words are crossed out, connect ~~virtually~~ the remaining sections this way.

- When words are crossed out and you're running to the next line, do it this ~~kind of mark~~ way, and make sure it curves all the way around as you see it done here, so that the "exit" and "entry" points are obvious.

- If you have a typo, like "*sinker* Rock Starr," you don't just fix the errant letter like this: sin*g*er. Correct the whole word, like this: ". . . ~~sinker~~ *singer* Rock Starr."

What's the Point?

The point is what I wrote at the beginning of this section: a script is like a roadmap. Make sure that if you have to manually mark a script before it's read on the air, anyone could find his way.

Corrections From the Front of the Class

The word "corrections" cuts both ways. It also refers to the corrections your instructor makes on scripts you turn in for assignments.

I've developed my own system of corrective marks, which I explain (in a handout) to students at the beginning of the semester. Then, instead of writing on every careless mistake something like, "Pay more attention to accuracy," or "Shouldn't you just round off this number?" or "Remember to hyphenate because it's actually three words when spoken aloud," I can just write (in these particular cases), A, RO, or H respectively. As you'll see, it's simply a series of letters, pointing to mistakes students make.

Each instructor's system is unique. But I'm showing you mine to underscore the variety of mistakes that turn up. They should have been caught by the writers in the proofreading process. *You* should catch them before turning anything in, especially when your job could depend on it!

A	ACCURACY is the most important thing in journalism. If you write well but are inaccurate, you're the world's worst journalist. Pay attention to facts. Don't get them wrong, and just as important, don't tell more than you know. If you have this letter on your script, it's because something is inaccurate.
AV	ACTIVE VERBS make the script come alive ("A man was killed by a bomb," versus "A bomb killed a man.")
C	COMMAS In broadcast copy they are not necessarily used for grammatical punctuation; rather, they can be used as a sign to the newscaster to pause. If there isn't a comma where there should be one, the newscaster might not know to pause. If there is one where there shouldn't be, the newscaster will pause where she shouldn't causing her to sound awkward. The only way to make sure you have it right is to proofread aloud with commas in mind. You wouldn't say, "Instructor, Greg Dobbs, told us this." It's "Instructor Greg Dobbs told us this." Likewise, in print you'd write, "In Lincoln, Nebraska, three men . . . " but in broadcasting you'd write, "In Lincoln Nebraska, three men . . . " because you'd say it that way.
CL	CLOSE should tell us where the story's going, or what it means, or wrap it up.
DIE	YOU CAN'T DIE "at 28." You can die at a party, or at home, or at the airport. If you want to give someone's age, then write it something like this: "Rock Starr died. He was 28." Or, "Rock Starr died at the age of 28."
DRQ	DON'T RAISE QUESTIONS you don't answer. Either answer the question in your script or don't raise it.
EC	EXTRA CLUTTER Is it necessary to name, for example, a police spokesman? No. The important thing is that "a police spokesman says the woman was drunk."
GA	DON'T GIVE AWAY THE SOUNDBITE with your lead-in.
H	HYPHENATE When we refer to a name with letters (like "FBI"), it's "F-B-I" because that's really three words. But here's an exception: U.S. is the proper abbreviation. (Remember, while NASA is an acronym, it's pronounced like a word, so you don't hyphenate it.)
JW	JUDGMENTAL WORDS Don't use them. Report, don't comment or editorialize.
L	LEAD INFORMATION must actually lead a story. If you bury a lead (somewhere in the body of the story), the audience may not stay interested long enough to hear you when you get to it. It should be the most important and/or the most interesting and/or the most immediate fact in the story. Keep it short and simple. It's the attention grabber.
LIU	LOOK IT UP if you don't know where or what something or someplace is. New, is about facts, not fiction.

LN	MAKE LARGE NUMBERS EASY TO READ, so if you have a big number like "$2.5 billion," spell out the word "dollar" instead of using the "$" symbol, and spell out the point, so it reads, "two-point-five billion dollars." Any number over eleven can be written as numerals. If it's a higher number like $23.5 billion, it reads "23-point-five billion dollars."
NA	NO ABBREVIATIONS Be particularly aware of common abbreviations like states, months, and units of measurement. Write out "New York" (not NY), "foot" or "feet" (not ft. or "), "government" (not gov't) and "international" (not int'l). The exceptions are: Mr., Mrs., Ms., Dr., and St.
NF	NO FLOW from the lead in into the sound bite.
NI	DO NOT INDENT for paragraphs. It's a news story, not a novel.
NP	NO PRONOUNCER Names (and other words) must be correctly pronounced. If there's any question about how to pronounce it, you've got to show it on the script! How do you know your anchor will know the correct pronunciation of "Champlain"? Or of "White House spokesman Chris Goldstein"? (Is it "Goldsteen" or "Goldstine?") Or whether the accent is on the first or the second syllable of "Perez"? Put phonetic pronunciation in parenthesis above or right after the questionable name, putting the emphasized syllable in ALL CAPS (for example, Sham-PLANE, GOLD-steen).
NS	NO SYMBOLS on scripts ($, degrees, %). Spell it out ("percent," "dollars," etc.)
P	PROOFREAD How? Aloud! (What you're writing is for the human *ear*, not the *eye*). If something's not proofread, it's sloppy. If it's sloppy, someone's going to screw up while reading it. If somebody screws up, the audience is distracted and you look stupid.
PA	PROOFREAD ALOUD and you'll catch mistakes that the eye won't always catch. You'll hear when words are overused. You'll catch embarrassing typos and tenses that don't match. You'll also catch things like, "He visited that dam project in Iowa."
PF	PRINT FORMAT doesn't cut it in broadcasting. A sentence such as, "'I didn't do it', the man said" must be written for radio and TV along the lines of, "The man said he didn't do it," or, "The man said, and I quote, 'I didn't do it.'" Remember, write like you talk!
PT	PRESENT TENSE Immediacy is most easily achieved by writing in the present tense, whenever possible. For example, it's better to write "The mayor says . . . " than "The mayor said. . . . . ." At least use the present perfect when you can. "A crippled plane has landed at the airport" is better than "A crippled plane landed at the airport."
PU	PUNCTUATION In making your correction, you left out (or left in) key punctuation that will confuse, embarrass, and ultimately foul up the anchorperson, which may be you.
Q	QUOTES must obviously be quotes! What this means is, if you just write: "The man said 'I didn't do it,'" the audience can't see the quotation marks on your script, and has no idea that these are the man's actual words. Someone might infer that the man is clearing you, the newscaster, of guilt. So

make it clear. In that example, therefore, you'd want to write something along the lines of, "The man said, and I quote, 'I didn't do it.'"

RM ROADMAP All the markings (connecting words after you've crossed something out, replacing one word with another, etc.) are your roadmap. Use the uniform markings you've been taught. They are basic and proven, and fairly universal.

RO ROUND OFF COMPLICATED NUMBERS Think about what's important from the standpoints of simplicity and understanding: "$2,037,292" or "more than two million dollars?" In a case like this, round it off.

SL SIMPLIFY LARGE NUMBERS like this: "43-thousand," not "43,000." Too many zeros for the anchor to read if there are distractions in the studio.

SLUG SLUG You need a slug in the upper lefthand corner. (You will learn about "slugs" in Chapter 16, "If the Shoe Fits, Write It.")

SN SPELL NUMBERS from 1–11, as in "one" to "eleven." So it's "two million dollars," not "2 million dollars."

SP SPELL IT RIGHT If you don't, it could end up misspelled on the bottom of a TV screen.

SW SIMPLE WORDS are better than longer more complicated words. It's not an "automobile," it's a "car."

T TRASH In other words, you just don't need this. It's extra words, extra time, makes everything harder for the audience to absorb. Shorter and simpler is better.

TS TRIPLE SPACE so you leave room for manual corrections. Yours or mine.

TW TOO WORDY because you gave too much information (TMI). Remember, it goes by your audience only once.

UO UNORIGINAL which means you just lifted words or whole phrases from your source. Come up with your own way of writing something. Depend on source material only for information.

W WRITE THE WAY YOU TALK One of the several times you proofread a piece, listen to how your script sounds. Ask yourself, is this the way I'd tell the story to a friend? If not, rewrite it.

Exercises to Correct Any Lingering Incorrectness

1. Rock Starr Returns

If you didn't see this one coming, you weren't thinking! The first time you corrected the Rock Starr story, it was with the benefit of earlier chapters but nothing else. The second time, you had the added benefit of alerts in this chapter to flaws that you might have missed the first time.

Now you know something else: how to properly make your corrections when required to do so. Making your corrections tests your proofreading skills as well as your use of corrective markings. This time, you should end up with something anyone could read, sight unseen, in a live broadcast.

Today sinker Rock Starr died at 28, and 11 people, 6 males and 5 females, were also killed too today when a US Airforce C5A transport carrying the singing sensation and the others tragically crashed today in NY's Long Island Sound. The plane, based at Lake Champlain Ill., had been flying at 43,000 ft. at the time, carrying the volunteer workers and supplies to an air base in Leningrad where a dam building project is underway with US help. Analysts conclude that altitude is a dangerous one is a dangerous one to fly at. The spokesman for the AF, Chris Goldstein, estimates that the loss to the govt from this mishap is estimated at $29,037,292. "We pride ourselves for our air skills, and we're flat-out shocked by the crash," the Air Force Chief of Staff told reporters at the Pentagon.

2. Same Thing, Different Story

The exercise here is just like the first one, except you haven't seen this story before. Trust me though, it needs just as much work as the first one.

Today 2 automobiles crashed during the blizzard on I95. According to state patrolman, Bob Worchester, who's patrol car arrived at the crash site just a few minutes after it happened, "One of the cars was weaving and crossed over the double yellowline; my guess is, 1 of the drivers was dead drunk." Both were were critical injured. Witnesses who saw it happen claim that the road was slick from the snow. "Anyone could crash in such bad conditions," said one. One of the vehicles involved in this awful crash was full of consumables from the supermarket, which already was beginning to spoil. The road just north of N.Y. was closed and still is while the wreckage is removed.

IV

Finding Out What to Write

12

News Hunters and News Gatherers

What You'll Learn

This chapter isn't specifically about how to write for broadcast news. But without this chapter and what it teaches you, you may have nothing to write about. The best broadcast writer in America is powerless if she doesn't know how to hunt down and gather the news.

It's not rocket science; it's really just a matter of using your natural human curiosity, and your capacity for persistence. Many people confronted with a news story wouldn't know where to start. A plane crashes, a murder is discovered, a legislative bill is defeated, a baseball player is injured. Where do you go for information to write your story? How do you research on the Internet? How do you work on the telephone? How do you pull off productive interviews? How do you know what to pursue and what to drop?

Let's begin with *you*. If you're standing still in a traffic jam and you can see flashing lights suggesting an accident a quarter mile ahead, will you sit in your car, turn the music up loud, and wait for the obstruction to be cleared? Or will you search for a radio newscast to tell you what's going on? Or ask the driver in the car next to you if she knows what the problem is? Or, if it's neither obstructive for other idle drivers nor dangerous, will you try to pull off the road and get out of your car and hightail it up to the accident itself so you can find out firsthand?

If you'd want to go there yourself, you have the instinct for news. You'd already be demonstrating your curiosity and your persistence, which are the personal qualities you really need to be a journalist. After all, the root of the word is "journal." When you try to see the accident for yourself, you're trying to gather the information you'd need to keep a journal, to write a story about what you've seen.

What you'll learn in this chapter is how to react to news. How to put those personal qualities to good use by learning who to talk to, where to go, what to look for when you're covering the news. The rules are the same for broadcast and print journalists alike. Follow your nose, don't give up!

The Terms of the Story

Shotgun Microphone   A long microphone, usually more than a foot long, shielded with a fuzzy-looking cover to filter out the wind. It only picks up the sound from the narrow direction in which it is pointed, so that superfluous noise from either side is minimized.

On Camera Standup   The reporter telling a portion of the story on camera anywhere in the piece—at the top, in the middle, or at the end—rather than just voiceover.

On Camera Bridge   An on camera standup somewhere in the middle of a story, between, or bridging, two other elements.

Feedpoint   The television facility, satellite truck or satellite pack, or any other place from which you transmit ("feed") your video.

News Release   A notice or memo put out by someone who wants journalists to know about developments within the organization for which he works.

Who Reports, Who Writes?

The first distinction you should understand is this: The production of a newscast or even a single story for radio or TV is a team effort. Everyone involved—the newsroom editors, the broadcast producers, the field technicians, the reporters on the street—is a journalist. Every one of them makes decisions that affect the coverage technically, logistically, creatively, or editorially. It doesn't really matter which specific field you personally have chosen to pursue; if you touch any piece of a story, you're a journalist. Just remember, you probably couldn't have done it by yourself.

Read these anecdotes about the importance of the whole team. You'll see what I mean. Everyone's a journalist. Everyone's part of the team.

"Unsung Journalists"

Two of the most successful stories in which I was ever involved—stories that won awards and acclaim—succeeded only because of colleagues who many people don't define as journalists. But I do, because without them and their persistence, one of these stories would have been unremarkable and the other, unseen. I tell them so you'll appreciate the entire team with which you work.

The first you've read about already; it was three days after the catastrophic earthquake in Italy, southeast of Naples. A couple of thousand people in several dozen villages had died, many because their humble homes collapsed on top of them during their Sunday supper.

For coverage like this, you want to find a fresh angle each day, and that becomes a challenge. Pretty soon the "big picture" stories are done, and your job as a journalist is to find the small stories, the personal stories that illustrate the big pain of the victims.

On day three after the earthquake, with a helicopter at our command, we bounced from village to village. But they *all* had casualties, they *all* were reduced to rubble. What would we do differently than what we had done the days before?

After a couple of hours of daylight we were in our second or third village, still empty-handed, when we heard a man shouting and saw him frantically gesturing atop a huge pile of rubble. He was shouting in Italian, but one member of our team knew the language and said, "He thinks he's found someone alive."

He had indeed. We scrambled with our camera gear to the top of the pile and spent the next six hours there. The rescuer who had shouted that first alarm had heard a squeal—just a tiny, weak squeal, but it sounded human. It was. It was a woman who, we learned before the end of the day, had been buried about six feet down, trapped by concrete and thick wood beams, the body of her dead sister on top of her.

For those six hours we watched and recorded as rescuers got her out. They had to work painstakingly slowly. This pile of rubble was a house of cards; if they moved the wrong stick or stone, the whole precarious pile could collapse, burying not just the survivor but the rescuers and, incidentally, us!

Over time, the squeal came more often, and eventually got louder. Rescuers delicately opening a passage were getting closer and closer. But in all those hours, we never saw the woman, we only heard her. And that's where Lenny Jenson comes in.

He was our sound man. He had a long shotgun microphone, and for six hours he held his arm fully extended into the ever deeper hole. For six hours he picked up the survivor's squeals, and the dramatic sounds rescuers made as they warily snapped thin twigs and lifted small stones, wondering whether each would be the one to cause this pile to collapse upon itself.

"*Somewhere down there is a woman named Lisa. . . .*" That's how our dramatic story on *World News Tonight* began, then it kept getting even better. "*This rescue worker cut up his face but said, 'I touched Lisa's hand, my blood doesn't matter.'*" In the story, we didn't see Lisa until the very end, when she was pulled from the hole and rushed to an ambulance waiting alongside the rubble, but viewers would hardly even notice, because we *heard* her. We heard every squeal, and every twig broken in the path to her crypt.

The story won an Emmy, for best spot news coverage on a network. I got a statue. So did the cameraman. But nobody at the National Academy of Television Arts and Sciences (which awards Emmys) recognized Lenny's incomparable achievement.

They should have. We sure did. Officially he was a sound technician, but it was his persistence—his instinct as a journalist—that made the story so special.

The second story was about the bloody fighting in early 1979 during the revolution in Iran, when forces supporting Islamic fundamentalist Ayatollah Khomeini pushed the American-backed Shah (like "king") of Iran from power. Because it had lots of oil and shared a border with America's Cold War rival the Soviet Union, Iran was an important American ally going down the drain.

It was a brush fire revolution. For months there had been brutal one-sided massacres by the Shah's soldiers against unarmed civilian dissidents. Hundreds died in downtown Tehran, the Iranian capital, in a single day. One Friday night in February, following yet another massacre, fighting broke out at a barracks between uniformed soldiers loyal to the Shah and the rebels and soldiers wearing the same uniforms, whose loyalty had shifted to the militant Ayatollah.

The fighting quickly spread to the streets. Within hours there was gunfire all over the capital, and soon after that, all over the country. Dissident soldiers (those who changed sides) were giving their weapons and ammunition to the rebels. For the first time, it was an even fight.

But the dissidents were scared. The fighting had spread so fast that the soldiers who had joined the rebels were still in their uniforms, easily identifiable if their pictures were taken and they probably would have been summarily court–martialed and executed, and they knew it. So word swiftly spread on the streets: if you see a camera, destroy it.

With my ABC News crew, we were in the middle of all this. We had spectacular footage illustrating the passion of the rebels and the fierceness of the fighting, but soon we learned about the ban on cameras. So we had to hide in storefronts along battle–torn streets, then dash out through their broken windows and grab a few shots and run somewhere else with a mad mob on our tails to temporarily hide again.

(continued)

"Unsung Journalists"   **Continued**

Eventually on that first day of fighting, we needed just one more element to make our coverage complete: the on-camera "standup." In a dangerous situation like that, you don't want to expose yourself any longer than necessary, so before you leap into the street and turn on the camera, you make sure everyone's ready, the camera's rolling, the microphone is activated, and the script is memorized. You probably won't get a second chance.

We jumped onto the street and the moment the cameraman was steady, I started talking: *"The battle started late last night when the Shah's Imperial Guard entered the Farahabad military base here in eastern Tehran. Fighting broke out, civilians started getting guns, and military mutinies began en-masse. And street fighters, to protect military defectors' identities, started turning on newsmen. Whenever we openly turned our camera toward the street . . ."*

At that point, just before the end of the on-camera bridge, someone spotted us. Someone with a gun. He turned and fired, and with the bullets whistling within inches of our heads, we all hit the ground, then as he and his compatriots came running, we jumped up and ran ourselves. By the time the gunman could carefully aim again, we had rounded a corner and disappeared into a maze of doorways.

It would be quite a television story, but the question was, how do we get it on the air? Because of the fighting, our regular feedpoint at Iranian television was shut down. Normally we'd then ship our tape on an airplane leaving the country, but because of the heavy fighting everywhere, the airport had tanks on the runways and was shut down too.

This leads to Maurice James. He was a sometimes-sound technician who more often served as courier for our ABC Paris bureau. He was in Iran for the coverage and with us that day simply because we needed an extra body to help haul supplies.

Maurice assessed the situation. We had remarkable video, but unless it found its way out of Iran, it would never make it on the air. So he made it happen. Amidst heavy fighting, he got through to the airport, searching for any route out of Iran. He pushed his way into the terminal, teeming with frantic people trying to escape, and spotted just one plane on the tarmac. But the doors from the terminal to the tarmac where the plane was waiting were locked and guarded, so keeping as low a profile as he could in the chaos, Maurice found the freight department, snuck through, ran toward terrified passengers scrambling up the airliner's steps, offered money and a convincing plea to whoever would carry our tapes, and got our story on the only flight out—to Tel Aviv. ABC had a bureau there, and that's where the piece was edited and fed to ABC New York.

As it turned out, this was the only video to make it out of Iran on this key weekend of the revolution. ABC News ended up feeding it via satellite to news syndicates all over the world. All thanks to Maurice. Did his I.D. card say "journalist"? No. Was he one? Yes. That day, he was the best.

What's the Point?

Even though your job description may not say it, if you work in a newsroom, or on a news team, you're a journalist. And if you never leave the newsroom, you're a journalist. You have to be. Few stories are the product of one person alone; in broadcasting, that is next to impossible. Whatever role you play, you make decisions that help shape stories. Curiosity, persistence, we're all born with them. It's up to you to activate them.

From the Melodramatic to the Mundane

There are a few things you need, of course, in addition to curiosity and persistence.

For starters, you should acquire some of the pocket-size tools—as books or software—that any good writer should not work without: an atlas, an almanac, a dictionary, and an encyclopedia. Pretty mundane? Yes, but also pretty irreplaceable. Why?

Imagine you have to write a piece from the newsroom about a nuclear reactor leak someplace in Russia called Chernobyl. You should at least tell your audience where in Russia this place is—northeast of Moscow, southwest of Moscow, a hundred miles away, a thousand miles? These are details that help viewers and listeners put the story into perspective. Find them in the atlas.

Or imagine that you learn ten minutes before your newscast that the president has been assassinated. Was he the forty-second or the forty-third? For a story of this magnitude, that's a perspective you'll want to include. The almanac has it.

Now imagine you've come up against a word you want to use in a story but you're not absolutely sure of its definition, or for that matter, its correct spelling (which is especially important if a script is displayed in a CG on the bottom of people's TV screens). Any decent computer these days has spell check and thesaurus tools, but sometimes your pocket dictionary still ends up being more efficient, and providing more information. Spell check won't catch the wrong spelling or volunteer the correct meaning of a word that's spelled more than one way (for example, "horse" and "hoarse," "sew" and "sow," and "to," "too," and "two").

Finally, imagine yourself charged with an assignment to write about a new discovery in the solar system, or about alligators in Florida, or about Communist China. There is no substitute for an online, software-installed, or single volume paperback encyclopedia.

Making Sure You're Wired

Those reference tools are indispensable, but they will not tell you what's going on in your world or your city today. The wire services will, often with more breadth and depth than you'll find anywhere else. So will other news organizations' web sites, as well as their regular daily output. So will news releases from people and organizations that want to attract your attention. And so will police and fire department and Civil Air Patrol and other emergency service radios (also known as "scanners"), to which a good journalist—and inescapably any assignment editor—must keep one ear attuned.

Perhaps the most important lesson to learn about all these sources of information is that they are just that: sources. They may or may not be accurate, and they may or may not be up-to-date.

What does this mean? Don't depend exclusively on sources, because their information may contain mistakes. The initial report of a plane crash with many casualties sometimes mercifully turns out to be overblown. The first word of an earthquake with "at least a hundred dead" sometimes sadly evolves as accounts trickle in to a total death toll in the

The assignment editor can never go far from the radios. Courtesy of KCNC-TV Denver.

thousands. The news release predicting one hundred thousand people at a demonstration sometimes self-servingly turns out to be a thousand percent inflated.

The 1999 shootings at Columbine High School in Littleton, Colorado, probably offer the most poignant example: the county sheriff himself publicly announced that the death toll might be as big as thirty. High as it was at thirteen, thankfully it wasn't half as high as the sheriff's indiscriminate prediction. Many Denver area TV and radio stations broadcast the sheriff's erroneous number in their live coverage (which was being linked to stations and networks nationwide), but thanks to newsroom veterans, some knew to advise their audiences that even though the sheriff said it, it might not be accurate. How did they know? From experience: the situation was still fluid, the school had not yet been secured, the sheriff could not substantiate his figure.

What's the Point?

Be careful. That's all, just be careful. Sometimes inevitably you have to trust your gut (such as when you have no time for personal research), but whenever possible, don't trust anyone or anything until you have checked it out yourself, firsthand.

During the war against Iraq in 2003, the coverage of an American family whose daughter, Jessica Lynch, was held as a prisoner of war until being dramatically rescued from an Iraqi hospital by fellow American troops, is an embarrassing example of misplaced trust. The reporter who wrote about the family for the *New York Times*, Jayson Blair, didn't really go to their West Virginia home as he claimed he did. He fabricated quotes, and even made up an erroneous description of the home itself. Ultimately he brought disgrace to the whole paper and was fired, but once his fraudulent reporting itself became a national story, reporters across the United States admitted that they'd incorporated information from the *Times* into their own stories.

Wired Language, Your Language

Another possible problem, particularly in the case of the wire services (and newspaper clippings), is that they may or may not communicate the news in language you want to use. First of all, they're usually written in a style fit for the eyes, not the ears (in Chapters 4 and 5, you read more on the difference between writing for print and writing for broadcast). That's a style you don't want to use. Second, and much more important, unless you personally know that the wire service reporter or newspaper writer has an unparalleled passion for accuracy and balance, not to mention a good sense for choosing the best lead, best words, and best information, why would you want to depend on them?

What does this mean? Look at the following leads for the same story, written by two different reporters who covered the end of a trial:

> *"Facing the possibility of serving in excess of 7 years in prison, Captain Joseph Hazelwood, skipper of the Exxon Valdez, which spilled millions of barrels of crude oil one year ago in Alaska's Prince William Sound, has been found not guilty of criminal charges relating to inebriation the night his supertanker collided with a reef, and he has been convicted by a jury in a state court in Alaska of just one misdemeanor charge, "negligent discharge of oil."*

Or:

> *SOT JURY FOREMAN: We the jury find the defendant Joseph Hazelwood not guilty of criminal mischief in the 2nd degree . . .*
>
> *NARRATION: Not guilty of any charge except the mildest misdemeanor: "negligent discharge of oil."*

Hopefully it didn't take you long to infer that the first lead is from a wire story, while the second lead is from our own story for ABC News, at the end of the trial of the captain whose supertanker was involved in the worst oil spill in history. Sure, by the end of both stories, all the same important information was told. But the wire service reporter didn't have to worry about people hearing his words just once and absorbing them; as a broadcast reporter, I did. So I didn't write a long complex lead like his, nor try to tell half the history of the disaster in a single lead as he did, and later in the TV story, there were no phrases like "in excess of" or words like "inebriation."

What's the Point?

What you already should know by this point in this book is that the style a print writer uses usually doesn't have a place in broadcasting. What you also need to know is if you lazily lift language verbatim from a print story—either sentences or single words—you run the risk of producing a piece that your audience won't be able to comprehend. Use the wires (and newspaper clippings) for information, not for language. Make your own decisions. Don't let another journalist make them for you.

The Final Indispensable Tool

Let's talk about computers and the Internet. At a pace that would have bedazzled journalists as recently as the early 1990s, a lot of information you'll need when researching stories not only is available on the Internet, but it's *only* available there. Already there are countless books to teach you how to do Internet research, with countless more in the works. So I won't try to provide chapter and verse.

But I will try to give you the general picture, and it is this: if a plane crashes, you probably can learn virtually everything you want to know—from its maintenance records to the date of the pilot's last health checkup—on the Internet. If a crime suspect is captured, you can probably learn everything you need to know about his background—from prior criminal history to employment record—on the Internet. You can learn about corporate records, political contributions, property tax obligations, and every word of just about every law.

If you have someone's phone number and want to learn the physical location, presto, go to an online reverse directory (which allows you to look up an address based on a telephone number). If you have an address and want to know what it's close to, presto, go to an online maps directory. If you have someone's Social Security number, go to the Social Security Administration's web site to find out from that number the state in which it was issued.

There are things that still aren't online, but wait long enough and they will be.

How to Use the Final Indispensable Tool

You don't use Internet search engines just to find the cheapest fare to Cabo San Lucas. You also can use them to get yourself started on story research. You might have to ask a search engine to lead you to a government site, but then, once there, the sky's the limit. It's just a matter of coming up with the right search terms, or "keywords," and to achieve that, you need to do just two things:

1. Learn the best ways to take advantage of the search engine you're using. Unfortunately, search engines don't have uniform rules; some will have you type search terms (keywords) in quotes; others will have you separate search terms and phrases with the words "and" or "or."

   So the rule to teach you here is to read each search engine's (and each web site's) search rules, or help tips. Sometimes they'll be printed right on the home page; sometimes you'll have to click on a help page.

2. Use your head. If one search term doesn't work, try a synonym, a variation.

   If you don't find what you want through search engines (perhaps because you're not coming up with the right search terms), think about a shortcut. Which means what? Think about the sort of web site that would have the kind of information you need. Then, instead of going through a search engine, try typing in URLs ("www" addresses) that make sense. It doesn't always work, but it doesn't always fail, either.

   And this final warning: what you learn about search engines today won't necessarily work well for you tomorrow. Search engine technology and superiority are fluid. The only solution is to be aware of this, and stay up to date.

Forever Changing the Final Indispensable Tool

It would take too many trees to produce the book that definitively lists the contents of the Internet. It keeps growing and changing. The growth is obvious, but the change may not be, so let me give you just this one example: the White House web site. When one president replaces another (such as the succession of George W. Bush after Bill Clinton back in 2001), the old White House web site (reflecting the eight years of Clinton's presidency) disappears, and a new one (reflecting the ongoing presidency of Bush) takes its place.

Apply this principle to whatever you're looking for. For example, the online roster of inmates at the Illinois State Penitentiary in Joliet changes, and temporarily relevant information is erased every time an inmate is released or a new one is registered. The online bill of lading for a cargo ship putting in at the port of New York is different for every voyage.

On the other hand, some records are permanent. Vital records, like births, marriages, divorces and deaths, can open the way to a wealth of information about people. Birth certificates, for example, can work wonders. If you find out where or when someone was born, perhaps you can confirm or contradict information you have from another source. Or perhaps you can use it to find out where someone went to school, and who his classmates were, and then, finding them, you can go in a hundred different directions to learn what you need to know.

But be aware of this important caution: the Internet is the ultimate populist tool. This means you must use your discretion about your source of online information, because depending on who provides it, some of it may be inaccurate. So, you shouldn't accept information as gospel just because it's on the Internet where anyone can post anything they like. What's more, if it's not on the Internet, that doesn't mean it's not credible. It just means it's not online. Think of the Internet as a useful research tool, but *not the only* research tool!

Also, search engines aren't the only way to get what you want online. Collections of information known as databases are another indispensable tool for your research. Perhaps the most frequently used online database is called Lexus-Nexus, where you'll find an abundance of full-length articles previously published in newspapers, magazines, and journals. Some databases require a subscription for occasional use, some require a single-use fee—payable online. The benefit of using a database is that you get access to cumulative and substantive research that others have done before you.

What's the Point?

The Internet is an indispensable research tool, but there is no single formula for every search. You simply begin by asking, what do I want to know about this person, or this company, or this *thing,* and what would I need to see to find out? Then you ask, how much do I trust this online source?

An Even More Indispensable Tool: The Interview

Now you've read about many sources of information on the printed page and the computer screen. But obviously those shouldn't be your only tools to hunt down and gather the news. Since a story basically consists of what you've seen firsthand and what you've learned secondhand, interviews are another tool at the heart of journalism.

When broadcasters refer to an "interview," they usually mean a conversation between a reporter or anchor and the interviewee, on camera or, for radio, on mike. They usually mean something that might yield sound bites for a broadcast story. But actually, an interview is much more than that, and often much more important.

To fully understand, consider the dictionary definition of the word (see how handy the dictionary is?): *"A meeting at which information is obtained from a person."* Hmmm. It doesn't say anything about an interview being *recorded.* That's because in many of the interviews you'll do, you won't be using a microphone. Why not? Because sometimes you won't be looking for a sound bite, you'll just be looking for information.

Not Every Interview Is a Blockbuster

So what is an interview? It is a conversation in which someone asks questions and someone else gives answers. It is a conversation in which, referring back to that dictionary definition, someone gives information. If you're doing a story about two trains colliding and you simply call a railroad spokesperson on the phone to get details, you're doing an interview whether you record it or not. If you show up at the scene of a public protest and you ask a participant what he's protesting, you're doing an interview whether you record it or not. If you run into the mayor in a city hall corridor and you ask her about some pending piece of legislation, you're doing an interview whether you record it or not. You're asking questions, and someone is giving you answers. Someone is giving you information.

Not surprisingly, the two qualities you need to do a productive interview are the two qualities I emphasized earlier in this chapter: curiosity and persistence.

The Curiosity Factor

Curiosity is critical because even if you personally don't care about the subject of a story, you must ask yourself what someone who does care would want to know. What would they ask? Those become the questions you ask.

For years, while based in Chicago for ABC News, I had to do a lot of farm stories throughout the Midwest. As a San Francisco native who always had been surrounded by pavement, frankly I knew little and cared less about farms. But time and again, I had to interview farmers about farm price supports from the government, irrigation techniques, the cost of tractors, and the price of wheat.

I could pull it off only because I asked myself, "What would other farmers want to know?" Eventually, by the way, I came to appreciate the intricacies and tribulations of farming, because I came to realize that without it, we wouldn't have much to eat!

The Importance of Persistence

Persistence is imperative because if your interviewee doesn't offer a direct answer to your question—or even just an indisputably clear answer (like a law enforcement officer referring to the undefined "hazmat" team that's on its way to clean up a chemical spill)—you must ask again, and sometimes yet again, until he does, or at least until it's crystal clear that he won't!

An example is an interview with the long-time leader of Libya, Colonel Mu'ammar Qaddafi. Terrorists had just attacked and killed western tourists, including five Americans, who were waiting in line for flights at airports in Vienna and Rome. United States intelligence traced the terrorists to Libya.

Like most major western news organizations, we flew to Tripoli and filed a request to see Qaddafi. After waiting for a few days in the hotel, we got an early Sunday morning call, which went to all western reporters who had come to town: "Be out front with your cameras in fifteen minutes. We are taking you on a tour of the antiquities around Tripoli."

All four of us from ABC News had seen the Roman ruins on Libya's coast before, but we knew of the Libyans' inclination for intrigue. So we went out front and got on the bus. As it turned out, we were the only westerners who did. That persistence paid off handsomely.

After driving out of town, we pulled up next to a field where an arrow-shaped row of tractors was plowing. The lead tractor—at the point of the arrow—had bodyguards holding machine guns running alongside, a pretty sure sign that the Qaddafi was in the driver's seat.

We ran through the field and sure enough, he was. It obviously was a setup, to show what a "man of the people" Colonel Qaddafi was, but that merely made our story all the more riveting.

Read this exchange near the beginning of the interview, and note the persistence to get a direct answer about Qaddafi's help for terrorists. Given what he probably was hiding, Colonel Qaddafi may not have fully cooperated, but you can't say we didn't try!

> ***DOBBS:*** *You have said one man's terrorist is another man's freedom fighter. How did you or Libya help the "freedom fighters" in Vienna and Rome?*
>
> ***QADDAFI:*** *As I told you, we support the freedom fighters everywhere, particularly our brothers, Palestinians. And we are not responsible for their attacks.*
>
> ***DOBBS:*** *Did they come from here, do you know?*
>
> ***QADDAFI:*** *No. You know, first of all, Palestinians are everywhere, even in America. They may come from America. There are thousands of Palestinians, refugees, are in America. They may come from America. That means Americans are responsible for these attacks.*
>
> ***DOBBS:*** *But did they come from here, is the question. These men, in Rome and Vienna?*
>
> ***QADDAFI:*** *Do you have any evidence?*
>
> ***DOBBS:*** *I'm asking you.*
>
> ***QADDAFI:*** *I ask you also.*

Eventually, persistence paid off, not necessarily with an honest answer, but with an answer:

> ***QADDAFI:*** *If they are here they can be my responsibility, but they are not here because they haven't—if they need, I will give them, I am not afraid . . . because they are freedom fighters.*

This was a case where between what the interviewee said and what he didn't say, the audience could reach its own conclusions.

Do Not Try This If It's Not **Your** *Home*

For those of you who hope some day to be "foreign correspondents," always bear in mind one thing. Our Constitution's First Amendment permits us to ask the most irreverent questions of our highest leaders, but it doesn't carry any weight beyond our shores. In other words, when interviewing a despot who can easily have you arrested and imprisoned on his whim—or in a broader sense, when breaking a dictatorship's arbitrary rules in the interest of getting your story—tread cautiously.

What's the Point?

An interview, whether or not you record it, can yield great information. If you do record it, it can provide a great dynamic too. Plus sound bites, of course!

A Few Tricks to Try at Home

One difference between the unrecorded and the recorded interview is that when you're recording, you want sound bites. Therefore, if you want to increase your chance of getting exchanges that flow and answers that are usable in your piece, learn these simple rules:

1. Do not ask "yes or no" questions.

   If you do, your interviewee may just tell you "yes" or "no." That may give you the information you need, but it won't give you the sound bite.

   Consider the following questions, and ask yourself which one is more likely to get someone to answer in the form you need:

   Were you happy to have your baby before the end of the tax year, so you could take a deduction on her?

   Shortest possible answer: "Yes!"

   What did you think about having your baby before the end of the tax year, so you could take a deduction on her?

   Shortest probable answer: "I was thrilled!"

   Or:

   Governor, are you going to run for reelection?

   Shortest possible answer: "No."

   Governor, what are your reelection plans?

   Shortest probable answer: "I'm not running again."

Maybe you'll get longer answers with either version of the questions, but your chance of getting one long enough to use as a sound bite is much greater if you phrase questions in a way that makes it hard to answer with just a word or two.

Intent on Silence

If a politician, or an entertainer, or a corporate executive who is used to speaking into microphones is your interview target, and he doesn't really want to talk, there may not be much you can do. The most amusing story is about President Calvin Coolidge, who was nicknamed "Silent Cal." It is told that a woman went up to his table at a White House dinner and said, "President Coolidge, I have bet $10 with my friend over there that you will say at least three words to me," to which Coolidge reportedly responded, "You lose."

2. Do not prepare for an interview by writing every question in advance.

Having a list of written questions can be fraught with risk. You may be so preoccupied with asking the next question on your list that it becomes a crutch and you aren't listening to the answer to the last question. It may cry out for a follow up question you hadn't planned.

What to do instead? Know before the interview what you want to talk about—a list of what you want to *cover* won't hurt—then *listen* to what the interviewee tells you and let the questions flow from that. Sure, if there's a key question that absolutely must be asked (like asking Colonel Qaddafi whether he helped the terrorists), by all means be prepared to do so. But once you're past the beginner's level of discomfort doing a recorded interview, avoid the "question list." It can paralyze you if the interview takes an unexpected twist.

One more point on predetermined questions. Often, when you ask someone to sit for an interview, they'll ask you for a list of the questions you plan to ask. It's a request you don't want to fulfill, because if you do, then any other question that logically flows from the conversation may be seen as a violation of the rules. So if someone asks you for a list of questions, tell them something like this: "Well, I don't actually write my questions down, but I'll want to ask you *about* (fill in the blank)."

3. Do not *discuss* your questions with the interviewee in advance.

Why not?

- The interviewee probably will think so hard about how she is going to answer the question—like a rehearsal in the mind—that the answer won't end up sounding spontaneous or natural.
- If the interviewee already has discussed something with you before the camera or tape recorder was turned on, he will likely answer the second time (when you are rolling for sound bites) with sound bite killers like, "I wanted to strangle him as I told you before but I was afraid I'd get caught."

- If the subject of the interview has an element of emotion or passion, it'll come across best the first time it is expressed. If that first time is *before* you're recording, well, you'll be sorry the second time.

These rules apply mainly to "amateur" interviewees, people most likely to feel some nervousness about the process. Politicians, entertainers, business leaders, professional athletes, and others accustomed to microphones and cameras are less likely to freeze up or otherwise foul up. As a general rule though, if you can do the interview without a "pre-interview," do so.

4. Be thinking about what you want to ask when the interviewee completes an answer—particularly when the interview is live on the air—but don't work so hard on forming the next question in your mind that you stop listening to the answer itself.

Like the second rule, your interviewee may use a term that requires, for your audience's sake, that you stop and ask for clarification—*"I think the CHP will issue its report by tomorrow."* Huh? The CHP? Ask your interviewee to answer the question again, but to explain what "the CHP" is (California Highway Patrol). Just like "hazmat."

Or, your interviewee may lay a bombshell at your feet—*"Yea, I killed her, but she deserved it"*—but if you're not listening carefully enough, you might miss the opportunity of a lifetime. It happens!

5. Listen for usable sound bites.

This doesn't mean just listen for clarity and for bombshells, or for sentences too convoluted to be understood. It also means listen for length. You don't want to sit there staring at your stopwatch while an interviewee is answering your questions, but you have to put that inner "mental stopwatch" to work and be aware of answers that are just too long to use!

So, if you've been given a minute and fifteen seconds for your entire story and an interviewee gives you a superb but long answer, it's perfectly okay to say something like, "That was right on the money, but it probably took too long to use on the air. Would you mind telling me again, but shorter?" Sure, it can be a bit embarrassing, but it's even more embarrassing if you don't get a usable sound bite at all.

Ask Before You Ask

Often for radio and sometimes for TV too, you'll want to record a telephone interview. That's fine, but be aware of the federal law regarding this: You cannot use someone's voice on the air unless he has given you permission.

What this means is, you should ask *before* you start taping an interview whether you have permission to use the conversation on the air. If you forget, you might be able to ask afterwards, but people who have been recorded without being told or asked beforehand are less likely to say yes after the fact. What's more, in some states retroactive permission is not legal.

And if you're talking about a live conversation on radio or TV, you *have to* ask first! If you don't, and you put someone's voice on the air without permission and they complain, the Federal Communications Commission can pull your station's license and, if the violation is egregious enough, put it out of business. Then you, personally, will be out of business for sure.

What's the Point?

A good writer, journalist, or reporter all need help. It might be reference books, Internet research, or outside sources of information. And it might be one-on-one interviews. Use them all. But without weighing their reliability, don't depend on any.

What They Call "Investigative Journalism"

Any journalist ought to be able to write a story about a fire, a merger, a ball game, or an election. Just watch, listen, and write. That's what fills most newscasts.

But what if there are rumors of arson behind the fire? Or embezzlement during the merger? Or illegal steroids on the team? Or bribes during the campaign? How would you find out? By asking yourself a few simple questions: Who might know something? What should I look at? Where should I go? Knowing all that is the difference between reporting and investigative reporting.

Every investigative story is unique. There is no single formula that applies to them all. But there are two qualities that are common to all, and they are the same two that you read about at the beginning of this chapter: use your innate human curiosity, and be persistent! Put yourself in the shoes of the investigator; in fact, *be* the investigator.

This makes the investigative journalist a theorist. It's a matter of filling in the holes, and looking for the contradictions. The investigative journalist is dealing not just with what is factual, but with what may *not* be.

What's the Point?

A story, any story, is good if:

- It's accurate (not wrong),
- It's clear (not confusing),
- It's dynamic (not boring),
- It's ready on time (newscasts won't wait).

An investigative story needs a few more elements, for the benefit of the audience:

- It's new (this ground hasn't been broken before),
- It's important (we care about what you've learned),
- It's exclusive (no one else has told us this).

Exercises to Hone Your Newsgathering Skills _____

1. Assume you are sent to interview the winner of a $100 million lottery, but because of her nervousness, she says you can ask only two questions, no more. Remember, you want good, long, fun sound bites! What are the best two questions you would ask?

2. You want to conduct a search on the Internet. The question is, how many handguns are in circulation in the United States, and in how many offices and homes? Make a list of at least 10 different keywords you might use to find your statistics.

3. Find out how many inmates are in the prison right now at Joliet, Illinois, with the last name "Jones." Find out how many (if any) are there with *your* last name.

4. To refresh yourself on how useful they can be, list five items you'll find in an almanac that could conceivably be necessary for a news story, and five in an atlas, and five in an encyclopedia, and five in a dictionary.

5. If you're doing an interview and the subject makes the following statements, write the followup questions you should ask in response to each:
   - "I thought I was going to die until the doctors performed an angioplasty."
   - "I saw one of the two cars that crashed weaving between lanes like the driver was drunk."
   - "We have determined that the plane crashed because of a faulty aileron."
   - "I found so much money in that dumpster that I figured I was set for life!"

6. List all the questions you'd ask if you were assigned to interview the coach of the team that has just lost the Super Bowl.

7. See how much you can learn about yourself on the Internet. Submit a list of facts (generalize if it's personal).

8. Go to the library. See how much you can learn about yourself, or your family, there. You might be surprised.

13

Running in Place

Not a day goes by that a TV or radio reporter doesn't get an idea for a story from a newspaper. Critics contend that the major networks couldn't even fill their newscasts if the *New York Times* weren't delivered. Maybe there's some truth to that. But these days, the same also is true in reverse. Every day, broadcast reporters come up with new story ideas, or sniff out new angles on old stories, that newspapers then copy. It's the way of the world, and no reason for anyone to hang their heads in shame.

But you ought to be ashamed if you're not trying to think of new ideas or new angles yourself. It's part of every journalist's job. Thinking, asking, pursuing, being as thorough as possible every day of the week. Thanks to the First Amendment to the U.S. Constitution, you have more freedom to write and report than journalists anywhere else on earth. By and large, American journalists show their recognition by busting their chops to be thorough.

One of the best books out there about how journalism is practiced is called *The News About the News*. It was written by Leonard Downie, Jr., who worked his way up to become executive editor of the *Washington Post*, and Robert Kaiser, who became its associate editor and senior correspondent. In an early passage, they define the scope of our uniquely American journalistic freedoms:

"In the formative years of the new republic, politicians, government officials and journalists jousted repeatedly over how far the press could go in challenging the politically powerful. Some of the same Founding Fathers who gave us the First Amendment also produced a sedition law that briefly threatened press freedom by punishing antigovernment journalism until it expired in 1801. Gradually over the next two centuries, American courts gave ever-greater protection to journalists and their work. The courts have barred government from imposing its will or prior restraint on the press, except for wartime censorship. The Supreme Court has made it difficult to punish the press after publication of hurtful or embarrassing information, absent malicious disregard for the truth. No other nation gives its journalists so much constitutional protection, and as a result, so much responsibility."

In more restrictive parts of the world, journalists who think out of the box—*responsibly*—find that the best apartments no longer are available to their families. Nor are the best jobs, the best schools, or the best medical care for their spouses and children. That's something we western journalists don't have to worry about, which makes journalistic lethargy almost a sacrilege.

So what you'll learn here is really pretty basic: run after stories, leave no stone unturned, don't turn your mind off. In other words, you're never really "off the clock."

The Terms of the Story

Press Pool (media pool)   A small group of journalists—sometimes just a print reporter, a broadcast reporter, a still photographer, and a television cameraperson—chosen to cover a significant event when there is not space for the entire press corps; the journalists included in the pool are obliged to share everything they have seen, heard, and recorded with all their colleagues.

Photo Op   Time designated for the media to take pictures or video of someone or something famous.

Running Down Tips

Here's a good question to start this section: what's a tip? Well, it might be an anonymous phone call letting you in on a secret. Such as, "A drug deal's going down at midnight tonight behind city hall." Or, "I saw the councilman checking into the Thunderbird Motel, and that woman on his arm was not his wife."

Those would be pretty easy to check out. To follow up on the councilman, you'd want to head out to the Thunderbird, and to contact the councilman's critics to see if you can confirm a pattern of adulterous behavior. On the drug deal, you'd want to be behind city hall yourself, and to consult with your superiors about bringing the police into the picture.

But a tip might be more vague: "Some of the nurses in the hospital's pediatric section have records of child abuse." You'll want to see the hospital's personnel records that, if the hospital doesn't want a tempest of bad publicity, it might show you, depending sometimes on how much damage it believes you can do to its image. Much of the time, public relations consultants will advise clients to deal with the media rather than ignore it, figuring they can always turn the statement you want to get into the message they want to give. Maybe you'll uncover sloppiness or negligence in the hospital's background checks. Maybe you'll get all the pediatric nurses' names, which you then can cross check with the state and see what names show up where they shouldn't be.

And sometimes a tip won't sound like a tip. Instead, you'll simply come across something that smells fishy. Say, for instance, that the civil service head of the city's parking division earns $75,000 a year, but you find out she lives in a million-dollar home, has a condo in Aspen, an apartment in Paris, wears silk suits, and drives a Ferrari. It could be family money, or the outcome of smart investments, but it also could be corruption. You won't know until you ask. So you ask. If the answers (and the evidence) aren't convincing, you dig around some more. Nothing wrong with going after a good juicy scandal if it's true.

Or, a tip might come from a source who says, basically, "What I'm telling you is off the record," which is like saying, "You can't use what I'm telling you." Don't worry. It's a tip. If you can confirm it with someone else, you can report it to your heart's content. You'll learn more about non-tip tips that are "off the record," or otherwise restricted, in Chapter 19.

When covering the Soviet invasion of Afghanistan (two decades before the war against terrorism in Afghanistan), I got a tip that wasn't even meant to be a tip, but it sent my camera crew and me off on an adventure that yielded news no one else had.

The big question early on was, how big is the invasion? How many soldiers, how many tanks, how many aircraft? Are Soviet forces fanning out all over the country, or just mobilizing to support their new puppet government in the capital, Kabul? We couldn't just show up at Soviet military headquarters and ask. They would just as soon have shot us as answered our questions.

So the job was to try to find someone who didn't have a direct stake in the invasion but might know something about its scope. That started with visits to a number of foreign embassies around Kabul, hoping for pieces of information that could be strung together to reach some sort of conclusion. In other words, I went out *looking* for tips! The trouble was, everyone's information was different. Every ambassador was trying to feed me information that served his own country's interest.

At the Saudi embassy though, after giving me his government's party line, the Saudi ambassador told a story. His cook, an Afghanistani woman, had just returned from a weeklong vacation in the northern part of the country, close to what then was the Soviet border. When she returned to Kabul, she told her boss—the ambassador—that her bus had been pulled to the side of the road and sat still for hours while hundreds of tanks rolled past, heading into the heart of Afghanistan.

Hundreds of tanks! That was a nifty nugget of information. I had to take into account the fact that the woman was not a military expert and like many citizens with no military background, might not know a tank (plenty of firepower, small crew) from an armored personnel carrier (protection for a company of troops, but limited firepower). So to overcome the language barrier, I drew a few pictures on a pad of paper, and could at least conclude that the machines she saw ran on treads, not tires. I also had to consider that as a maid in Afghanistan, perhaps she never had gone to school and didn't know how to count. But it was a starting point, and as it turned out, fairly accurate.

In fact it compelled us to sneak out of Kabul and see for ourselves. Sure enough, there was a constant column of Soviet armored personnel carriers heading into the country, which meant tens of thousands of troops at the very least. And for good measure, we spent several hours lying in the tall grass around the Baghram Air Base (which became the main staging point for American forces during the war against terrorism there that began in 2001), counting Soviet airplanes and helicopter gunships landing and taking off.

We could conclude—and report—that it was a major invasion. All thanks to a tip, that wasn't even meant as a tip.

What's the Point?

If you get wind of a story, or a new take on a story, you have to run it down. Think of everything as a tip worth pursuing. Sometimes it'll be a dead end, but when it's not, you'll look in the mirror and say, "I'm a real journalist."

For a Common Cause

You already read at the top of this chapter that newspapers and broadcast news organizations "share" information. They share it literally, in some cases, where they have entered into increasingly popular and productive partnerships. But even where the information–sharing arrangement isn't formalized, practically speaking it is necessary. A newspaper staff that isn't watching TV might be depriving its readers of a solid investigative scoop caught on camera. And since newspapers typically have bigger news gathering staffs than broadcasters, broadcast journalists who aren't reading newspapers probably aren't covering all the news that their audiences need. Sure, everyone can read news releases and listen to police scanners, but the stories that someone had to think up ultimately deserve the broadest possible exposure. It's the way of the world.

Here's a simple example. *The Denver Post* did a story in late 2002 about a young man from Mexico, Jesus Apodaca, whose family had illegally come to the United States six years earlier. He had just graduated with honors from his suburban Denver high school, and having been accepted to the University of Colorado (which was legal), he was trying to get in-state tuition (which, because he was an illegal alien, was not).

A local congressman named Tom Tancredo, who made his mark as one of the nation's leading crusaders against illegal immigration, read the story and brought it to the attention of the U.S. Immigration and Naturalization Service, suggesting deportation. Not because Apodaca or his parents and siblings were bad people, but because they had plainly and publicly admitted to illegal entry.

This led to a progression of coverage in radio, TV, and print. Stories were about the impact of illegal immigrants on the economy, on education, on the healthcare system. It led to dialogue about the worth of illegal immigrants, and the efficiency of sealed borders, and the cumbersome process of trying to enter the United States legally. It made politicians and citizens alike take sides. It even motivated Congressman Tancredo to announce that because he had become a leader in the movement to crack down on immigration, he would break his previous pledge to serve just three terms in the House of Representatives. That led to a renewed debate on term limits for elected officials.

The Denver Post started it. All news organizations in Colorado (and several national) picked up on it and found novel angles with which to elaborate on it. Everyone was the better for it. Including, for better or worse, the congressman.

What's the Point?

There's a good reason why, even though you work for a radio or television station, you should read the newspapers too. Not to regurgitate their reporting, but to use it as a jumping off point for your own.

If You Don't Like That Reason, How About This One?

What do you do if you don't like sports? Or can't conjure up any interest in business? Or are bored by what has come to be called "reality" television? Ignore it? Use that section of the newspaper to line your cat litter box? Only at your peril!

Why? Because unlike the average reader who is willing to live in ignorance about particular topics, that very story you chose to ignore might be the very story on which you're assigned today to report.

Say you walk into your newsroom and the assignment editor shouts, "Get down to the football team's training center and find out who's going to be the quarterback this Sunday. And hustle. You're already late." Unfortunately, you won't get away with saying, "Send someone else. I hate sports."

Equally unfortunately, you'd better not ask, "Why's there a question about it?" or, "What's happening on Sunday?" let alone, "What's a quarterback?" You're a general assignment reporter and you're expected to know a little bit about everything. You'd better. You're going to have to ask intelligent questions when you get where you're going, and make some sense of the story after you leave. What's more, you'll have to write it with the enthusiasm of a real fan.

So how do you avoid the problem (and potential embarrassment) of disinterest? By reading the papers before you come in. Every word, in every section, like it or not.

What's the Point?

Consider the newspapers as your briefing papers. If the news director or the broadcast producer or the assignment editor reads them, you'd better too. Remember the Boy Scout motto: Be Prepared.

Seeing Every Color, Every Hue

One of my most embarrassing and unprofessional moments was when I failed to notice the president's tie. That's right, President Ronald Reagan's necktie.

I was covering a mostly benign four-country presidential trip, and we were in Lisbon, Portugal. Truth be known, while once a mighty colonial power, Portugal's not a big player anymore on the world stage. But the President of the United States dropped in anyway, and I was selected to be the broadcast reporter in a very small press pool during his meeting with Portugal's president (whose position is just ceremonial because a prime minister runs the government). The press pool had to be small. The two presidents sat shoulder to shoulder on a couch that took up a good third of the floor space of the whole room.

The five of us in it—a video cameraman, a sound technician, a still photographer, a print reporter and me—crouched at the presidents' feet for the two or three minutes we were permitted in the room. Although I furiously scribbled in my note pad to capture every inconsequential word exchanged between the two, there was really nothing interesting to report.

Wrong! When I got outside and met with the crowd of reporters with whom I was obligated to share my information, I dutifully briefed them on what I'd heard.

Then I asked the reporters still listening, "Any questions?" There was only one: "What was the design on the president's tie?" My first response was, "Which president?" although it didn't really matter; I hadn't noticed either one. She said, "Reagan," and I had no choice but to say, "I don't know." I should have known. I was supposed to be everyone's eyes and ears. I was supposed to note the room's color and temperature and whether the

American president was seated with his back to a window and, yes, the design of his necktie. This reporter wanted to know, because she was with a cable TV show that was doing a series on. . . . yep, presidential neckwear.

I hadn't been a very good reporter that day. I'd focused on the dialogue, such as it was, and ignored the environment. The colorful details might not be the most important part of the story, but for someone in the media (and sometimes that'll be *you*), they are a part. Even a critical part. That's why, even if you aren't naturally any more observant than I was, you must consciously force yourself to take everything in. When you're in an auditorium for instance, note the color of the walls, and whether there's a curtain on stage, and how many seats there are for the audience and, of course, how many are filled. When you're outside, note how hot or cold it is, and if it's quiet or noisy nearby, and whether there's wind. Note every sight, every sound, every smell. You never know when something like that will be a useful, if uncritical, piece of color for your story.

What's the Point?

Here's the simplest point in this whole book: notice everything, because it might come in handy.

Questions When They're Not Allowed

People turn into celebrities in this country for the funniest reasons. Sometimes it's because they're accomplished. Other times it's simply because they're famous. In other words, all it really takes to become a celebrity is to be, a well, a celebrity.

Does fame make some important? No. For that matter, neither does money, or title, or reputation. Those things may get them the best table at the best restaurant, but as a journalist, you shouldn't treat these people with deference simply because they're celebrities. Respect, perhaps; deference, never. That certainly applies to singers, dancers, actors, athletes, and also extends to your city's mayor, your state's governor, and even the President of the United States.

For example, the media spokesperson for a chief executive might invite you and your station's camera into the office for a "photo op." You might be told, explicitly or implicitly, that during the photo op, you're only to observe the sights and sounds, but you cannot ask questions. Huh? Here's this elected official, this *servant of the people*, and they're saying "No questions"? If not now, when?

That's when you have to do your job, even if some of the chief executive's aides—and perhaps some in your audience—think you're disobedient and rude. Your justification's easy though: "There's an issue out there on which this mayor (or governor, or president) hasn't yet commented, and it's my job to ask him!" As often as not, even though you've broken the rules, you'll get an answer. The chief executive, after all, doesn't want to look evasive or inaccessible.

Anyway, just because you ask, the chief executive (or other "Very Important Person") doesn't have to answer. Having already mentioned President Reagan in this chapter, I'll tell you another thing about him. Every time Mr. Reagan walked toward or away from his helicopter on the White House lawn, one particular reporter named Sam Donaldson, who had contempt for the "rules" of the photo op, shouted a question at him. Typically, the President cupped a hand to his ear and shouted back, "Sorry Sam, can't hear you over the helicopter." But every once in a while, evidently because he figured it served his purposes, the president shouted out an answer. And Sam came that much closer to holding the nation's most powerful leader accountable on the issue of the day. All because he treated him as just another man, not as a celebrity.

What's the Point?

There's a reason for the cliché about famous people putting their pants on just like the rest of us, "one leg at a time." They're born the same as you, they'll die the same as you. And in between, they're no more important than you are. Remember the rule: treat everyone with respect, but leave your deference back in the classroom.

Exercises to Help You Run in Place _____

1. Run Till You Drop
   Treat each bullet point below as a "tip." Explain in each case how you would "run it down."

   - A stranger sends you an email saying, "I work at City Hall, and just about every week, Judge Jones has a drunken party for friends in his chambers, complete with illegal gambling."
   - You get a call from a woman who you know is a tenured professor at the top university in the state. She tells you, "Two of the other professors in my department are selling exam questions to students for cash."
   - The chief auditor at a major local company meets you in a dark parking garage and reveals, "My CEO has been cooking the books. He has insisted that we camouflage our losses so that investors won't be scared off. I questioned the policy and was told I'd be fired if I didn't go along."

2. Read Till You Drop
   Walk into the next session of class prepared to answer any question about anything in the newspaper, from the sections with news, business, sports, culture, and anything else to which you might be assigned as a general assignment reporter. (In fact, walk into class *every* day prepared to answer such questions!)

3. Watch Till You Drop
   The next three times you walk anywhere—to a class, to a job, to a market—make mental note, then written note, of everything you see. *Everything*. Note the sights, the colors, the temperatures, the people, the light, the sounds, the smells. Submit that list to your instructor. It's what you'd use if you were writing a story about the place through which you walked.
   Then, write that story. A forty-five second voiceover for television or radio.

14

Letting It All Hang Out

What You'll Learn _____

Whenever someone says, "Picture this," I want you to picture *this*: a news story told with nothing but pictures. No words, no interviews, just video. Video good enough, illustrative enough, to tell the story without a script. Video that needs no explanation. Or, for radio, the same thing but with sound—sound from the scene of the story that requires no elaboration.

Such opportunities are few and far between. Video of people sunning themselves can easily enough communicate to viewers that today was a beautiful day as video of people under umbrellas conveys a different story. But even excellent video of a fire, or a political demonstration, or a plane crash, which might seem to stand on its own and need no amplification, doesn't answer all the questions that come up.

For example, a colleague who worked for a TV station in Chicago once was casually shooting a small airplane lifting off from a lakeside runway in the city when the plane suddenly flipped upside down and went into a spiral and, within seconds, plunged into Lake Michigan. We needed no explanation of the event itself: a plane took off, turned over, and fell. But what had caused the crash? Was it wind gusts, pilot error, engine failure, maybe a heart attack? Who was at the controls? An experienced pilot or a novice? Someone local, or from out of town? Was anyone else onboard? (Thankfully, no.) Did the pilot have a chance to say anything to the control tower before hitting the water? (Evidently not.) Had he lived or died? (He died.) Although the fundamental fact of the story was obvious to everyone watching, only words could answer the questions we all asked. For that matter, only words could answer an obvious question about the footage itself. How did the cameraman happen to capture the plane crash? (He was testing a brand new camera on his day off.)

So even in the best of circumstances, pictures and/or sound alone will rarely suffice. But—and this is the key to what you'll learn in this chapter—the best broadcast stories are the ones in which the words support the pictures or sound, instead of the other way around. Every story is different, and some just don't have the ingredients you need for a good broadcast story. But almost always, you can use video or audio to illustrate *something*. Almost always, you can let the video and audio make a point that you don't make with words. In this chapter, you'll learn how, but I'll give you a big hint right now. If it's for TV, don't write a word—not a single word—without having some notion of what picture will be on the screen when the word is spoken. That's how the best television news writers work.

This chapter is primarily about television, but many principles apply to the use of audio for radio, too.

The Terms of the Story _____

Long Shot Same thing as a "wide shot."
File Video Video clips from the station's, the network's, or someone else's archives that are used in stories.

How a Rose Tells the Story

Let's start with a typical city council meeting. Why? Because there's just about nothing more dull than a typical city council meeting! Not just because the topics run the exhilarating range from sewage to property taxes, but because the pictures run no range at all. Almost always it's a bunch of council members, sitting side by side at a long curved counter, talking or listening. Whoopie!

But wait! Dull though it may be, maybe there's still a way to use this video to communicate something. What if the council chamber is filled to overflowing, standing room only? If you show it, you don't have to say it. What if the council is discussing the issue of unequal pay for female city employees? If the audience is almost all women, that'll help you drive home that point. What if a member of the council falls asleep during a debate? Well, it might not shed a whole lot of light on the issue being debated, but it sure will be funny, and might in fact illustrate just how dull the debate is. None of these hypothetical scenes is exciting, but at least they'd help you use *television* to tell your story.

Or at the other extreme, think about a picture that's truly worth a thousand words. One of the best examples in my memory is from coverage of a terrible tornado in South Dakota. It tore out hundreds of homes and wiped out dozens of lives in its path. But fairly typical of tornadoes, it touched down, then leaped in the air, then touched down elsewhere again. Some structures stood untouched, despite devastation all around them.

So the story began with a rose. A closeup shot of a single rose, poking out of the ground. The opening line was:

The tornado didn't destroy everything.

Then, as the cameraman began a slow pullout from the closeup of the rose, revealing the scattered bricks and broken lumber of homes that had been destroyed on either side, the narration continued:

Some flowers survived . . . some homes survived . . . some people in this otherwise devastated town survived too.

Then, of course, the story went on to describe—in pictures and words—how harmful the tornado had been, and how much of the town had *not* survived. But that opening shot set the stage. By the time it pulled out to its widest angle, it was a striking symbol of the random nature of the tornado, and the lucky people whose lives and homes weren't ruined.

And, there was the story of Canadian hero Rick Hansen. He was a paraplegic, paralyzed in a car crash. For several years he sat in his wheelchair and felt sorry for himself. But then he decided to make the best of his new life. He would push himself around the world *in his wheelchair*, raising money along the way for medical research on spinal cord injuries.

We shot his triumphant departure from his home town of Vancouver—triumphant even at the outset because Hansen had struggled mightily to raise the funds and assemble the team he'd need to support him for the two years and two months his venture would take. We also arranged to have cameras record his chairbound trek along different difficult portions of the trip, through exotic parts of Yugoslavia, Israel, China, Australia. Finally, we hooked back up with Hansen during the last few days of his worthy two-year-plus mission, westward through the Rockies in British Columbia, his last leg to Vancouver.

The crowds along that final couple of hundred remote miles of the route—with not a single good sized town between him and his destination—were as thick some places as a New York crowd cheering the Yankees in a victory parade. To Canadians, Hansen was every inch a hero. In my mind I likened the scenes to what I've read about the ticker tape parades that greeted Charles Lindbergh after he became the first man to fly alone across the Atlantic. Every inch a hero.

But those dramatic, cheering, proud, adoring crowds didn't make the story special. The shots of Rick Hansen did. The long shots, taken across a canyon from the end of a curve in the road as he approached the beginning, highlighting the small scale of one man laboriously pushing his wheelchair up the highway against the massive backdrop of the Canadian Rockies. That's how the story started, with the long shots running long, to let it all sink in:

> *It took Ferdinand Magellan three years to go 'round this earth, Yuri Gagarin—the first to do it in space—89 minutes. But no one, ever, has had to provide all his own propulsion, with the sheer force of his arms. No one, 'til Rick Hansen.*

Then, this sound bite with Rick (which was moving, in more ways than one):

> *For me it's been the struggle of my life. There will never be anything after this as difficult . . .*

Then the closeups, taken from the tailgate of a station wagon about twenty feet ahead of Hansen, showing how much stronger he was than when he had started, but with his chest still heaving, his breath still short, his skin now tanned and cracked by so many months of exposure.

> *For two years, two months now, he has struggled, pushing himself every inch of 25-thousand miles. 29-year old Rick Hansen, paralyzed by a car crash in his teens, has pushed himself all the way around the circumference of the earth.*

You could have turned down the sound and still grasped the soul of the story. No, you might not have known how Rick Hansen ended up in a wheelchair, or why he was completing this round-the-world trip. But you would have understood that right there on your television screen was a man with almost unimaginable tenacity, indomitable determination, and bottomless inspiration. The pictures alone told that part of the story. Nothing in print could come close.

Here's a good use of pictures in a different way, during our coverage of a potentially catastrophic flood in Minot, North Dakota. As the Souris River swelled from the spring thaw and threatened to rise above its banks through the heart of Minot, the city's hearty citizens went to work filling sandbags and building the riverbanks higher. And higher. And higher. We covered the story for five days and each day, as the river rose, the sandbagged riverbanks rose with it.

Minot's saviors always managed to stay about one sandbag above the rising water and to save their city, which was dramatic. But the pictures each day looked just like the day before: shovels loading sand, human assembly lines, and the water just below the top of the ever higher sandbag wall, until the day the river crested.

Then, employing a technique we had planned from our first day of coverage, we showed a scene from Day One, when they laid out the first layers of sandbags, then dissolved to a scene shot from precisely the same place and composed the same way on Day Two, then dissolved to the same thing from each successive day until the crest. Once again, even without any audio, a viewer could see in that 20-second sequence how successfully the people of Minot, North Dakota, had kept their sandbagged city dry.

What's the Point?

Some stories don't have self-explanatory visual elements. But when one does, use your video for all it's worth. Let the video do what words cannot equal. That's pure television.

When There's No Rose Left Alive

Sometimes of course, you might be happier writing for a newspaper, because you can't imagine what to show in the story you're covering for TV! I don't mean a story like the South Dakota tornado where, even without the rose, the destruction would have been easy to illustrate. But maybe a story like that typical city council meeting mentioned earlier, without a standing-room-only crowd, an all-woman crowd, or a sleeping councilman.

Creative writing helps, of course. Not fancy, not fictional, just creative, to connect the viewer to what's on the screen. For example, a story about funding that was withheld from local sewage treatment plants if they didn't comply with new federal regulations. We went to the country's biggest plant, which was in Detroit. (It treated the sewage from the city and 39 suburbs. Who says a reporter's job isn't glamorous?) I don't have to tell you what the primary picture was for the story, do I?

If your only shots are at a sewage treatment plant, then excuse the pun, but there's no way to clean them up. For that matter, there's not much chance for variety either. So without much choice, we started our story with an unexciting shot of the plant, and wrote the opening line this way, to connect the viewer:

Most of those that have not complied are like this one, the sewage treatment plant at . . .

It could have said, "Most of those that have not complied are like the sewage treatment plant at . . ." But that extra little thought, "*like this one*," made a difference. It directly addressed the viewer, and helped pull the viewer into the story.

Another example is an experimental welfare plan in Milwaukee. Not only were there few things to shoot, but we didn't have much time to shoot them. So the story started with a lot of faces from the county welfare office. Pretty ordinary. But again, a couple of extra words justified them:

When people like these apply for welfare here in Milwaukee. . .

People "like these." Contrast that with the slightly shorter, "When people apply for welfare in Milwaukee. . ." That could be written by anybody, anywhere. Adding "like these" sends the viewer a message: our reporter is *there*, reporting *firsthand*. Suddenly the faces, however mundane, are the heart of the story. Suddenly, the extra few words help *connect* the viewer to the story.

There are simple ways to use simple words or phrases to connect your viewer with your video. Sometimes it's your way of signaling the audience, "We're really at the scene of the story, not just rescripting a story someone else covered."

Probably the most obvious is the word, "here."

Disconnected: The oil spill in Alaska has destroyed more than. . .
Connected: The oil spill here in Alaska has destroyed more than. . .

Disconnected: In Houston's City Hall, the demonstrators. . .
Connected: Here in Houston's City Hall, the demonstrators. . .

Disconnected: It is hard to find support for the peace treaty in Cairo.
Connected: It is hard to find support for the peace treaty here in Cairo.

Another is, "like this" or, "like these."

Disconnected: An S-U-V consumes twice as much gas as. . .
Connected: An S-U-V like this consumes twice as much gas as. . .

Disconnected: The governor announced that all horses in the state will have to be tested. . .
Connected: The governor announced that all horses like these in the state will have to be tested. . .

These little tricks are useful in just about every story you write, whether the video is any good or not! They are useful for the viewer, and if you want to go from a small market to a bigger one, useful for you too.

Creative camerawork helps too. This means, use your imagination—either because you're shooting the video yourself, or working with whoever is. Get down low to look up at the council members sitting around their podium. Go to the side of the citizen who's testifying—everyone else will shoot her from the front, whereas the side profile has more inherent interest. Shoot the audience "in compression," which means we'll see several faces in an angled side shot, looking closer together than they are. Get behind the council members, to see the meeting as they see it. Maybe take a long shot from outside the opened council chamber doors, to show the whole environment of the meeting, framed by the entryway.

What's the Point?

Connect with your audience. With pictures or words. Make them feel like they're right there beside you.

Wallpaper, Instead of a Rose

Unless you want a plain, indifferent, uninviting look in your home, you put something on your walls to cover the raw, unadorned surface: paint, paneling, wallpaper. Television is the same. Unless you want a blank screen, you put something on it to cover every second of a story. When you have sensational video, the screen doesn't seem big enough! But when you have lousy video, you still have to fill the screen, even if the video doesn't illustrate much of anything. The word for that video is "wallpaper."

You'll see wallpaper in economic stories more than anywhere else, in stories about unemployment rates, consumer confidence, median income. The narration inevitably is about "Americans," about as generic as you can get. And what video fills the screen? You've seen it a hundred times: a crowd shot, often looking down a city sidewalk during rush hour. Wallpaper? Absolutely. Remember, this is where the camera must be particularly creative, because the subject matter isn't.

Or how about a story on taxes! Now before reading on, stop for a moment and ask yourself, what pictures could you shoot for a story on *taxes*? Think. *Think.*

Tough, isn't it? Well, there are tax forms, and people filling out tax forms, and accountants checking tax forms, and books and booklets on tax law, and items on which we pay taxes, and the people who pay taxes, which means everyone. So you're not dead in the water, you can find these scenes for your story. But they're all "wallpaper."

However, if that's all you have to work with, work with it. I once did a story about new complications in the federal tax code. The script started this way:

> *The I-R-S commissioner himself said it, right on the front of your book of instructions: "Completing your return this year could be more difficult."*

That made the visuals simple enough: we'd open on a medium shot of the tax brochure sent to every American household, then go in for a closeup of the commissioner's printed warning. It was wallpaper, but it served the purpose. And notice the personalized writing: ". . . the front of *your* book of instructions." Something to which every taxpaying viewer could relate. That's another indispensable trick to connect the viewer to video that is—as you know by now—just wallpaper.

Another economic story full of wallpaper was about American labor unions pricing themselves right out of their workers' jobs. We went to a Zenith television factory near Chicago, where roughly a quarter of the workers were losing their jobs to cheaper workers overseas. All we really could shoot were the workers, and the televisions they were making (which soon would be made instead in Mexico and Taiwan).

So we started with faces. One face after another on the assembly line. Soon-to-be-unemployed faces. The script read this way:

> *The faces on the TV assembly line here tell the story: American faces, all members of an American labor union, all earning comfortable American wages. . . which just can't compete with lower pay scales overseas.*

Once again, wallpaper. But the script justified it, and helped viewers relate to the kinds of people the story was about.

What's the Point?

Unless your camera broke and your video library burned (destroying all your file video), you always have something to fill the screen. The challenge is to use it to its best advantage, no matter how dull.

Fight to Avoid a Fight

A viewer doesn't dedicate part of his attention to what he sees and another part to what he hears. He can't. You know that because *you* can't. So the operative phrase for this short section is, "Don't let your words fight your pictures."

This is bad:

VIDEO

Business leaders meeting inside convention hall.

NARRATION

More than a thousand demonstrators shouted in protest outside the convention hall.

This is better:

VIDEO

Business leaders meeting inside convention hall.

NARRATION

While the leaders met in the convention hall, demonstrators outside were shouting in protest.

This is best:

VIDEO

Demonstrators outside convention hall.

NARRATION

More than a thousand demonstrators shouted in protest outside the convention hall.

The principle is obvious. Your words and your pictures should match or, if they can't (because you don't have video to show what you're talking about), your words should be crafted to reflect the video you're showing (as in the middle example above). What you don't want is your words fighting your pictures.

Think about that story about sewage plants, used as an example earlier in this chapter. To refresh your memory, the story actually wasn't as much about sewage plants as it was about federal funds that were withheld from them. But the best (and only) pictures we had were of Detroit's sewage plant. Therefore the words would have fought the video if the story had started like this:

The federal government will not release the money for a higher level of sewage treatment if. . .

That's why, instead, it started like this:

Most of those that have not complied are like this one, the sewage treatment plant at. . . .

One more thing: if you have video of two cars that have collided—one red, one blue—you don't have to write, "The two cars that collided, one was red, the other blue, were totaled." We can see it! Likewise, if you are covering a fire and you shoot video of a woman covered with blood and crying uncontrollably, you obviously don't have to write, "A woman was covered with blood and crying uncontrollably."

That's the beauty of television. Whether it's minor detail or major emotion, pictures can tell at least some of your story. If you write what the pictures already show, you might be letting the words fight the pictures. Don't.

What's the Point?

Making sure your words don't fight your pictures is something print writers don't have to worry about. Lucky them. You do. Don't ignore it.

When There's Better Sound Than Just Words

You've just learned about another burden you have that print writers don't. But you also have learned in this book about some tools that you have and they don't, to make your story effective, illuminating and memorable. You have read references to it elsewhere in the book, but now you'll get some solid examples. It's "Natural Sound," which we usually just call "NAT SOT."

I've already told you about the stirring video of the man who pushed himself around the world in his wheelchair, Rick Hansen. But you haven't yet read about the story's NAT SOT, which was just as important.

The moment we hooked up with Hansen, we attached a wireless microphone to his shirt so we could *hear* him, not only for our interview (I rode a bicycle alongside for about fifteen minutes, the crew shooting from the tailgate of our rented SUV), but before and after our talk, to capture his huffing and puffing up the last mountain passes of his trek. If those seconds of NAT SOT in the stories didn't tell the tale of one man's determination despite his disability, nothing could! In fact, we opened the story (meaning I stopped talking) for NAT SOT several times—to hear Hansen huffing and puffing, to hear crowds along his route cheering as he pushed past, and to hear his exchanges with his support team in a van sometimes rolling just ahead of his wheelchair.

Another story where NAT SOT was critical was about a therapy program, run by a guy named Wayne Michael, an inmate at the State Prison in Stillwater, Minnesota. Three times a week, he got twenty-five maximum security prisoners to sit in a circle for what they called a "game," but in fact it was a confrontation: twenty-four against one. The purpose of the confrontation was for the twenty-four to force the "one" (who had to sit in the middle of the circle) to admit to the behavior that put him in prison in the first place, to recognize the behavior that made him an outcast, and to force him to confront his own self-destructive defenses. They'd shout at him, accuse him, shame him, badger him.

NARRATION

Wayne Michael, therapist, helping people to handle stress, by facing it.

NAT SOT (from inmates in circle, shouting):

You never been no good, you never done no good, you nothin' but trash . . .

Then, later:

NARRATION

Then the game moved to Vernon Scott, a murderer, confronted for simply overeating.

NAT SOT (from another inmate):

*You are fat, you're ugly, and you're always gonna be an outcast 'cause you don't give a **** about yourself.*

(Scott, head in his hands, weeping): No no no no no no no. . .

The NAT SOT portions of the story told it all. Viewers could feel the embarrassment, the shame, and the conversion. My only job with the narration was to fill in the holes.

Another example of a different kind is a feature story about a traveling ballet company. It was called "Ballet West" and went places in the Rocky Mountains that otherwise never got treated to cultural performances like ballet.

As you'll see from the script, viewers were never far from the sound of the story. Here's how it started:

NAT SOT

Swan Lake music (from film about Russian ballet dancer Rudolph Nureyev)

NARRATION

When Rudolph Nureyev made his "grand jeté," his giant leap to America, ballet was strictly for the highbrow. Fewer than a million seats were sold nationwide for professional ballet back then. . . two thirds of them in New York.

NAT SOT ("uncultivated" man from a TV commercial promoting the touring ballet company) Ballet? Ha ha ha ha ha ha ha.

As you can see, we started with NAT SOT (over video of Nureyev, then of characters dancing in the ballet commercial) and, after two short sentences, returned to it. Each time, we then continued the music from the NAT SOT "under" the narration that followed, so that it never completely disappeared. The second section of NAT SOT was followed by similar construction, which set the tone of the whole piece:

NARRATION

This is a TV commercial for a Salt Lake City company called "Ballet West". . .

NAT SOT (more music from same TV commercial)

NARRATION

Using a man who quite obviously is hardly a highbrow, the commercial makes a point.

NAT SOT (same man now watching contentedly, from commercial)

Ballet West. One performance can make the difference.

After a couple of sentences explaining that the ballet we were showing (and hearing) was being performed in the unlikely town of Rock Springs, Wyoming, the feature continued at the same pace.

NARRATION

Ballet West came, to dance in a high school gym. They had to bring their own floor. . . and, their own music.

NAT SOT

Music (over shot of reel-to-reel audio tape recorder, from which the music played)

And again, after more narration about touring troupes, intercut with sound bites from delighted Rock Springs residents:

NARRATION

Ballet has finally reached the masses. . . and the masses, love it.

NAT SOT

Music continues (over shots of Rock Springs residents, intercut with ballet closeups)

At this point, as we faded out the music from the ballet, we faded in music from a ballet class in Rock Springs where little children were learning.

NAT SOT

Music from ballet school

NARRATION

If the past is any guide, then tomorrow's audiences, like tomorrow's dancers, will continue to grow.

This was a story about dance. A story about dance should be full of music. It was. Viewers were never far from the sound the people heard in Rock Springs, Wyoming.

What's the Point?

Each example in this section used NAT SOT to pull the viewer into the story. Anyone watching actually had a sense of what it was like to be at the prison in Minnesota. And in the high school gym in Rock Springs, Wyoming.

Microphones and Cameras Where They're Not Allowed

There is no uniform rule about microphones and cameras in a courtroom. Some judges allow them when both sides in a dispute (criminal or civil) say it's okay (although the judges usually still have the discretion to keep them out). Some permit them whether participants like it or not. In some courts, a single camera and mike—for the media pool—are allowed, the camera in a fixed position somewhere behind the dock (where the defendant sits), so that the chief partakers in the legal action aren't recognizable if they don't turn around. And some (including all federal courts) ban microphones and cameras no matter what!

I am aware of only two exceptions in federal courts. For the trial of Oklahoma City Federal Building bomber Timothy McVeigh, a camera and a microphone were installed to send a closed circuit broadcast to a site in Oklahoma City, so that hundreds of survivors and family victims could witness the proceedings without traveling to Denver, where the trial itself was held. And even more notably, in recognition of the public's overwhelming interest, the U.S. Supreme Court made an unprecedented exception to the federal courts ban by allowing remote microphones in its chamber during arguments by lawyers for both presidential candidates, Vice President Al Gore and Texas Governor George W. Bush, after the disputed election of 2000.

Your job? Always fight to get your camera and microphone in the door. Even in federal courts, even when the idea may be summarily shot down. Why? Because arguably, a policy that prohibits cameras and mikes, forcing you to cover a legal proceeding for your station armed only with paper and pencil, discriminates against broadcasters. Reporters with pads and pencils, and even courtroom artists, are almost always included; the only exception is usually in a trial where national security issues may be discussed. Magazines and newspapers can thrive within restrictions like these because paper and pencil are the only tools they really need. TV and radio obviously need more. Our tools are video and audio. Deprived of these tools, we are at a disadvantage, which means our audience is too.

Of course you must be mindful—as judges are—that electronic equipment like cameras and microphones can alter participants' performances, and thus alter justice. You may not remember it, but the murder trial of former football star O.J. Simpson proved this. Almost everyone involved, including the judge himself, apparently adjusted their demeanor for the camera. Whereas the federal trial of Timothy McVeigh, who was convicted of bombing the Oklahoma City Federal Building and killing hundreds inside, was considered a model of proper justice. Cameras and microphones for the general public's consumption had been prohibited. You don't want to influence the proceedings of the court, which is a risk you take if you record them electronically. But you don't want to deprive your audience of a thorough report on those proceedings either. You must walk a fine line.

Personally, I was twice involved in petitions to get our camera and microphone into a prohibited place. Once we went before the Utah Supreme Court. The other time we went to a federal appellate court. Both times—related to a prison interview we'd arranged with convicted double-murderer Gary Gilmore—we lost. But on our audience's behalf, we tried. You should too.

Two organizations have informative guidelines that pertain to the use of and rules about recording equipment in court. They are the Radio and Television News Directors Association, and the American Bar Association.

What's the Point?

If you don't try to get recording equipment into a courtroom because the judge or the rules don't allow it, you are accepting decisions that put you and your audience at a disadvantage. But if you try and succeed, take every conceivable precaution not to influence the performance of participants, or the outcome.

Exercises to Put the Angels in Your Work _____

1. What the Video Doesn't Show
   Remember the story in the introduction to this chapter, about the plane that crashed in Lake Michigan? Use the honor system; challenge yourself. Do *not* go back and re-read it. Just pic-

ture the video I described: "A small airplane lifting off from a lakeside runway in the city when the plane suddenly flipped upside down and went into a spiral and, within seconds, plunged into Lake Michigan." Now, the exercise is this: List all the questions the video does *not* answer.

This time, try the same thing on the following piece of video: A body lies prone in a park, while about a dozen uniformed police are down on their hands and knees on all sides of it, combing through the tall grass. Again, list all the questions the video does not answer.

2. Connecting the Viewer
   Pretend you are reporting from the scene of the following stories and have video to illustrate what you're talking about. Picture that video in your mind, then add one or two (or three) words to each of the following sentences to help connect viewers to what they're seeing:

   - The hurricane blew cars a hundred yards from where they were parked.
   - The mayor's speech at the Public Library lasted more than two hours.
   - Elementary school students were locked in the schoolyard.
   - McCaffrey broke his leg on a play where he wasn't even covered by a defensive end.
   - The manager of the restaurant says his customers were scared.
   - Jumbo jets have failed safety tests twice this year.
   - The rain at our downtown weather station has set a new record.

3. Hanging the Wallpaper
   Here's an economic story. Your job is to list the shots you'd collect to cover it and then to rewrite it to connect the viewer.

   Three out of every five workers in downtown Middleville are spending more for lunch this year than they did last year. And for parking. And for gas. The cause? A successful economy. There are no office vacancies in Middleville. Downtown stores report that business is so good, customers have to stand in long lines to pay. Buses from the suburbs are running full. The mayor had a news conference today in the main plaza downtown and announced a program to fight inflation, so that workers won't look for jobs elsewhere where daily costs are lower.

4. Stopping the Fight
   Read below about the video you have to work with, then rewrite each narration so the words don't fight the pictures:

   VIDEO

   Bodies on the ground, their faces covered

   NARRATION

   The dam burst open and the river rose above its banks in the middle of the night. First it flooded downtown Minot, then it spread to Minot's most expensive homes. By daylight, 26 people had been found dead.

   VIDEO

   A race car slamming into a concrete wall going into a turn.

   NARRATION

   Jon Jeffreys was one of the most popular drivers on the racing circuit. He had helped many younger drivers get their start, and had created a foundation to find safer ways to build race cars. That made his death even more poignant. When Jeffreys' car hit the wall, the driver's cockpit wasn't strong enough to protect him. He apparently died instantly.

VIDEO

Governor giving a speech to an outdoor rally after having a pie thrown in his face.

NARRATION

At first it seemed like every other campaign appearance: the governor met in private with major financial supporters, then dropped into a meeting of party leaders, then went to the rally organized for his reelection. That's where a man in a Lone Ranger mask pushed a pie in his face.

5. Hearing the Fight

    Let's use a hypothetical fire for an exercise. Your job is to take the written story that follows, then look at the NAT SOT below it that is available to use, and insert it where it makes sense. Don't rewrite the story, just show where you would open it up for NAT SOT.

    NARRATION

    All four floors of the medical building burned. Glass was blown out of windows, bricks fell from the outside walls. It's not clear where the fire started, but the worst explosions came from a medical lab on the top floor. A woman who escaped says that's because of chemicals kept there in a storage room. As alarms continued to sound, firefighters responded from every fire house in the city. Their first job: to rescue a woman trapped on the balcony directly above the building's entrance. They all stopped fighting the fire for just a moment and cheered when she was lowered safely to the ground.

    Here is the NAT SOT you have as a part of your video:

    - Fire trucks pulling to a stop, sirens blaring
    - Firefighters cheering successful rescue
    - Bricks falling to the sidewalk
    - Woman screaming on balcony
    - Explosion from top floor

6. Waging the Fight

    In 100 words or less, as if you're appealing directly to a reluctant judge, make the best argument you can make to have cameras and/or microphones in a courtroom.

15

A Picture is Worth a Thousand Words

_____

The popular maxim (attributed to Fred R. Barnard) in this chapter's title sums up what you learned in the last chapter. Pictures are an integral part of television news.

If you end up in television news, you'll either shoot video, edit video, or work with someone who does. So it's important to understand the basics of shooting and editing video tape. That way, even if you don't know how to turn on the camera or the editing equipment, you'll know a little bit about what can (and should) be done with them, once *somebody else* turns them on.

That's why, while not highly technical, this chapter will deal with some of the fundamental mechanical requirements of television news. Like so much of the business, shooting and editing are not governed by hard and fast rules. But because of the limits of our viewers' eyes and ears, these rules are *wise* to follow, most of the time, anyway.

The first thing to remember is, you are not creating music videos; you are creating news stories. They must be fair and accurate, simple, credible, and clear. Equally important, remember that they usually go by the audience just *once*. So any kind of camera move or abrupt edit that jolts your viewers does them a disservice. Any kind of story that's dull when it could be dynamic does them a disservice too.

In this chapter, you'll learn a few simple techniques about how to shoot and how to edit. I'll talk about how to make your video construction dynamic and how to make your audio transitions seamless.

Practice makes perfect, and while you won't necessarily be practicing these creative skills in this course, you'll have a few fundamentals in your head about what to practice!

The Terms of the Story _____

Zoom Lens   A single lens that permits the cameraperson to press an electronic button, making the shot evolve from a wide shot to a medium shot to a closeup, or vice versa.

Video Pad   Several seconds of a shot held static both before and after activating the zoom lens and before and after panning.

Dissolve   The transition from one shot to another in which the end of the first shot slowly (over half a second, a second, two seconds, whatever feels right) fades from view as the beginning of the second shot comes into view.

Pan   Moving the camera from left to right, or right to left, to follow some action (like a plane landing) or to reveal, for example, the front of something when you started on the back.

Jump Cut   The transition between consecutive shots where the same person or the same action is in both shots but without a logical sequence (for example, she's walking at the end of the first shot, then abruptly standing still at the beginning of the second shot).

Cutaway (cut shot)   A shot used for just a few seconds to cover a jump cut, typically some other scene in close proximity to the person or the action in the jump cut.

Zooming to Dizzying Heights

Motion picture film and video cameras really weren't meant to have zoom lenses. In fact originally they didn't. Instead, they had three different lenses mounted in a triangular pattern on a metal plate (called a "turret"): a telephoto lens to bring distant objects closer (the closeup), a wide angle lens to capture a panoramic view (the wide shot), and a third lens in between (the medium shot). If you were using the telephoto lens and you wanted to switch to wide angle, you manually rotated the plate.

Eventually someone came up with the idea of eliminating the manual rotation by enabling the film maker instead to "zoom" from one focal point to another. That was its sole original purpose. However, film makers started using the "zoom" also in the body of their shots, so that they could start with, say, a wide shot of a political demonstration, then "zoom in" to a closeup of one demonstrator's sign. Or vice versa, starting with the closeup.

It wasn't long before they began to abuse their new tool. Some used the "zoom" to push into or pull out of something in just about every wobbly shot, which then had to be edited into the story (because the cameraperson gave the editor no choice). For the viewer, the result was slightly less dizzying than a roller coaster ride.

There's nothing wrong with pushing into or pulling out of something *if it serves a purpose*. The president speaking from a stage to a huge rally of excited supporters in an auditorium (start on the president and pull out to reveal the crowd, or start on the crowd and push in to the president). A terrorist holding a hostage in a window (wide shot of the terrorist holding a gun to the hostage's head, then push into a closeup of the frightened hostage, or, start on the hostage closeup, then pull out to a wide shot to reveal the terrorist holding the gun to her head). You might want to push in from a medium shot to a closeup when the person you're interviewing starts to cry. Or from a wide shot of demonstrators to a closeup when a single protestor starts shouting.

But something is wrong with using the zoom lens when it doesn't add anything: zooming from a closeup to a medium shot of the president giving an economic speech, or from a panoramic view of the desert to a single cactus, or from a wide shot of a building to a closeup of its front door. In each of these examples, your shots usually will be more effective if you use the zoom to capture both, but in the editing process, you *cut* from a wide shot to a closeup or from a closeup to a wide shot or from a medium shot to anything else. In other words, utilize the zoom all you like, but only to change your focal point. Used sparingly, it can enhance the drama or mystery of a story. Used commonly, it can give the viewer a headache.

What's the Point?

Just because you have a zoom lens doesn't mean you always have to use it. Viewers don't want to be taken to dizzying heights. A steady static shot still is the easiest shot to watch.

Zooming Cuts Both Ways

Now that you know *not* to make your viewers go insane with a zoom lens, here are two tips to keep you sane when you do use it.

- Zooming in *and* out

    If something seems worth zooming into while you're shooting, then make sure you zoom out of it too. Alternately, if it's worth zooming out of, then it's also worth zooming into. Why? Because when you're covering a story, you don't always know precisely how you're going to edit it. You might think you'll want to start on a closeup and then pull out to a wider look at the same scene, or alternately, start on a wide shot and then push in to either a medium shot or a closeup. But you might change your mind later. It happens all the time!

    Let's say you're covering the apartment house fire used as an example earlier in this book. A woman is on the fourth floor balcony of the burning building, holding her baby and screaming for help. While you're still at the scene of the fire, you think you'll start your story like this:

    > *This woman was holding her baby and screaming for help. They were stranded on a fourth floor balcony. Firefighters didn't know how many people were trapped inside the burning building, but rescuing the woman and her baby became their first priority.*

    Perfect. The sequence is obvious. You'll start on a closeup of the woman, then pull out to reveal how stranded she and the baby are on the balcony. Therefore you only shoot it that way. After all, why waste video tape?

    But when you start editing the piece, you decide it would be more effective to begin instead like this:

    > *The whole building was burning. Firefighters didn't know how many people were trapped inside. But they could see one woman trapped outside—one woman and her baby, stranded on a fourth floor balcony. Their rescue became the firefighters' first priority.*

    The trouble is, you only shot it the other way—closeup, then wide shot—which locked you in. If you had given yourself the insurance of shooting it both ways, you would have given yourself the option of changing your mind. After all, it's only video tape. It's the cheapest tool you have.

- Holding still, too

    When you use the zoom lens, don't just turn on the camera and start zooming. Instead, turn on the camera and hold it steady on whatever you're shooting for a few seconds. Then, start your zoom. Likewise, when you have completed the zoom (from closeup to wide shot *or* from wide shot to closeup), hold it steady at the end of the shot, too.

    This serves two purposes. First, holding the shot steady at the beginning lets the editor hold it that way for a few seconds while the viewer's eye settles on the scene before it starts moving. Sometimes this isn't important, but if you're shooting a busy scene, it is. Second, holding it steady at the beginning and at the end gives you some video pad for the insertion of special effects.

    What does this mean? The full answer is for some other course, but for the sake of simplicity, it means if during your edit, you're dissolving (or "fading") from one shot to another (a basic special effect) instead of abruptly cutting from one shot to another, you don't want to use up half the zoom at the top of the new scene before the old scene completely disappears from view. Instead, you begin the dissolve over the steady part of the shot—that's the video pad—before the zoom starts. You might not understand this yet, but trust me, you need that extra video pad, and you get it by holding a shot steady both before and after you activate the zoom lens.

What's the Point?

What may make sense while you're shooting a story may not make sense when you're editing it. So give yourself insurance. Insurance means flexibility.

Panning for Gold

Panning means moving the camera from left to right, or right to left. If you're videotaping a tractor plowing a field from right to left, you'll pan from right to left to keep it in the frame. Or maybe it's demonstrators running past the front of the White House, in either direction. Or, the subject might not be moving, but there's reason to pan anyway. If you have the justices of the Supreme Court lined up in front of you for example, you might want to pan across their nine faces, from one end to the other, even though they themselves are stone still.

Now, this might be the shortest section of the book. Why? Because the rules that you've already learned about zooming also apply to panning:

- Pan when it serves a purpose, but too many pans can be dizzying.
- If it's worth panning from left to right (for instance, the example of the Supreme Court justices), then it's worth panning from right to left too, because it maximizes your options during the edit.
- Because you want the viewer's eye to settle on the subject, and because you might want to go into or get out of a shot with a special effect, hold every pan steady for a few seconds at both the beginning and the end.

What's the Point?

Although sometimes the subject of your story demands movement, movement for movement's sake alone serves no purpose. If you're panning, only pan for gold. This is true when you shoot and equally true when you edit.

Now, one exception to everything you've just read. Sometimes, particularly on a feature story, the senior producer or news director will *want* you to create a lot of movement—maybe pans and zooms, maybe a "walking" shot where the cameraperson is walking while shooting or the reporter is walking while talking—and maybe he'll even want shaky shots, which give the impression of "real time," and which can capture the viewer's eye specifically because they're different from the norm.

The Story's in the Background

When a reporter covers a story for television, the final package usually has a standup, which some people call the "on-camera" part. Whatever is said, wherever it is done, something has to be in the background, behind the reporter. Likewise, if it's a live shot, the reporter has to be standing in front of something (the one and only exception is coverage in a blizzard).

Choosing your background is important. Not only because you want something interesting, but because you want something relevant. If you've covered a bad traffic accident, you want the accident behind the reporter. If it's a protest march, you want the marchers behind the reporter. If it's a candidate campaigning for election, you want the candidate speaking, or chatting, or shaking hands in the background. The point is, you want the background to *reinforce the theme of the story,* a reminder to the viewer of what the story is about.

A great background isn't always available though. If you cover a news conference with the mayor, you may have to put the dull (and predictable) background of city hall behind you, and sometimes you may have no choice. This is where you get creative. What was the mayor talking about? Cutting down dead trees in the city park? Then go out to the park and do the standup there, which puts the *subject* of the story behind the reporter. Doubling the charge at downtown parking meters? Go downtown and lean on a parking meter for the standup. Use your imagination, so the viewers won't have to use theirs.

The most illustrative standup I ever did accomplished more than just reinforcement for the viewer. It helped tell the story.

An oil tanker had burst a leak on Lake Huron. We went into the oil slick in a small motorboat. The oil was as thick as tar, but while you could see on the surface that it was shiny, you couldn't tell that it was thick. So I took a boat paddle from its brackets and, while describing the thick polluting oil, I dipped the handle into the slick, then after only a second or two, pulled it back up. The oil literally pulled up with the paddle, like thick toffee from a pot. That video told more than I ever could have done verbally.

You have to think about backgrounds far more often than just when the reporter is on camera. You also have to decide what to put in the background of an interview. Typically, if it's with a politician, the city or state or American flag serves the purpose. If it's an economist, a computer screen. An athlete? The playing field. A factory worker? The assembly line.

Many interviews are done indoors, which is limiting, and many are done at the convenience of the interviewee. But whenever possible, apply the same principle to interview backgrounds as you do to standup backgrounds: use the background to reinforce the theme of the story.

What's the Point?

It's worth repeating: whether an interview or a standup, choose a background whenever you can that reminds viewers of the story's theme.

I Was Framed!

Here's something that's true whether you're taking still photographs or video tape, in fact it's true for painters too. How you *frame* your picture might make the difference between something mediocre and something extraordinary.

Do you remember the rose from the previous chapter, the rose that stood after the tornado tore through South Dakota? Here are three ways that rose might have been framed in the story's opening shot:

There is no formula to tell you which of these is best. But there is common sense. The first one has the rose squeezed way off to the edge, with nothing but empty space filling the rest of the frame. Not good, because the viewer's eye won't automatically go to the edge of the frame first. The second has the rose near the middle, but so small that its significance is lost; the viewer has too much else to look at. The third frame is most likely to catch the viewer's eye and maintain his interest. The rose is front and center, and when the shot pulls out to either a medium or a wide shot, revealing destruction all around the rose, its very survival is all the more amazing.

This applies no matter what you're shooting. It may be a beautiful new civic auditorium that's being built. If so, you probably want to frame it to exclude the construction dumpster sitting just off to one side. It may be a range of mountains. Frame it so you don't cut off the highest peaks.

The worst framing I ever saw was in a standup from Washington D.C. Pretty clearly, the cameraman wasn't fond of the correspondent. With the United States Capitol as a backdrop, the correspondent was commenting on a big debate in Congress, but because of how he was framed, few viewers could have paid much attention to what he was saying.

Simply put, the cameraman had disembodied the reporter. Instead of shooting him the usual way, pretty much from the belt up, he shot only his head above the bottom of the frame and, what's more, didn't fill the screen with it. The correspondent's head was down at the bottom of the screen, like a soccer ball waiting to be kicked. It was like a skit from *Saturday Night Live,* but it wasn't funny. It was distracting.

What's the Point?

Just because something in front of you looks good to your naked eye, it doesn't automatically look good on video tape. Your job is to place it in the best part of the frame, so the viewer's eye goes straight to it, and so the background—basically, anything else in the shot—doesn't overwhelm it.

Cut Away for a Cutaway

When you're editing a speech, a news conference or an interview, never take the speaker's words out of context.

Having said that, sometimes the speaker says something meaningful, then something meaningless, then something meaningful again, and you have to edit out the meaningless part and join the meaningful parts together to make them comprehensive and clear.

You may remember this from Chapter 5. You're covering a murder, and a detective has just told you this:

> *Well, the fact of the matter is, we can't really, uh, I mean, we can't find the gun, which we need to nail our suspect, so even though we've got him behind bars right now, we're gonna have to let the guy go. But believe you me, and I was telling my wife this very thing earlier this morning, or maybe it was yesterday, but the one thing for sure is, we're going to keep looking for that weapon and when we find it, you can bet your life we're going to arrest the guy again and put him away for life so he will never again roam the streets.*

There's some meat in there somewhere, but there's a lot of trash, too. Wouldn't it be better if he had said it this way, which doesn't change his meaning but makes it shorter and more interesting to hear?

> *We can't find the gun, which we need to nail our suspect, so even though we've got him behind bars right now, we're gonna have to let the guy go. But we're going to*

keep looking for that weapon and when we find it, you can bet your life we're going to arrest the guy again and put him away for life so he will never again roam the streets.

Unfortunately that's *not* how he said it, but you can fix it. Go back and compare the first version with the second. What you'll see is, only two sections have been eliminated:

At the top:

Well, the fact of the matter is, we can't really, uh, I mean . . .

From the middle:

. . . believe you me, and I was telling my wife this very thing earlier this morning, or maybe it was yesterday, but the one thing for sure is . . .

Both of these sections are wasted and meaningless. You haven't changed the context or meaning of the detective's statement by taking them out.

From a pictorial point of view though, you have had to edit his video. It doesn't make a difference at the top; you just begin the sound bite later. But in the middle, it'll be obvious to the viewer that you have edited the sound bite; they'll see what's called a jump cut. This means, for example, on his final word from the first shot, "*go,*" his head may be facing slightly to the left, or he might be gesturing with his hands, while on the initial word from the second shot, "*but,*" his head may be facing slightly right, or his hands might be at his sides.

There are two simple ways to deal with this:

1. Dissolve from the first shot to the second. This is a signal to the viewer that you've made an edit and aren't trying to hide anything.
2. A cutaway shot (some just call it a "cut shot"). What's a cutaway? Typically it's a shot of the audience at the speech or news conference, or of the reporter *listening* during the interview (even if the shot of the reporter is taken by turning the camera toward the him and recording the cutaway after the end of the interview itself).

    You edit in a cutaway shot to cover the place where you joined the two parts of the sound bite together, and keep it up only two or three seconds. It almost looks like you have a second camera in the room, trained only on whoever's in the cutaway.

    But note I said that in the case of the interview cutaway, the reporter is "listening," not "reacting." There's a big difference. "Listening" means a benign expression on the reporter's face, a minimum of body language. "Reacting" means nodding assent, or showing skepticism, or contempt. Reporters shouldn't do this when the cutaway shot is being recorded, since it might not accurately reflect the reporter's reaction at the time the interviewee was talking. It only adds to the public's perception of bias.

    There is, of course, a third way to deal with an edit of sound bites:
3. Illustrative video. If the mayor is talking about dead trees in the city park, and you want to cover an edit of sound bites, show the mayor for a few seconds, then dissolve

into video of the dead trees. Maybe you return to a shot of the mayor a few seconds before she finishes speaking, although if the video's good enough, maybe you don't. Either way, you have covered the edit, and made the story more visually interesting.

The jump cut will show up in another context too. Let's say you're videotaping an airplane coming in at the airport. It's a jump cut if one shot shows the plane just touching down on the runway, then the next shot shows it taxiing to a stop. That's not a natural sequence. So you use a cutaway between the two shots: possibly someone watching the plane, the ground crew signaling the plane, or the control tower.

What's the Point?

When you shoot stories, especially when they include news conferences, speeches, and interviews, shoot cutaways. There are other ways to cover jump cuts, including just dissolving between them, but have a cutaway in your pocket in case nothing else works well.

Proving the Reporter Is There

The piece of the TV package where the reporter appears on camera usually is called either the "on-camera" or the "standup." "Standup" is what I've used in this book. A standup is shot for a few reasons:

1. Protection. Saying something in a standup (shot while you're still at the scene of the story) that you may not have good pictures to cover.
2. Familiarity. This is how the station can bring the "personality" of its reporters into viewers' homes. It's important because television is a personality-driven business.
3. Credibility. It proves that the reporter really covered the story (or at least showed up before it was over).

When the story package is sandwiched between live standups, which are used more and more these days, the pre-taped standup isn't an issue.

But when the whole package is going to be edited before the show, the question you face is, do you do your standup for the top of the piece (a "standup open"), for the middle (a "standup bridge," which bridges from one part of the story to another), or for the close (a "standup close")? The answer is, it depends! Four factors help you decide.

1. The formula. Do you, and all reporters at your station, usually do a standup close? If so, mix things up in the next story you produce with a standup bridge, or a standup open. Or vice versa. Be unpredictable, if your news director gives you that kind of discretion. If not, do it the way the news director wants it done.
2. The video. Do you have good video for everything *but* your close? Then make it a standup close. Do you have a key point to make somewhere in the middle of your story, but lousy video to cover it? Make it a standup bridge. Is it a picture–challenged story from top to bottom? Is it important, for that matter, to show the audience at the

very top that the reporter was right there at the scene of the story? Then maybe you want a standup open.

The standup bridge is harder to figure out how to do (before you've written the rest of the story) than the standup open or close. For the open, you only have to know how you want to start your story. For the close, you only have to know what comes before the standup. For the bridge, you have to know what comes both before it and after it. In other words, you have to plan a key part of the story's structure in advance.

3. The background. Sometimes you end up doing the standup at the first stop you make while covering the story, simply because you know it's the best background you're going to see all day. For example, you might be covering an auto accident, and that's your first stop. Maybe you're still going to go to the hospital, the home of the victim, and the police department. But you want the accident behind the standup. Depending on how you think you'll build your story, this helps determine whether you do a standup bridge or a standup close.

4. The sound. Wherever you're doing a standup, there might be sound in the background, like an airplane flying overhead, or traffic passing by, or children screaming in a nearby schoolyard. That's known by the remarkably high-tech term, "noise!" The issue isn't whether it drowns out the reporter because if it does, you shouldn't shoot the standup there.

No, the issue is how it's going to sound edited up against the narration, which has been recorded in a nice quiet studio (and probably with a different microphone that produces different tonal qualities). Remember, the standup bridge has to be edited to narration on both ends, often meaning significantly different sound quality as you go from narration to standup to narration. The standup open or close has to be edited to narration only once.

The good news is, there is a way to mitigate that awkward audio transition. Whenever possible, don't just butt your narration right up against your standup (whether it's a bridge, an open or a close). Rather, at the end of the narration, open up your audio track for one or two seconds of NAT SOT (its duration depending on how interesting it is). The music from the parade, the birds chirping in the trees, the airplane taking off from the runway. Or, if it makes sense in the telling of the story, insert a sound bite where the audio's altogether different. Then when you get to the standup (or also, in a bridge, back to the narration), the audio difference isn't nearly so blatant.

What's the Point?

Usually, if there's halfway decent video for your story, the standup is not going to be the most important part, because it's best to start and end with good picture. That's one reason why bridges make sense. But because of audio issues, sometimes closes sound better. Of course if your station has a policy dictating what kind of standup to do, alternatives might be moot.

And don't forget this lesson from Chapter 9: if it's a standup close, then it should wrap up the story, or tell the viewer where the story goes next, or summarize what it all means.

Where You Make It or Break It

No matter how good the video from the field, lousy editing means a lousy story. But good editing can make even lousy video shine (well, sort of). Anyway, editing is more than just an afterthought. Earlier parts of this chapter have dealt with some editing issues. There are more.

As you read in Chapter 6 there are two schools of thought about how to choose your first shot. One says, choose something interesting but save your best stuff so you can build to a climax. So what might the opening shot be? An "establishing" shot; for example, a wide shot of the building, or the parking lot, or the hillside on which the story takes place. The other school of thought says (and personally I prefer this one), start with your best stuff. Grab the audience's attention. Snag your viewers. Make them hope for more. I think choosing your lead shot is like writing your lead sentence: if it's an attention grabber, you're more likely to succeed.

From the top of the piece to the bottom, every shot you insert also requires a decision about timing. Sometimes a shot shows continuing action, like a demonstration. If so, leave it up as long as it tells the story. But when a shot is more static, sit on it only long enough for the viewer to absorb what there is to see, but not long enough to turn boring. If there's something to read in the shot (like a demonstrator's protest sign), make sure you leave it up long enough to be read.

You'll usually end up with long shots (I use the terms "wide shots" and "long shots" interchangeably), medium shots, and closeup shots. Mix them up. Nothing but medium shots, for instance, would become a tedious formula for the viewer's eye. However, don't change shots and shot composition arbitrarily; if you go from a long shot to a closeup of something in the long shot, make sure the long shot and the closeup match. In other words, if the quarterback is waving his hands in the long shot, you can't cut to a closeup where his hands are at his sides.

In the last section, I told you about using interesting video to cover sound bite edits. What I didn't tell you is, sometimes it's a good technique even if you don't have an edit to cover. For instance, to use the example one more time of the mayor talking about dead trees, you can let the mayor start speaking on camera, but once the viewer has established that it is the mayor, cover the rest of the sound bite with video of the trees. Once the viewer has established that it's the coach talking about the team, or it's the snowplow driver talk-

Long shot
(sometimes written as "l/s").

Medium shot
(sometimes written as "m/s").

Closeup
(sometimes written as "c/u").

ing about the blizzard, or it's the police officer talking about the accident, cut or dissolve to the team, or the blizzard, or the accident.

Finally, the subject of music. The rules about music are very clear: it belongs in a news story only if it's an integral part of the story. Obviously if you're reporting on a rock band, there'll be music throughout. If you're covering a parade, we expect to hear the marching bands. But not music from some other source. Do *not* insert music from another source, just to spice up a story. Leave that to Hollywood.

Does this mean you'll never hear unrelated music in someone's news story? No. But just because some newsrooms do it doesn't make it right.

What's the Point?

Editing can make or break a television news story. It's a visual medium. Use every tool you have.

Exercises to Put Pizazz in the Picture

1. Don't Let the Critics Pan You
   You are covering an air show, where the U.S. Air Force is landing its newest one-man-crew fighter jet. The plane circles over the airfield, then lands in front of the audience of VIPs, then taxis to a position right in front of them, with the pilot crisply saluting as he rolls to a stop. Write a brief essay answering the question, when are zooms and pans appropriate in the shooting and editing of this story, and when are they not?

2. The Background of Your Story
   Assuming realistic expectations about what you'll be able to video tape, what's the best background you can think of for standups on the following stories:

   - A plane crash
   - A flu epidemic
   - A school shooting
   - An election defeat
   - An economic recession
   - A blizzard

3. Sounding Good
   You are doing a story about the opening of a new truck stop at the north end of the city. Noisy big rigs are coming and going constantly. Explain how to ease the awkward transition from the sound of narration, recorded at the station, and the sound of a standup, recorded at the truck stop with unavoidable background noise.

It's All Part of the Show

16

If the Shoe Fits, Write it

What You'll Learn _____

Television and radio scripts aren't uniform from one newsroom to another—among other reasons, they use different scripting software. What's more, formats are different depending on their use: at the station, or in the field. This chapter is strictly about use inside the station (generally, the field reporter can scribble the script on her hand, as long as she can read it, although that's *not* recommended). As you'll learn in the final chapter, "Holding Onto Your Dream," you might have to learn an entirely new format at every new station you enter.

But certain basics apply everywhere you go, no matter what software you use. Well, *almost* everywhere (I assiduously stick to the prospect that at some point, you'll end up working at a station that is the exception). Although there are several kinds of script formats, I'll tell you what remains the same, almost wherever you work. It'll certainly be based on the style I'd want if you worked for me!

Why does it matter? Because the whole purpose of a script is to be *readable,* and uniform to all who see it. That means not only readable language, but a uniformly (within the station) readable format. You're working with a team, and everyone on the team—anchors, writers, producers, graphic artists, control room technicians, studio technicians—everyone needs the same information, in the same language. Everyone needs to know what's supposed to happen as the story airs. Furthermore, as you already have learned in this book, all the good writing, reporting, and editing you do can go down the drain if the anchorwoman stumbles on the script, because that will distract the audience and quite possibly be all the viewer or listener remembers.

The Terms of the Story _____

Incue   The first few words of a sound bite, included on a script so everyone in the studio and the control room knows what will be said.

Rundown   The list of stories, including the length of each, that will air in the newscast, in their planned logical sequence.

Slug   A code specific to each scripted story, making it easy for anyone to quickly identify the title, the writer, the date, and newscast for which it is written.

The Shape of Your Script

The fundamental difference between scripts for television news and for radio news is simple: a TV script (depending on the software) has an imaginary line (and sometimes an actual printed line) down the middle of the page, usually just a bit left of center (making roughly a forty/sixty percent split). *Only* technical information for directors, producers, and technicians goes on the left side, the script of the story itself (and sometimes some technical information useful to the anchor) goes on the right side. When a teleprompter is used, just the part on the right side shows up.

Here is an example:

Mayor resigns—4 Jul—6pm—Dobbs	:55 Page 1/1
Jennifer o/c Cam 2 CG: Jennifer Jakes/7News	(JENNIFER) The mayor this morning dropped a bombshell. She will resign in a month.
Jason o/c Cam 1	(JASON) Why?
Jason VO Tape 3	(JASON VO) At her regularly weekly news conference she wouldnt say, but her official spokesman dropped a hint afterward.
SOT Tape 3 CG: Larry Law/Mayor's Spokesman 8 seconds Outcue: "…job in Washington."	
Jennifer VO Tape 3	(JENNIFER VO) As longtime local citizens know, Mayor Martinez is the daughter and granddaughter of senators, and early in her political career, she said there has never been any question in her mind that the United States Senate is her ultimate political goal.
Jason o/c Cam 3 CG: Jason Jeffreys/7News	(JASON) Of course this raises a different question: who will succeed her at City Hall? The city has no formal procedure to select a successor without a special election. The Clerk of Elections says that will be costly.
SOT Nancy Nigh/City Treasurer 5 seconds Outcue: "…of half-a-million dollars."	
Jennifer o/c Cam 1	(JENNIFER) The City Treasurer says that right now, there's no money for that.

If a station has the software, as most do, then a script for TV can be typed out from the left margin of the page to the right margin, and the software can convert it to the left-side/right-side format.

A radio script usually doesn't have a line down the middle. Instead, it is written the way you write almost everything else: from the left side of the page to the right side, with technical information inserted wherever it falls in the script and often indented to distinguish it from the words that are read on the air.

Here is an example:

```
Mayor resigns—4 Jul—6pm—Dobbs          :55                          Page 1/1

The mayor this morning dropped a bombshell.
She will resign in a month.
Why?
At her regularly weekly news conference she wouldnt say, but her official spokesman,
Larry Law, dropped a hint afterward.

                    SOT #4
                    8 seconds
                    Incue "Mayor Martinez has a long history…"
                    Outcue: "…job in Washington."
                    Summary: Mayor has history with Washington politics, always wanted
                    to work there.

As longtime local citizens know, Mayor Martinez is the daughter and granddaughter of
senators, and early in her political career, she said there has never been any question in her
mind that the United States Senate is her ultimate political goal.
Of course this raises a different question: who will succeed her at City Hall?
The city has no formal procedure to select a successor without a special election.
Nancy Night, the Clerk of Elections says that will be costly.

                    SOT #2
                    5 seconds
                    Incue: "Typically this kind…"
                    Outcue: "…of half-a-million dollars."
                    Summary: Special elections typically cost half-million dollars

The City Treasurer says that right now, there's no money for that.
```

What's the Point?

If you go to work in a newsroom and don't know the difference between a script for radio and one for TV, you might not lose your brand new job, but you'll wish you'd learned the difference before getting there.

The Look of Your Script

Should you type your scripts in ALL UPPER CASE LIKE THIS, or in Upper and Lower Case Like This? Single spaced, double spaced, or triple? It's a matter of personal preference. The news director's or the anchor's personal preference, not yours. How about indenting sentences? Some newsrooms do it, others don't. How much potentially distracting technical information should you provide on the portion of a script that the anchor must read live? Some think everything ought to be noted, some think almost nothing.

So I won't purport to tell you the *right* way and the *wrong* way to do these things, because there's a good argument for each. (The best argument may be that if the news director wants it a certain way that is how you'd better do it!) But I shall tell you what *I'd* want in *my* newsroom, and why.

1. Upper and lower case versus ALL CAPS
   Say you write a sentence like this:

   The limo driver, Matthew Miles, says he has the first Lexus in Lubbock, and he loves it.

The anchor may be able to read it more easily in upper and lower than if you write it in ALL UPPERS like this:

THE LIMO DRIVER, MATTHEW MILES, SAYS HE HAS THE FIRST LEXUS IN LUBBOCK, AND HE LOVES IT.

This is even more important, I believe, when you have consecutive sentences. Bearing in mind that the anchor has many distractions while reading and cannot simply stare at the script, upper and lower case helps him distinguish between the end of one sentence and the start of another. In other words, it helps prevent confusion.

For example? Look at the paragraph you just read about consecutive sentences. It is duplicated below, word for word, in the same size, the same spacing and the same font, but in ALL CAPS:

THIS IS EVEN MORE IMPORTANT WHEN YOU HAVE CONSECUTIVE SENTENCES. BEARING IN MIND THAT THE ANCHOR HAS MANY DISTRACTIONS AND CANNOT SIMPLY STARE AT THE SCRIPT, UPPER AND LOWER CASE TYPING HELPS HER OR HIM DISTINGUISH BETWEEN THE END OF ONE SENTENCE AND THE START OF ANOTHER. IN OTHER WORDS, IT HELPS PREVENT CONFUSION.

Which one seems easier to read? Upper and lower case in my opinion, although many news directors disagree. You'll work for them, not for me, so do it however they want it.

2. Single versus double or triple spacing

Let's take a look at the last paragraph in both single and double spaced formats:

Which one seems easier to read? Upper and lower case in my opinion, although many news directors disagree. You'll work for them, not for me, so do it however they want it.

Which one seems easier to read? Upper and lower case in my opinion,

although many news directors disagree. You'll work for them, not for me,

do it however they want it.

Now imagine the paragraph in a teleprompter, or only on the right side of a television news script. There's probably no real consensus on single versus double spacing. In my experience, double spacing is better, simply because with all the distractions confronting whoever's reading this on the air, the eye will find the next line in the script more easily if the script is double spaced.

3. Indenting versus not indenting

You're writing a news script, not a novel. Each story begins at the top of the page and, if it's long enough, continues onto the next page (and each page after that) until the end. There are no paragraphs and, therefore, my preference is no indentations, although here too, some news directors (and anchors) prefer indentations. In any event, you start each story on the left-hand margin of your script section.

Here is an example for TV, first, *with* indentations:

> *The mayor this morning dropped a bombshell. She will resign in a month. Why? At her regularly weekly news conference she wouldn't say, but her official spokesman dropped a hint afterward: the mayor has her eye on the United States Senate.*
>
> *As longtime local citizens know, Mayor Martinez is the daughter and granddaughter of senators, and early in her political career, she said there has never been any question in her mind that the United States Senate is her ultimate political goal.*
>
> *Of course this raises a different question: who will succeed her at City Hall? The city has no formal procedure to select a successor without a special election. The Clerk of Elections says that will be costly, something like half-a-million dollars. The City Treasurer says that right now, there's no money for that.*

Now, the same story *without* indentations:

> *The mayor this morning dropped a bombshell. She will resign in a month. Why? At her regularly weekly news conference she wouldn't say, but her official spokesman dropped a hint afterward: the mayor has her eye on the United States Senate. As longtime local citizens know, Mayor Martinez is the daughter and granddaughter of senators, and early in her political career, she said there has never been any question in her mind that the United States Senate is her ultimate political goal. Of course this raises a different question: who will succeed her at City Hall? The city has no formal procedure to select a successor without a special election. The Clerk of Elections says that will be costly, something like half-a-million dollars. The City Treasurer says that right now, there's no money for that.*

Both examples look fine, and in fact you might glance at them both and think that in the example *with* indentations, it is easier to distinguish one paragraph from another. But there's the rub: it's all one story, so there shouldn't be any paragraphs to distinguish. (As you'll see in a moment, the insertion of a sound bite will create its own natural separation.)

So if you shouldn't write in paragraphs, how can you help the anchor see a clear distinction between one sentence and another? By starting each sentence on a new line. Like this:

The mayor this morning dropped a bombshell. She will resign in a month.
Why?
At her regularly weekly news conference she wouldn't say, but her official spokesman dropped a hint afterward: the mayor has her eye on the United States Senate.
As longtime local citizens know, Mayor Martinez is the daughter and granddaughter of senators, and early in her political career, she said there has never been any question in her mind that the United States Senate is her ultimate political goal.
Of course this raises a different question: who will succeed her at City Hall?
The city has no formal procedure to select a successor without a special election.
The Clerk of Elections says that will be costly, something like half-a-million dollars.
The City Treasurer says that right now, there's no money for that.

Remember too, for a TV anchor, this probably will be on a teleprompter, which means she will be reading from a mirror reflecting the script in front of the camera lens. It'll scroll by the center point of the lens just one line at a time, possibly with each sentence starting on a new line, but without paragraphs.

4. Being clear about where the sound bites fall

Although formats differ (as with different scripting software), every script, for a radio or a TV newscast, requires a clear, visible, identifiable break so the anchor knows to stop for a sound bite.

Let's use the same story about the mayor's surprise announcement that she is resigning. But this time, there will be a sound bite. As you'll see in the television format below, no matter what else might be distracting the anchor, there can be no doubt while reading this on the air about when to stop, and when to start again.

SOT
Larry Law/Mayor's Spokesman
8 seconds
Outcue: "...job in Washington."

The mayor this morning dropped a bombshell.
She will resign in a month.
Why?
At her regularly weekly news conference she wouldn't say, but her official spokesman dropped a hint afterward.

As longtime local citizens know, Mayor Martinez is the daughter and granddaughter of senators, and early in her political career, she said there has never been any question in her mind that the United States Senate is her ultimate political goal.
Of course this raises a different question: who will succeed her at City Hall?
The city has no formal procedure to select a successor without a special election.
The Clerk of Elections says that will be costly, something like half-a-million dollars.
The City Treasurer says that right now, there's no money for that.

Sometimes, the kind of information that is printed on the left side above will be in that break, the empty space, between narration sections. That allows the anchor to see it too, although usually either a floor director or a control room executive can give this information to the anchor through the earpiece.

5. Too much versus too little information

Note the information on the left side of the script, above: a sound bite (SOT), the name of the speaker (so it can be turned into a CG), and the bite's length and out-cue (so both the control room and the anchor know when to expect it to end).

Now, just to be clear, here's the story one more time, but with *two* sound bites built in. As you'll see, the principle is the same whether you have one, two, or twelve. But I'll add another element: the names of the anchors on the right side, and whether they are doing a voiceover (VO) covered by video, so if two anchors share reading duties, they'll know who is supposed to read what, and whether they are on camera or off.

```
                                    (JENNIFER)
                                    The mayor this morning dropped a
                                    bombshell.
                                    She will resign in a month.
                                    (JASON)
                                    Why?
                                    (JASON VO)
                                    At her regularly weekly news conference
                                    she wouldn't say, but her official spokesman
                                    dropped a hint afterward.

          SOT
          Larry Law/Mayor's Spokesman
          8 seconds
          Outcue: "...job in Washington."

                                    (JENNIFER)
                                    As longtime local citizens know, Mayor
                                    Martinez is the daughter and
                                    granddaughter of senators, and early in her
                                    political career, she said there has never
                                    been any question in her mind that the
                                    United States Senate is her ultimate
                                    political goal.
                                    (JASON)
                                    Of course this raises a different question:
                                    who will succeed her at City Hall?
                                    The city has no formal procedure to select a
                                    successor without a special election.
                                    The Clerk of Elections says that will be
                                    costly.

          SOT
          Nancy Nigh/City Treasurer
          5 seconds
          Outcue: "...of half-a-million dollars."

                                    (JENNIFER)
                                    The City Treasurer says that right now,
                                    there's no money for that.
```

There also might be information typed or penciled in on the left side about which computer or tape machine will be used to play the sound bite, although like a few other pieces of information for the lefthand column of a script (like which camera to use, and what else to generate as a CG on the screen), that is strictly for the control room's use and is often added by the director or producer.

6. Information notations in radio scripts

As you saw earlier in this chapter, the radio script typically isn't arranged in a "left-right" format—it is done "above-below"—but the principle of ensuring visual clarity by separating narration from information is the same.

What's more, you want a bit more information for radio. For instance, the "incue" is a good idea, so the anchor knows right away if a careless finger or a technical snafu has triggered the wrong sound bite. And the "summary," so the anchor can extemporaneously paraphrase the sound bite if it doesn't play at all. Not all radio stations require this, but I think they should.

The mayor this morning dropped a bombshell.
She will resign in a month.
Why?
At her regularly weekly news conference she wouldnt say, but her official spokesman,
Larry Law, dropped a hint afterward.

SOT #4 (referring to the station's system of cataloguing sound bites)
8 seconds
Incue: "Mayor Martinex has a long history..."
Outcue: "...job in Washington."
Summary: Mayor has history with Washington politics, always wanted to work there

As longtime local citizens know, Mayor Martinez is the daughter and granddaughter of senators, and early in her political career, she said there has never been any question in her mind that the United States Senate is her ultimate political goal.
Of course this raises a different question: who will succeed her at City Hall?
The city has no formal procedure to select a successor without a special election. Nancy Nigh, the Clerk of Elections says that will be costly.

SOT #2
5 seconds
Incue: "Typically this kind..."
Outcue: "...of half-a-million dollars."
Summary: Special elections typically cost half-million dollars

The City Treasurer says that right now, there's no money for that.

---

7. The long and the short of it

As you learned earlier in the book, if you're given forty seconds to tell a story, the producer doesn't want thirty-five seconds and she doesn't want forty-five. Furthermore, people helping produce the newscast need to know how long it is, but might not have a copy of the rundown.

Some scripting software actually times scripts according to the preprogrammed normal speed at which the anchorman or anchorwoman reads. It will post the timing on the script itself.

Otherwise, at the bottom of each story, you should either type or pencil in the total running time (TRT) of the piece.

Some do it formally: *TRT :40*

Some do it informally, just putting *":40"* or *"40 sec"* at the bottom of the page and circling it.

What's the Point?

The choice between upper and lower case letters and ALL CAPS, and between indenting or not indenting, is up to your superior in the newsroom. But arguably, it isn't just a matter of looks, it's a matter of visual clarity. Likewise, clarity and specific information are critical when you show a sound bite.

Slug Every Script

The last thing you want to do when you're in a hurry—which is usually the last half hour before a TV newscast and the last ten minutes before a radio newscast—is have to read through a script on a computer screen or a piece of paper to find out what it's about—or if someone else wrote it and you have a question, to find out who to ask—or to see if it has been used before.

That's why you write a slug horizontally along the top, or in some newsrooms vertically in the upper left corner, of each new script.

What specifically do you include? By now you shouldn't be surprised to learn that there is no uniform answer. As in almost every other area of script writing, different stations require different elements in the slug. Uniformly though, they require a name for the story. On the story about the mayor resigning, for instance, it probably should be:

> *Mayor resigns*

You want to keep the slug name to a word or two if possible. "Mayor resigns" is just enough for a producer frantically stacking the stories in the right order at the last minute, and anyone else needing to be certain they're on the same page, to know precisely what the script is about without having to read through it.

Be careful not to be too vague when you choose the name. If you use "Mayor news conference" or "Mayor talks" rather than "Mayor resigns," it could be mistaken for *another* story from the mayor's news conference the same day.

I think three other elements are useful in a slug: date, time (the time the story airs, not the time it's written), and the writer's name.

Here's a brief rationale for each:

- DATE By listing the date, someone checking the archives while writing a followup or a related story will know how long ago the original story took place.
- TIME By noting the time of the newscast in which the story aired, you make it clear to whoever is producing a show later that same day, or the next day, that this script needs updating or rewriting or removal for fresher news. In other words, how *old* the story is.
- WRITER'S NAME This is how someone with a question about the story can quickly figure out who to ask.

So, here's the slug I'd want to see along the top, or in the upper left corner, on the first page of the story about the mayor:

Mayor resigns – Jul 4 – 6 pm – Dobbs

Or:

Mayor resigns
Jul 4
6 pm
Dobbs

Finally, some stations include a "designator" at the top—a code that includes the nature of the package being read: whether it's a voiceover (VO), whether it includes tape (SOT), whether it involves video, a photo, or an illustration behind the anchor (for example, CHYRON, which is an image projected behind the anchor), or other such elements.

Also, some scripting software programs will automatically give you page numbers, updating them as new ones are inserted.

What's the Point?

The slug isn't important, until you need to know information, and there's no slug. The slug can answer a handful of questions in a single moment.

Exercises to Fit In _____

1. Below are the elements of a story. You must write a 45-second voiceover version for television, and a 20-second version for radio. Put each in an appropriate script format, with appropriate information, for its medium.
   - Two street gangs
   - Names: "Feeders" and "Riders"
   - Housing project 10 blocks west of downtown
   - Each side has guns
   - Day after mayor announces new terminal for airport
   - Shooting from opposite sides of playground
   - Fourth gang-related shooting in city this year
   - Girl shot on swing
   - Mayor releases IRS forms
   - Girl died on way to hospital
   - Mother pushing her
   - Mother injured
   - Girl four years old
   - Project residents demonstrate for more police protection
   - Police have descriptions of shooters
   - Police have no suspects
   - Mayor names new police chief

2. Below are the elements of another story, including sound bites. Write one version for television, a minute and ten seconds long. Write another for radio, 50 seconds long. Include at

least two sound bites in each, and put each piece in an appropriate format, with appropriate information, for its medium.

- 2 trucks collide head-on
- 7:15 a.m.
- On eastbound I-80 just west of Main St exit
- 1 driver killed
- Dead driver had pickup truck
- Dead driver's name unknown
- Other driver ran from scene
- Other driver had oil delivery truck
- Driver who fled wearing red jumpsuit, long hair
- Male friend from dead driver's car hospitalized, then released
- Traffic stopped 2 hours
- Oil all over road
- Governor trapped in traffic jam, late to park dedication
- 3rd highway death in town this month

SOT: Jack Johnson, friend of dead driver, hospitalized then released

"Don't know where the guy came from, we were just driving along, kinda slow because of rush hour, then bam, he hits us on the left side of the truck and the next thing I know, I wake up and my buddy's slumped over the wheel." *(Make this 13 seconds long)*

SOT: Bernice Brown, witness

"I'm right behind this oil truck when he starts skidding, then bangs into the pickup, and I see the guy jump out his door. He's wearing this bright red jumpsuit and he's got real long hair, and I hope they catch him fast!" *(Make this 8 seconds long)*

SOT: Sgt. Tom Tapper, first officer to respond at the scene

"When I got here, the suspect was long gone. But we've got a good ID on the guy and we'll get him." *(Make this 5 seconds long)*

17

Fitting It All In

What You'll Learn

Television and radio newscasts have one thing in common if you're putting together a show for either medium: you need a good rundown (which some call the "lineup"). In other words, a good lead story, a good closing story, and lots of good stories in between. Furthermore, you need a logical order for your stories, so that you don't follow a piece about a house fire with a piece about a dog that laughs, nor do you follow the dog story with a piece about a raucous city council meeting on crime.

And that's not all. Your newscast has to be well written so that one story flows with a smooth transition into the next. And, the newscast has to be well paced, meaning every anchor voiceover isn't 12 seconds long and every reporter's package piece (the story told by a field reporter) isn't two minutes. On top of all that, the whole thing has to be timed out perfectly, because you're in trouble if it runs short and you have nothing worthwhile to fill the extra time, or if it runs long and you cut into the beginning of the next program.

So putting the newscast together requires objective decisions because, like a statistician, you have to squeeze a lot of material into a finite space, and to decide how long each story and each anchor transition should be. But it also requires subjective decisions, because you have to choose the story that shines above all others to open the newscast, the stories that get buried in the middle, and the piece that ought to play last, the one most viewers will likely remember.

What you'll learn in this chapter is how to make those decisions, which means how to think about them. The rest—actually creating a good rundown—then should come automatically.

The Terms of the Story

Reader   A short story the anchor covers without production elements such as sound bites or reporter packages.

Backtime   Timing the pieces at the end of a rundown, so you know near the end of the show whether you have enough, not enough, or too much material left to cover.

Taking the Lead, Closing It Out

The first thing you should do when putting together your rundown is choose the lead story. Almost without exception, it should qualify as news, rather than a feature. (Actually, I can't think of any exception. But like so many rules in newswriting, the exception probably will come up some day.)

Beyond knowing to choose news, how do you choose your lead? The same way you choose a lead sentence in an individual story: decide what's the most important event of the day, and/or the most interesting event, and/or the most recent (breaking news). Although the examples in this chapter will focus on television, the process is precisely the same for radio, but without any consideration of course for video.

If one story stands out above the others for all the reasons you just read, plus it is a good picture story, then it's a no-brainer; you have figured out how to lead your rundown. But what if you have two equally compelling possibilities, and one's a good picture story while the other isn't. I'd say that's a no-brainer too; go with the picture story first, because it'll grab the attention of the audience.

However, what if you have to choose between two obvious leads, and both are good picture stories, or else *neither* is a good picture story? Then go to the next set of criteria: is one story local, the other not? If it comes to that, go with the local story first. Why? Because at least subconsciously, when viewers turn on a newscast, typically they want to know first and foremost, "Is my home safe?" Then, "Is my community safe?" Then comes the question, "Is my nation safe?" and only after that, "Is my world safe?" Think of your viewers' motivation in those terms and you'll rarely fail to figure out how to prioritize your newscast.

To get you thinking about choosing a lead, consider the following hypothetical possibilities as if they are your choices one night:

- Earthquake in Pakistan.
- Nation's Gross Domestic Product announced in Washington. No change.
- Our mayor, with millions of dollars in his pocket after embezzling the city's emergency funds, dies in flames as city hall burns to the ground. The money burns up with him.
- Weather tomorrow will be sunny with a high of 65°.

Okay, this one was easy; the third option has all the elements you want in a lead story. But that's the point: choose the story that has those elements, or at least as many as possible. They won't always be so obvious.

Your next task is *not* choosing your second story, then your third, your fourth and so forth. You certainly want to create some flow from the lead story to the second story (or, if there are two good lead story possibilities, from the first lead to the second lead), but that will come soon enough.

Instead, after choosing your lead, your next task is choosing your close. The process is different than choosing the lead. For one thing, having good pictures in a closing piece is probably even more important than in a lead piece. After all, if a story is critical enough to lead a newscast, then the information usually supercedes everything else. But if you want viewers to remember the closing story and talk about it the next morning with everyone at work, good pictures enhance the chance that they'll remember it.

So what are you looking for in a good closing piece? It's easier to say what you're *not* looking for. To begin with, "importance." If a story is important, you'll be wanting to position it higher in your rundown. (The exception to this is when a lead story is so big that you want to repeat it at the end of the show, just to make sure people who tune in late don't miss it.)

Secondly, you're not looking for anything dour or depressing. Closing stories aren't chosen because viewers "need to know"; they're chosen, frankly, to leave viewers upbeat, if possible within the context of news, to "leave 'em laughing." You're not looking for something dull or complicated. What you want is a story that makes an audience laugh or cry, ideally, tears of joy.

What's the Point?

Some days a single story jumps out as the lead. Other days, nothing does. The only constant is, there has to be a lead story on every newscast. And a close. Although you might make a different choice than a competitor, if you use the criteria you have learned here, you can't go wrong.

Filling in the Holes

Okay, you have chosen your lead story and your closing story. What's left? Oh, nothing much—just *the rest of the newscast.* This becomes a challenge on several levels, because you want to deliver stories that people need to know. But also you want a rundown that flows and won't lose anyone's attention.

One key to success is in the decisions you make about sequence. For example, if you have two farm stories for your newscast—one about apple growers and the other about orange growers—is there any doubt that you'll run them back to back? Of course not. They are *related.* It sounds like the most logical decision of the day. You have a *sequence* of stories about fruit!

But what if your piece from the apple farm is about the price of apples dropping below cost, while your piece from the orange grove is about unseasonably early frost killing most of the crop? Does it make more sense to pair the two "fruit" stories together in your rundown, or to pair the apple story with a related story about the economy (in the "economy" section), and the orange story with another about bad weather (in the "weather" section)?

The answer is, you can justify either decision. Where you put your stories in the rundown depends partly on what other stories you want to run. What's important is to group stories together that have a common thread. What's important is continuity.

In other words, look for ways in which stories are related and group them logically together. Put all the crime stories together, all the political stories together, all the international stories and all the economic stories and all the weather stories together. That's a good start, but not foolproof: sometimes, as with the above examples of apples and oranges, a

Jeff Gurney   7/23/03 13:04:49   [KCNC]RUNDOWN.10PM.TODAY. 1
14:59 under

P	PG	SLUG	TAL	PRODUCTION	GRAPHICS	GRAPHICS#	CA	VT
		changes:						
		10p 2003		bill/molly/larry/steve		prod: anania 6325		
=	001	HEADLINES 59:10	MH/BS	C21		Dir: Woody 6469		
=	001A	1)		VO				7
=	001B	2)		VO				8
=	001C	3)		VO				9
	002	4) 2 shot		L2 FULL		(HOLD MUSIC)		
=====	======	================	======	============================	===============	=====================	=====	=======
		M1 @						
	A01	OPEN	======	AP				
				L2-ZOOM				
	AX	SUPERTEASE	MH/BS	LB		DC-1	2	
	AX1	1)		PKG				
	AX2	2)		VO<				
	AX3	3)		VO<				
	AX4	4)		VO<				
	AX5	TALENT/REOPEN	======	C30				
AZ		BREAK 1 ======	======	===========================	10:11:15	=====================	=====	=======
		BUMPIN		C35				
		WEATHER	M/B/L	L3z/WCK(st)/CC+			2/3/1ck	
		MORE WEATHER	LARRY	WCK(wxc)/L3			1ck/2	
	BX	TEASE 2	MH/BS	L2		DC-1	2	
	BX1	1)sports		VO<				
BZ		BREAK 2 ======	======	===========================	===============	=====================	=====	=======
	C01	SPORTS ANIMATI	======	C15				
	C30	TOSS TO SPORTS	B/M/S	L3(super steve a)			2	
	C35							
	C40							
	C45							
	C50							
	C60							
	C70							
	C80							
	C90	TOSS BACK	S/M/B	L3			3	
	CX	TEASE 3	BS/MH	L2		DC-4	2	
	CX1	1)kicker		VO<				
	CX2	2)weather		CC<				
CZ		BREAK 3 ======	======	===========================	===============	=====================	=====	=======
	D10	LAST WEATHER	LARRY	WXC/L3			3	

At KCNC-TV in Denver, page 1 of the rundown for the 10 o'clock evening newscast has more empty holes than committed decisions at 1:04 in the afternoon.

story will fall into *two* categories. For example, if you have a story about car theft, but it's about car theft *in France,* you can put it either in your crime section or in your international section.

Or, better yet, structure your rundown so your international stories follow your crime stories, then let the French car theft story act as the transition between the two. In other words, let the story on car theft in France be the final "crime" story, which also makes it the first "international" story (or vice versa). Thinking like this actually helps you figure out how to construct your whole rundown.

What's the Point?

What matters most is that the sequence of stories and of *sections* of stories in a rundown should be logical, and the transitions related and meaningful.

Bridging the Gap

The fruit stories you just read about—apple prices dropping below cost, while early frost kills most of the orange crop—lend themselves to good written transitions.

For example, if you choose to pair these pieces together because they're both about locally grown fruit, you can write a transition that *connects* the two stories, something like:

> *While our area's apple growers are suffering from high costs, the region's orange growers are suffering from bad weather. Jane Jackson reports.*

On the other hand, if you pair the apple story with another economic story, you have a substantive looking economic "package" within the rundown, which might make more sense and make for a simple transition. Ditto for pairing the weather stories:

> *Now that you've seen how the ice storm tied up tonight's rush hour traffic, we're going to show you how it hurt our region's orange growers. Jane Jackson reports.*

But now deal with a tougher transition challenge. Pretend your rundown has a story about auto pollution, followed by a story about high school cheerleaders (*you* never would have constructed the rundown this way, but someone else did and you're stuck with it). Not a perfect choice, but here is how you might manufacture a transition:

> *Speaking of automobile exhaust, eight girls at our high school today were exhausted, after three hours working out some new dance routines. . . . .*

Ouch! That *sounds* manufactured, contrived, a "stretch." On the other hand, you don't want to just end one story (and sequence) cold and start another, as here:

> *. . . . . and everyone caught without an emissions inspection sticker will be fined fifty dollars. Eight cheerleaders at our high school were bone tired today after. . . . .*

So how do you deal with the transition? The immediate answer is, *try something else.* Don't build such a disconnected sequence into your rundown if you can help it. The emissions story could be paired with news about money, or pollution, or cars. The cheerleader story could be paired with news about health, or education, or sports. Usually there'll be *something* to work with.

Then again, sometimes there isn't. Sometimes you have a story that you must tell, even though it doesn't logically flow into or follow from any other story in the rundown.

There's still a solution. Use a simple transition word, or sentence, like these:

Meanwhile, today at our high school . . .
Some news today from our high school . . .
It's not related, but eight cheerleaders at our high school . . .
On a different note . . .

They're not pretty, but they provide some sort of continuity.

What's the Point?

The first place to build flow is in your choice of stories. The next place is in your sequence of sections. After that, it's up to the writing. Good transitions can help you connect disconnected stories without almost anyone noticing.

Change Your Pace

Now that rundown construction seems logical, here's something to make it hard again. *Pace.* Let's say you have twenty stories to run in your newscast; eight of them are reporter packages, three more have video for anchor voiceovers. The rest are simply read by the anchor with nothing more visual than, say, a photo or a graphic over the anchor's shoulder.

Even if your most important *and* interesting *and* recent stories happen to be the eight reporter packages, you can't just put them in positions 1 through 8 in your rundown. Why not? Because while the top of the show will be dynamic, after that it'll be anchor voice followed by anchor voice followed by anchor . . . you get the idea. The rest of the show would be boring.

So on top of all your other decisions, you have to figure out how to respect the other priorities you've learned in this chapter, yet observe the utmost priority of a good production. How? By spreading those picture stories—the eight reporter packages and the three video–covered voiceovers—through the newscast. Then place the other pieces accordingly.

There's no set formula for this. But it doesn't have to alter your key decisions. You choose your lead story based on the story. You choose your closing piece the same way. What's left gets put in the big hole in-between, compromising between a logical sequence and a logical pace. This doesn't mean radically shifting your story order. It only means sprinkling your video—the reporter packages and the anchor voiceover video—throughout the rundown.

Jeff Gurney   7/23/03 21:53:22

0:01 over

[KCNC]RUNDOWN.10PM.TODAY. 1

P	PG	SLUG	TAL	PRODUCTION	GRAPHICS	TIME	BKTIME	WR	ANCH
		changes:				0:00			
						0:00	21:59:10		
		10p 7/23/2003		bill/molly/larry/steve		0:00	21:59:10		
=	001	HEADLINES 59:10	MH/BS	C21		**0:20**	21:59:10	##MH	bsmh
=	001A	1) NY Shooting		VO		0:00	21:59:30	=	
=	001B	2)Denver City Hall		SOT		0:00	21:59:30	=	
=	001C	3)Thornton Shooting		VO		0:00	21:59:30	=	
	002	4) 2 shot		L2 FULL		**0:00**	21:59:30	=	
=====	================	=================	======	======================	==============	0:00	21:59:29	==	
		* Note L1(sk) @ A50				0:00	21:59:29		
	A01	OPEN	======	(Married)		**0:10**	21:59:29	##	
=	A15	COLD OPEN	BILL	PKG		**0:20**	21:59:39	##AA	BSMH
=	A20	NY SHOOTING INTRO	BS/MH	L2/2X1	2X1	**0:20**	21:59:59	##AA	MHBS
=	A21	NY SHOOTING LIVE	SCOTT	RF		**0:20**	22:00:19	##	
=	A22	NY SHOOTING PACKA	SCOTT	PKG		**1:30**	22:00:39	##	
=	A23	NY SHOOTING TAG	M/B/S	RF/2X1	2X1	**0:15**	22:02:09	##	
=	A30	OUR CITY HALL INTRO	MH/BS	2X1(hotswitch)	2X1	**0:15**	22:02:24	##	MHBS
=	A31	OUR CITY HALL LIVE	ERICKA	RF		**0:15**	22:02:39	##	
=	A32	OUR CITY HALL PACK	ERICKA	PKG		**1:10**	22:02:54	##el	
=	A33	OUR CITY HALL TAG	ERICKA	RF		**0:15**	22:04:04	##el	
=	A36	SHOOTING WRAP	BILL	L1/SS	MAP	0:15	22:04:19	##	BS
=	A40	THORNTON KILLING I	MOLLY	LB/SS	SHOOTING/MAP	0:22	22:04:34	##sb	MH
=	A41	THORNTON KILLING LI	BOYD	RF/VO/SOT/SS/RF	MUG	1:00	22:04:56	##sb	
=	A42	THORNTON KILLING T	MOLLY	L1		0:10	22:05:56	##sb	MH
-\	A50	IRAQ LATEST	BILL	L1(SK)		0:27	22:06:06	##	BS
=	A55	HUSSEIN SON LATEST	BILL	VO/SOTVO		**0:35**	22:06:33	##	BS
=	A60	FORT CARSON DEATH	BILL	LB/SS/VO	COLORADO TRO	0:31	22:07:08	##AR	BS
=	A65	CHILDS MTG	MOLLY	LB/VO/SOTVO/LB	CHILDS/CHILDS	**0:36**	22:07:39	##kj	
=	A70	ESCALATOR TEST	MOLLY	LB/VO/SOT/L1	ESCALATOR	**0:45**	22:08:15	##cy	MH
=\	A73	PINEWOOD SPRINGS	BILL	LB/VO(sidekey map)	SPRING GULCH	0:23	22:09:00	##	BS
=	A76	CO ARSONIST	BILL	SS/L1	MAP	0:24	22:09:23	##ar	BS
=	A80	NUNS TO JAIL	MOLLY	L1/VO		0:19	22:09:47	##	
=\	A81	ROCKY TEASE	MOLLY	CG		0:06	22:10:06	##	MH
=	A90	DAVIS RECALL	BILL	LB/VO<	DAVIS RECALL	0:18	22:10:12	##ar	BS
	AX	SUPERTEASE	BILL	LB	SENIOR DRIVIN	**0:45**	22:10:30	##	MHBS
	AX1	1)senior driving	BILL	VO<a	* music late *	0:00	22:11:15		
	AX2	2)boulder lights	MOLLY	CC<b		0:00	22:11:15		
	AX3	3)weather	LARRY	SC1<a		0:00	22:11:15		
	AX4	4)ice cream	MOLLY	VO<b		0:00	22:11:15		
	AX5	TALENT/REOPEN	======	C30		0:10	22:11:15	##	
AZ		BREAK 1 ==========	======	=====================	===========	**3:10**	22:11:25	====	=====
	B15	BUMPIN	=====	C35		0:10	22:14:35	##	
=	B20	HAWAII CRASH	MOLLY	L1		0:15	22:14:45	##AA	MH
=	B25	SENIOR DRIVING	MOLLY	LB/VO/SOT/L1	SENIOR DRIVIN	**0:40**	22:15:00	##kj	MH
=	B30	WEST NILE LOVELAN	BILL	LB/VO/SOTVO	WEST NILE	**0:35**	22:15:40	##AA	BS
=	B35	BONFILS RESULTS TO	BILL	LB/VO<	WEST NILE	0:23	22:16:15	##kj	BS
=	B40	BOULDER LIGHTS	MOLLY	LB	LIGHT POLLUTIO	0:22	22:16:38	##ar	MH
=	B50	WEATHER	M/B/L	L3/L1/WCK(st)/CC+		**3:00**	22:17:00	##	BS
=	B50a	MORE WEATHER	LARRY	WCK(wxc)/L3		0:15	22:20:00	##	
=	B60	OZONE ALERT	BILL	L1/VO(timelapse)		0:19	22:20:15	##kj	BS
=	B65	CANCER TEST	MOLLY	L1/VO/SOTVO		**0:45**	22:20:34	##kj	MH
=	BX	TEASE 2	MH/BS	L2		**0:15**	22:21:19	##	MHBS
	BX1	1)sports		VO<		0:00	22:21:34		

It's just seven minutes before show time. If nothing changes, this is how the show will look.

What's the Point?

Just as a newspaper tries to make itself *look* interesting with a layout (and with photographs) that keep the reader's interest, you want to make your newscast look and sound interesting from top to bottom. The formula is to *avoid* any formula!

Ending Your Show

If rules were made to be broken, so were rundowns. You might have something timed out on paper that fits perfectly into your allotted time. Great, until an anchor takes another five seconds to chat extemporaneously about the story that just ended, or perhaps until a technical failure means a piece you're counting on doesn't play and suddenly you've got another ninety seconds to fill. Now multiply each snafu by several times per newscast. Inevitably it's going to end up with too much material, or not enough. You just won't know until you're near the end.

For a producer, this can be the stuff of premature gray hair. But it doesn't have to be, because you should build both possibilities into your rundown.

Too much material? The solution is, plan to cut something from the end. But not your closing story; you've counted on that one since you first created your rundown. Instead, "backtime" the show. Know the timed-out length of the last few "readers," the pieces the anchor tells without accompanying video. When you're near the end of the newscast, if other items have taken longer than they were supposed to in the rundown, you'll have a pretty good idea how much time you need to cut.

So if you get near the end of the newscast and it's running ten seconds too long, kill a ten-second reader near the end. If you need twenty-five seconds and your last few pieces before the closing story run ten, twenty, ten, and fifteen seconds respectively, take out one of the ten-second stories and the fifteen-second story. Suddenly, thanks to backtiming, you're back on schedule. Make sure, of course, that everyone—the director, the technical director, the audio technician, the studio floor manager, and most of all, the anchors—knows.

If you have too little material perhaps because a piece doesn't come up, or a story you were counting on doesn't come in, or someone just miscalculates, the solution is backtiming in reverse. Have extra stories ready to fill the extra time—stories you don't actually plan to run, stories that the audience can live without if you never get to them. Then, when you find yourself ninety seconds short near the end, you've got these extras to bail you out. As before, know their length so you can calculate the best combination to fill the hole.

Teasing Your Audience

To most people, "teasing" an audience would mean making fun of them. But not in broadcast news. "Teasing" for us means a short clip of either an anchor or a reporter appealing to the audience's interest even before a newscast is on the air, or before going into a commercial break, to promote a specific story that's coming up. It's meant to hold their attention so they don't pick up the remote control and stray to another station.

A popular film made many years ago called *Kentucky Fried Movie* had a parody of television teases, which went like this:

I'm not wearing any pants. Film at 11.

Well, that probably would achieve its purpose, but I don't have to explain why you can't use it in the real world.

What can you use? Something that tells people that you're going to have a story worth watching or hearing, without giving away all its vital elements.

Assume a wing broke off a plane while it was taking off from your airport this afternoon. The plane crashed, killing all one hundred and ten people on the plane, and forcing the cancellation of all other flights for the balance of the day. If you do a tease like this, you haven't left anything new and critical for the newscast itself:

A plane crashed this afternoon at the airport when its wing broke off during takeoff. It killed all 110 people aboard and forced the cancellation of all other flights for the rest of the day. Details at 11.

Details at eleven? (Yes, yes, in the Central and Mountain Time Zones, for most major stations you'd say "Details at ten.") You've already *given* the key details. It's enough to do a simpler tease like this:

A fatal plane crash at the airport. Many are dead, flights are cancelled. Details at 11.

Some teases, though, are too simple. Like,

Something horrible happened today at the airport. Details at 11.

It's too simple because you have to tell people *something,* since even a tease should convey some *news.* And, you have to give the audience as much reason as you can for making sure they catch the story, which is why these next teases aren't good enough either:

A plane crash today at the airport. Details at 11.

Viewers might assume it's a light plane with a single pilot, sad, but not compelling.

110 people die today. Details at 11.

How? From a plane crash, or ptomaine poisoning?

A wing breaks off an airplane. Details at 11.

Okay, by now you know why this isn't quite enough.

Exercises to Line Up Your Rundown _____

1. The Easy Way
    You're producing tonight's newscast and you have the following stories to work with in your rundown:

    *   Tiger escapes from city zoo, still at large
    *   3 cars crash in front of police headquarters, one driver hospitalized
    *   State's unemployment rate drops by 1/2%
    *   Today is 10th anniversary of opening of first video game parlor in city
    *   Washington High School track squad loses star sprinter
    *   Water restrictions imposed locally because of drought
    *   Inflation reaches 20% in Great Britain
    *   Million people in Iran protest American foreign policy
    *   New chairman selected for city opera company
    *   Policeman fired from force for false credentials
    *   Monsoons cause oil spill in Sea of Japan
    *   Fire in abandoned department store downtown, no one hurt
    *   New sculpture goes up in front of City Hall
    *   Young man still holding girlfriend and four members of her family hostage at gunpoint in crowded terminal at city airport
    *   State university dental school loses accreditation
    *   Mayor announces expansion of City Hall
    *   State university football team has first workout of season
    *   Temperature reaches new high for the date at airport
    *   Local developer announces plan to build new 16-unit apartment building
    *   Local baseball team sold to city's biggest employer
    *   Local widow leaves estate to her four cats
    *   Terrorist bomb kills four people on subway in Paris
    *   55 employees at local software firm laid off
    *   Santa Claus makes early appearance at Childrens Hospital
    *   Price of parking meters downtown goes up by 10¢ per hour
    *   World Series winners visit President in White House
    *   State legislature passes law requiring five disabled parking spaces per every hundred spaces at supermarkets and shopping malls
    *   FBI reports slight drop nationwide in violent crime
    *   Cold front coming to area by weekend
    *   Local striptease club loses license for serving alcohol to minors
    *   School board announces cut in financial subsidies for textbooks

    Now, by applying your best news judgment, and by grouping stories together into a logical sequence—and the sequences into logical sections—create a rundown.

2. The Hard Way
    Now it is harder. Create a good rundown from the same list of stories, but this time you have to take pacing into account. The stories done as "reporter packages" are in **ALL CAPS and BOLD,** and the stories for which there is video for an "anchor voiceover" are just in **bold.** All the rest have nothing more visual than a photo or a graphic over the anchorperson's shoulder.

[handwritten in left margin: Combine #1 with #2]

- **TIGER ESCAPES FROM CITY ZOO, STILL AT LARGE**
- **3 cars crash in front of police headquarters, one driver hospitalized**
- State's unemployment rate drops by 1/2%
- Today is 10th anniversary of opening of first video game parlor in city
- **WASHINGTON HIGH SCHOOL TRACK SQUAD LOSES STAR SPRINTER**
- Water restrictions imposed locally because of drought
- Inflation reaches 20% in Great Britain
- **Million people in Iran protest American foreign policy**
- New chairman selected for city opera company
- Policeman fired from force for false credentials
- **Monsoons cause oil spill in Sea of Japan**
- **Fire in abandoned department store downtown, no one hurt**
- **New sculpture goes up in front of City Hall**
- **YOUNG MAN STILL HOLDING GIRLFRIEND AND FOUR MEMBERS OF HER FAMILY HOSTAGE AT GUNPOINT IN CROWDED TERMINAL AT CITY AIRPORT**
- State university dental school loses accreditation
- Mayor announces expansion of City Hall
- **State university football team has first workout of season**
- Temperature reaches new high for the date at airport
- Local developer announces plan to build new 16-unit apartment building
- **LOCAL BASEBALL TEAM SOLD TO CITY'S BIGGEST EMPLOYER**
- Local widow leaves estate to her four cats
- **Terrorist bomb kills four people on subway in Paris**
- 55 employees at local software firm laid off
- **SANTA CLAUS MAKES EARLY APPEARANCE AT CHILDRENS HOSPITAL**
- Price of parking meters downtown goes up by 10¢ per hour
- **World Series winners visit President in White House**
- State legislature passes law requiring five disabled parking spaces per every hundred spaces at supermarkets and shopping malls
- FBI reports slight drop nationwide in violent crime
- Cold front coming to area by weekend
- **CONTROVERSIAL LOCAL STRIPTEASE CLUB LOSES LICENSE FOR SERVING ALCOHOL TO MINORS**
- School board announces cut in financial subsidies for textbooks

3. The Necessary Way
   Below you'll see four different "pairs" of stories from the list above. In each case, write a transition from the first story to the next.

   - 55 employees at local software firm laid off
   - **SANTA CLAUS MAKES EARLY APPEARANCE AT CHILDRENS HOSPITAL**

   - Water restrictions imposed locally because of drought
   - Cold front coming to area by weekend

   - Price of parking meters downtown goes up by 10¢ per hour
   - Inflation reaches 20% in Great Britain

- **Fire in abandoned department store downtown, no one hurt**
- State university dental school loses accreditation

4. The Final Way

   Here are more stories from the list (which has been pared down). This time, you'll see the projected length, in seconds, of each. Assuming your closing story is on this list (choose the best one), figure out what you'd drop if you suddenly had to cut 75 seconds at the end of the show.

   - **TIGER ESCAPES FROM CITY ZOO, STILL AT LARGE** (50)
   - **3 cars crash in front of police headquarters, one driver hospitalized** (25)
   - Today is 10th anniversary of opening of first video game parlor in city (10)
   - **WASHINGTON HIGH SCHOOL TRACK SQUAD LOSES STAR SPRINTER** (80)
   - Water restrictions imposed locally because of drought (15)
   - **Million people in Iran protest American foreign policy** (05)
   - New chairman selected for city opera company (10)
   - **Monsoons cause oil spill in Sea of Japan** (15)
   - **Fire in abandoned department store downtown, no one hurt** (30)
   - **New sculpture goes up in front of City Hall** (10)
   - State university dental school loses accreditation (10)
   - **State university football team has first workout of season** (15)
   - Temperature reaches new high for the date at airport (05)
   - Local developer announces plan to build new 16-unit apartment building (15)
   - **LOCAL BASEBALL TEAM SOLD TO CITY'S BIGGEST EMPLOYER** (60)
   - Local widow leaves estate to her four cats (20)
   - 55 employees at local software firm laid off (20)
   - **SANTA CLAUS MAKES EARLY APPEARANCE AT CHILDRENS HOSPITAL** (50)
   - Price of parking meters downtown goes up by 10¢ per hour (15)
   - **World Series winners visit President in White House** (10)
   - State legislature passes law requiring five disabled parking spaces per every hundred spaces at supermarkets and shopping malls (25)
   - Cold front coming to area by weekend (10)
   - **CONTROVERSIAL LOCAL STRIPTEASE CLUB LOSES LICENSE FOR SERVING ALCOHOL TO MINORS** (55)
   - School board announces cut in financial subsidies for textbooks (25)

18

Even More Ways for Radio

What You'll Learn

Radio is a pure medium. What this means is, you have to capture the listener with only one tool: sound. That probably sounds limiting but it isn't. Sound is sound, but how you edit, package, and present it can make every piece different. Sometimes it might seem that the reporter's voice is the most effective way to convey the facts. Sometimes the words of the newsmaker do it best. Sometimes it's the sounds recorded at the scene of the story itself—the bulldozer knocking down a house, the water rushing under the bridge, the woman screaming on the balcony.

Within those categories of sound, you have a variety of options. If you choose just the reporter's voice, do you want a pre–written carefully delivered narration, or do you want the reporter to describe something extemporaneously? If you have both a reporter at the scene and sound from the scene, do you combine them into some sort of packaged report? If there's an interview, do you include the reporter's questions, or run only the newsmaker's answers?

What you'll learn in this chapter is how to produce each of these in a radio news story, and how to create a mix of sounds so your radio newscast has all the dynamic, flexible, unpredictable elements it needs to be interesting.

You'll also learn a bit more about writing. Namely, how to write a radio report that brings the listener into the story, rather than just delivering the story to the listener. And how to help the listener understand what he is hearing, so that in the absence of television's visual cues, distracting questions don't come up.

Finally, because radio is more likely to have one or even two newscasts every hour (unlike the typical three or four per day on TV), you'll learn how to make each newscast fresh, so the listener doesn't start to think the stories sound stale.

All in all, writing for radio is tougher than writing for TV. You have to squeeze more information into less time, and you don't have pictures to support your words. What's more, you usually have to produce more reports for radio than for TV, because radio usually has more newscasts. But the reward is what you read at the top of this section: radio is a pure medium, which often makes it a pure pleasure.

The Voice of Authority

Nothing is as credible as firsthand coverage, whether the reporter writes and narrates a story that she personally has covered or the anchor takes the reporter's facts and weaves them into a "reader" from the studio. The facts are just as accurate either way. Everyone in the newsroom knows that. But listeners don't. Just as television news stories often include a standup to "prove" that the reporter was really there (which raises the audience's comfort level with regard to credibility), radio news stories often include a report from the scene.

But how does the radio reporter convince the listener that she was really there? Well, with nothing to work with as indisputable as video, the answer is to verbally place oneself in the story. How?

Sometimes with a single word. Since I was responsible for pieces on ABC Radio News while I covered stories for ABC TV News, I often put that single word at the very top of a radio piece written in tandem with a package for TV:

> *Here above the Arctic Circle, oil companies ceaselessly, purposefully pump nearly two million barrels of oil, every long Arctic night . . .*

Or, deeper in the lead sentence:

> *The good old days for smokers here at Denver's airport have gone up in smoke.*

Or, deeper in the story:

> *Military spokesmen say that according to their first reports from the battlefield, the field is silent. Whether surviving Iraqi units actually got word from Baghdad—there is some question about whether lines of communication still exist—or whether they just stopped shooting because they weren't being shot at, nobody here at the Pentagon knows.*

That one word, "here," sends a message. Reread the examples without that word, and think about how much less "eyewitness" credibility they have.

Sometimes another way of placing oneself at the scene works better. Read the following portions of radio reports I wrote during the Gulf War in 1991, and you'll see how different words *personalize* the pieces:

> *Vice President Quayle got his longest and loudest applause when he told the wives and children of F-one-eleven crews now fighting in the Gulf, quote, "We will hold Saddam Hussein and his henchmen personally accountable for their actions." No F-one-elevens have been shot down so far, but these families are painfully aware that it can happen any day.*

> *As he walked into the United Nations, I asked the Kuwaiti ambassador for his reaction to Saddam Hussein's speech. His response, and I quote, "Back to square one!"*

> *A Pentagon spokesman told me that 27 of Iraq's 42 fighting units are now, for all intents and purposes, out of business.*

> *From my conversations with diplomats at the United Nations, it appears that Iran will keep the Iraqi airplanes on the ground. . .*

And, of course, sometimes you combine "personalizing," first-person references:

Some of the Iowans I interviewed think it can be costly to help the Soviets. Some think it can be costly not to. Businessman Roger Stetson says if we help them, we help ourselves, because we create another strong market for American goods. But Carl Bales, director of a homeless shelter here, disagrees.

I spent the better part of a day just watching people walk into police stations here in St. Louis, bearing bagsful of rifles, shotguns, handguns, whatever firearms they wanted to sell to the city for 50-dollars apiece.

For the last 30 years here there has been an almost ceaseless flow of lava from Kilauea, one of the world's most active volcanoes. For the last 15 years, defying the laws of nature, some of this lava has flowed right back. We saw dozens of packages of lava, mailed back from tourists who took home more than just memories.

What's the Point?

It's important to make it clear that you're not just rewriting a wire service story or just reporting secondhand information, but that you spoke personally with the newsmaker, or witnessed the news event firsthand.

Shifting Your Lead

If you're covering a major story, your radio station might want the story on every newscast—which could mean *twice every hour.* But you don't want to report it precisely the same way each time, because it'll sound stale to listeners who've already heard it before.

If there are new developments, coming up with a different lead for every newscast is easy if you simply make the newest development your new lead. But sometimes the story isn't changing, yet you still have to vary your lead. It shouldn't be too tough, because there's no single "best" way to write a story. In fact, sometimes you'll welcome the opportunity to use more than one of your good ideas.

For example, a blizzard in the Midwest. Here was the lead in my first spot for ABC Radio News:

Forecasters here predicted only one to three inches of snow. It is more like an inch an hour.

Then later:

Forecasters here got it wrong. They had predicted only. . .

Then:

At its peak, the snow fell here at about an inch an hour. Nothing like the forecasts . . .

Then, later still:

All told, almost two feet of snow fell here. . . almost two feet more than forecasters had predicted!

In other cases, the challenge won't be how to come up with a new top to the same hard news story, but how to come up with different approaches to a softer story so that each radio spot stands alone. But it shouldn't be hard because, as I said before, there's more than one good way to write a good story.

Here are three examples from a story about a controversy over whether Japan should be represented at the fiftieth anniversary observance of Japan's attack on Pearl Harbor:

> *No one here at Pearl Harbor said "over my dead body," but they came close. The question was, should Japan play a role in the fiftieth anniversary of its attack here?*

> *The attack on Pearl Harbor, 50 years ago today, still is vivid for many Americans: the surprise, the irreversible call to war.*

> *Every day, there seem to be as many Japanese tourists paying their respects here at Pearl Harbor as Americans. But not today.*

Finally, remember that sometimes you'll cover a story at, say, 8 o'clock at night that still will be newsworthy the next morning. So if you prepare more than one version, you will want to change the time reference. For example, your first report might say:

> *The plane crash tonight has left two children without a father.*

Then, for the morning newscast:

> *The plane crash last night left two children without a father.*

What's the Point?

In radio news, you sometimes have several reports to prepare on the same story, and you have to keep them sounding fresh. Freshening your lead is the best way to do it.

Let Us Count the Ways

As you read at the beginning of this chapter, there are many ways to use sound to present information in a radio newscast. We'll refer to them as:

- Actuality
- Voicer
- Wraparound
- ROSR
- Q&A

Actuality

This is the sound from the story itself. Sometimes we just call it ACK (rhymes with "back"). In some newsrooms it is called NAT (for "natural sound"), WILD (for "wild sound"), or RAW (for "raw sound"). For the rest of this chapter, we'll stick with ACK.

What is it? Maybe it's the sound of flames crackling from a burning building, or of the firetruck's siren as it races to the scene. It also might be sound from an interview with a victim, or with the firefighter who rescued her. Or from the fire chief at a news conference after the fire has been put out.

How might you use ACK in a radio news story? Here's a hypothetical example, where the anchor reads the intro:

ANCHOR: A fire destroyed a home this morning just a block from the high school.

Then, using the possibilities listed above, you might insert:

- ACK of flames crackling from the burning building
- ACK of firetruck's sirens as it races to the scene
- ACK of the victim screaming
- ACK of the firefighter describing how he rescued the victim
- ACK of the fire chief at a news conference afterward

Each one requires a setup, of course. So, here is how you might set up each one, using your words to help identify and reinforce the actuality:

ANCHOR: A fire destroyed a home this morning just a block from the high school. The sound of the flames told the story: the house burned to the ground.
ACK: flames crackling from the burning building

ANCHOR: A fire destroyed a home this morning just a block from the high school.
ACK: firetruck's sirens as it races to the scene

ANCHOR: A fire destroyed a home this morning just a block from the high school. Jennifer Jones was trapped inside until firemen rescued her.
ACK: the victim screaming

ANCHOR: A fire destroyed a home this morning just a block from the high school. Firefighter Sam Smith ran inside right away and saved the owner.
ACK: firefighter describing how he rescued the victim

ANCHOR: A fire destroyed a home this morning just a block from the high school. At a news conference afterward, Fire Chief Barb Blank explained why the house could not be saved.
ACK: fire chief at a news conference afterward

After the ACK, usually it's a good idea to re-identify what the listener has just heard. Therefore, each example above might be constructed this way:

ANCHOR: *A fire destroyed a home this morning just a block from the high school. The sound of the flames told the story: the house burned to the ground.*
ACK: *flames crackling from the burning building*
ANCHOR: *Those flames took firefighters 20 minutes to put out.*

ANCHOR: *A fire destroyed a home this morning just a block from the high school.*
ACK: *firetruck's sirens as it races to the scene*
ANCHOR: *A firetruck got there in enough time to rescue the owner, but not to save the house.*

ANCHOR: *A fire destroyed a home this morning just a block from the high school. Jennifer Jones was trapped inside until firemen rescued her.*
ACK, victim: *I thought I was going to die in my own kitchen.*
ANCHOR: *The home's owner also says her kids had just left for school five minutes before the fire started.*

ANCHOR: *A fire destroyed a home this morning just a block from the high school. Firefighter Sam Smith ran inside right away and saved the owner.*
ACK, firefighter: *I knew there was a woman inside because I could see her through the window.*
ANCHOR: *The firefighter says saving the owner's life made this his best day ever on the job.*

ANCHOR: *A fire destroyed a home this morning just a block from the high school. At a news conference afterward, Fire Chief Barb Blank explained why the house could not be saved.*
ACK, fire chief: *The flames spread through the insulation, and burned through the walls in every part of the house, all at once.*
ANCHOR: *Fire Chief Blank promises she'll try to convince City Council to outlaw the kind of insulation used to build that house.*

Voicer

This is the reporter's narrated report, pretaped or live. As you now know, it should include some kind of reference such as the word "here" to convey to the audience that the reporter actually is covering the story. Also, it should include information that you'd only know by actually being there.

A voicer does not contain ACK, but if you have ACK from the scene of the story—"natural sound" in the television sense of the phrase—you can use it in the background. Or, if you write and record the voicer (or call it into the station) with the sound in the background, better yet. For instance, if it's a story at an airport, it's effective to include the sound of airplanes taking off in the background (but only if they're recorded while you're covering the story, meaning don't fake it). If it's at a fire, it's effective if the listener hears the crackling flames.

Wraparound

This is a combination of voicer and ACK. We usually abbreviate it to just a "wrap," because you "wrap" the reporter's voice around the actuality.

We'll use the fire again as an example.

REPORTER: When the firetruck got here, the first firefighter to jump off the back, ran into the burning house.

ACK, firefighter: I knew there was a woman inside because I could see her through the window.

REPORTER: The firefighter pulled her through the burning doorway and saved her life.

Also, a wrap can have more than one piece of ACK. For instance:

REPORTER: By the time the firetruck got here, the whole house was burning.

ACK: crackling flames

REPORTER: The first firefighter to jump off the back of the truck, ran into the burning house.

ACK, firefighter: I knew there was a woman inside because I could see her through the window.

REPORTER: The firefighter pulled her through the burning doorway and saved her life.

When doing a wraparound, just like when you're using ACK as a standalone element for the newscast's anchor, identify the speaker again afterward. The radio listener doesn't have the advantage the television viewer has, seeing the name on the screen. And, use words to reinforce what the audience is hearing, like "firefighter" both before and after the ACK with the firefighter in the examples above.

ROSR

This one is fun. ROSR stands for Radio On Scene Report. You say it as if it is spelled "roser," rhyming with "dozer." It's useful whether you're doing radio or TV, because it is what its name implies: an "on scene report," but unlike a voicer, which is written and re-hearsed, a ROSR is extemporaneous. What this means is, you look at the scene in front of you, then you think of a few key points you want to cover, then you just talk, into a recording device, a live line, or a telephone.

A ROSR doesn't serve any purpose if you're covering a mayoral news conference, but it works well when there's some kind of action in front of you. It might be a political demonstration, where you simply describe what you see:

About a hundred people are running toward City Hall, and I'm watching maybe a dozen policemen chasing them, and now a woman who was running has just tripped on the steps, and it looks like she's hurt—she's holding her leg and crying...

Or it might be a flood in the middle of a town:

I'm just high enough on a bluff to be above the water, but about 30 feet in front of me, a man and a woman are perched on the thick limb of a tree... I think it's an oak tree... and there's a woman in a rowboat trying to get to them, but from here it looks like the current is carrying her too far from the tree...

A ROSR isn't just about the facts; it's a chance to tell how it *feels* to cover the story. It's the best device to make the listener feel like he is right beside you.

Q&A

Q&A means "question and answer." It's like ACK from an interview or a news conference, but it includes the reporter's voice.

So in the fire we've been using as an example, instead of just running a sound bite of the firefighter as ACK, you might run it as Q&A:

REPORTER: Why did you go running into the house the moment you jumped off the truck?

FIREFIGHTER: I knew there was a woman inside because I could see her through the window.

If the next Q&A set is good, you might continue it:

REPORTER: Why did you go running into the house the moment you jumped off the truck?

FIREFIGHTER: I knew there was a woman inside because I could see her through the window.

REPORTER: But didn't you know you could get trapped inside with her?

FIREFIGHTER: Sure, but I'm trained to save lives, and saving hers made this the best day I've ever had on the job.

Of course you might also want to omit the first question and write into the Q&A, starting with the first answer:

ANCHOR: Firefighter Sam Smith told reporter Andrea Asbury that he ran into the burning house the moment he got there.

FIREFIGHTER: I knew there was a woman inside because I could see her through the window.

REPORTER: But didn't you know you could get trapped inside with her?

FIREFIGHTER: Sure, but I'm trained to save lives, and saving hers made this the best day I've ever had on the job.

Different news directors have different preferences for how to use Q&A. There are a few good arguments for using it:

1. It is another way for the station to prove that the reporter was actually there.
2. It helps put the listener in the reporter's shoes ("Gee, that's what I wanted to ask"), and pull the listener into the story.
3. It is a departure from the formula of sound bites.
4. It allows for clarification, if the reporter asks a question to help the listener understand a point. For example:

> *FIREFIGHTER:*   We were concerned that the hazmat team would be too late.
>
> *REPORTER:*   The hazardous materials team?
>
> *FIREFIGHTER:*   Yea, because they were already on another dicey job and couldn't get to this fire until they were through there.

Who's Talking

In many television newsrooms, an anchor or a reporter doesn't have to identify the newsmaker coming up in a sound bite. It's not a bad thing to do, but the name will be up on the screen visually as a CG for the first three or four seconds of the sound bite, making verbal identification unnecessary. A cautionary note: many stations require the verbal ID anyway. The upside is, it serves as reinforcement. The downside is, it takes a few more precious seconds of narration.

Radio's different. If you don't identify the speaker before we hear him, we may not have a clue who's speaking. Some stations like to "surprise" the listener with a sound bite, then identify it after we hear it. Yuck.

If you are covering an auto accident and have ACK of someone describing how it happened, but you don't explain before the sound bite who that person is, the listener doesn't know whether it's the driver of the car, a passenger, an eyewitness, a police officer at the scene, or a police spokesman who's not at the scene. It leaves the listener distracted, wondering who he's hearing, instead of listening to what's actually being said.

So always identify the speaker beforehand and, if you can, again after the sound bite plays. In fact, about the only exception to the rule is when you have a sound bite from the President of the United States. People who don't know the president's voice probably won't be listening to the news anyway.

Exercises to Sound You Out about Sound

1. Tell Them You're There
    By either changing or adding just a few words, rewrite the following radio spot three different ways, making it clear each time that you've actually been at the scene of the story. To fulfill the assignment, you must do more than just insert the word "here" in three different places.

Witnesses say the driver of the blue car was weaving when he collided with the truck. He concedes that he was eating his lunch while driving, and walked away with just scratches, but the truck driver collapsed at the wheel and was taken to the hospital. The highway where it happened, Interstate 70 at its intersection with I-55, was closed for an hour. Traffic was backed up for almost five miles. It only got back to normal when the road reopened at two this afternoon.

2. Tell Them More Than Once
   Now, take the three spots you just wrote, and on a new page, make each one appropriate for a particular newscast: 4:00 this afternoon, 9:00 tonight, and 6:00 tomorrow morning.

3. Tell Them More Than One Way
   This time, take the original spot, which is printed again below, and tell it three different ways, so the same listener could hear it all three times and find it interesting each time.

   Witnesses say the driver of the blue car was weaving when he collided with the truck. He concedes that he was eating his lunch while driving, and walked away with just scratches, but the truck driver collapsed at the wheel and was taken to the hospital. The highway where it happened, Interstate 70 at its intersection with I-55, was closed for an hour. Traffic was backed up for almost five miles. It only got back to normal when the road reopened at two this afternoon.

4. ACK-to-ACK Communication
   In the section about actuality, you saw a basic anchor leadin (which also could be the leadin for a reporter's wraparound), then five different ways to set up five different kinds of actuality.
   You're going to do the same thing yourself now. What you'll see below is the basic leadin, then three possibilities for ACK plus a Q&A between a councilwoman and a citizen. What you have to do is modify the basic leadin for each specific piece.

   ANCHOR or REPORTER: The City Council heard fourteen witnesses, all with the same complaint: the rail yard in their neighborhood keeps them awake at night.
   - ACK of railroad yard, including whistles, metal wheels on tracks, cars noisily connecting
   - ACK of neighbor (Noah North) from interview after city council meeting ("I don't get more than four hours sleep at night.")
   - ACK of neighbor testifying to city council ("If they don't stop working at night there, I'm going to be ill.")
   - Q&A between councilwoman and neighbor (Councilwoman Meyer: "How seriously do the trains affect your life?" Neighbor: "If they don't stop working through the night there, I'm going to be ill.")

5. On Scene Communication
   Either on your way to class or from class, do two ROSRs about whatever is happening on campus, or in your neighborhood, or on the street. Record them. Make each about thirty seconds long. If anyone seems to think you're strange, walking along talking to yourself, just smile. The beauty of a ROSR is that you can do it just about anywhere, and you should. It's good practice if you're going to be a broadcast journalist.

VI

Being the Right Kind of Journalist

19

Holding onto Your Sources

What You'll Learn

Thanks to the First Amendment and various state and local laws, you have a thick coat of protection against frivolous complaints about what you write and report. That doesn't mean you won't be the target of complaints; arguably, if you're not, you're not doing your job. But aside from your employer, there is little to hold you to account for the kind of job you do, except your adherence to the ethics of the business, and your own self-esteem.

In other words, your greatest fear might be losing your job, which should be incentive enough to behave honestly. But even worse might be losing the public's trust, because without that, you're just an empty suit. If you pay attention to the lessons learned earlier in this book about fairness and accuracy and balance, you should be safe. And if you pay attention to the lessons in this chapter about playing by the rules with your sources, you should be successful.

In this short chapter and the next one, you'll learn what those rules are, and how to ensure that you're carrying them out correctly.

Hold On

Sometimes sources will "embargo" information. What does this mean? Typically, a government agency or a company or organization will tell you that something's going to happen, but only on the condition that you don't report it until the day and time they designate.

For instance, the mayor's news secretary might send you a news release like this:

"Tomorrow at 4 o'clock in the afternoon, the mayor will hold a news conference at city hall to announce that she is firing the city fire chief because of poor responses by the fire department to two major fires in the past three weeks. This information is embargoed until 3:00 PM tomorrow."

Why is the news secretary giving you advance notice?

1. To make sure the news assignment editor reserves the resources—camera crew (if it's for TV), reporter, possibly a satellite truck—to cover the story
2. To allow the reporter to do some advance research on the story

3. To allow the show producer to pull up video from the two major fires
4. To make sure the producer leaves sufficient space in the lineup to report the story

What are the rules of the embargo? Pretty simple: you have been given advance notice as a helpful courtesy, but you must keep the story confidential until the time the news secretary has designated for its release.

What happens if you break the embargo by reporting the story before the designated time? The mayor's news secretary, and probably anyone else in city government who finds out that you broke an embargo, won't trust you in the future. Maybe that means you won't get embargoed information any more. Worse, it could mean you won't get cooperation from the mayor's office at all any more.

But what happens if another news organization breaks the embargo? Is your station supposed to continue to respect the previously designated time to report the story? No. Once one news organization has prematurely reported an embargoed story, all news organizations are permitted to report it immediately. That's the rule of the game.

What's the Point?

Breaking an embargo means a station gets a jump on its competition. But the competitive advantage doesn't last long, while the damaging consequences do.

When You're Told Not to Tell

From time to time, usually in connection with stories about crime or politics, a source will give you information, then turn around and tell you that you can't use it. The phrase for that is "off the record," and it's one of a handful of ways a story source will put you in the loop without compromising his or her own position. So let's look at each one, and explain what each means.

Off the Record

When someone tells you that something is "off the record," it means you can pursue the story, but can only report it if you can verify the information you have been given with at least one other source. What's more, if you can verify it and decide to report it, you cannot even vaguely identify the original source, the one who gave you the "off the record" information in the first place.

If you read the classic book *All the President's Men* by *Washington Post* reporters Bob Woodward and Carl Bernstein, you'll learn that they got their most damning information about President Nixon, who ultimately resigned because of their reporting, from an "off the record" source who never has been publicly identified beyond the nickname "Deep Throat." Because the information was accurate, we know in retrospect that Deep Throat was someone who worked at a fairly high level in either the Nixon administration or the Nixon re-election campaign. The only other thing we know is that periodically Deep Throat left a coded signal for Woodward to meet him late at night in a Washington D.C. parking garage, where Deep Throat apparently felt safe about protecting his identity.

Why bother cooperating with a reporter at all? Because pretty obviously, Deep Throat didn't like the secretive and evidently unlawful ways Nixon and some of his associates operated. Why not act in the open? Because pretty obviously, Deep Throat still had ties to the White House, perhaps still actually worked for the White House, and feared the ramifications if the leaks were traced to him.

Sometimes a source's motives might not be so noble, if indeed Deep Throat's were. But still, although you might find it helpful to consider a source's motive for revealing information without allowing its unencumbered disclosure, by and large the information will be helpful and worth hearing, motive notwithstanding. For no matter what the motive, or how limited you are by the terms of its source, it will help you focus your search for a story . . . and perhaps put you on a story you hadn't even known to research.

However, try whenever possible to persuade your source to give you information either on "deep background" or "not for attribution," both of which you'll learn about next. If you accept something "off the record," you could conceivably end up with a blockbuster piece of information, and no way to use it. The worst thing that can happen when you ask is, the source tells you, "It's off the record or nothing!"

Deep Background

Unlike "off the record" information, you can report information someone gives you on "deep background," but you cannot identify the source, not even in the most general terms. You simply must be satisfied to attribute your information to "a source." Perhaps you can find a second source to confirm it, one who is willing to be identified.

What this means is if you have something on deep background, you cannot say where it came from.

So if, for hypothetical example, the governor's news secretary has told you on deep background that he has seen the governor writing checks from the state ledger for personal expenses, what can you say in your story about the news secretary?

Try these, and figure out which one is right:

Lindy Moore, the governor's news secretary, told me today that the governor has been writing checks for personal expenses from the state ledger.

Nope, can't do it. You've named the source.

The governor's news secretary told me today that the governor has been writing checks for personal expenses from the state ledger.

Nope, still no good. You haven't used his name, but his identity is obvious.

An aide to the governor told me today that the governor has been writing checks for personal expenses from the state ledger.

No better, really. There may be a few aides in the governor's office, but it might not be hard for the governor to figure out which one leaked the report, or to fire the whole lot! For that matter, maybe the governor knows that the news secretary is the only one who has seen him writing the checks.

> *A source at the state capitol told me today that the Governor has been writing checks for personal expenses from the state ledger.*

Still no good. Partly because there may be just a handful of workers at the capitol who know what the governor's doing, and the governor knows that. But mainly because your source—the news secretary—wanted it on deep background, and that means you don't identify her at all.

> *A source in state government told me today that the governor has been writing checks for personal expenses from the state ledger.*

No, and I hope that by now, you know why not.

> *We have learned that the governor has been writing checks for personal expenses from the state ledger.*

Yes. Beyond the fact that the news secretary exposed his identity to you in the first place, this is obedient to his wishes, and the only way you are allowed to report the story, unless, as you already have learned now, you can confirm it with someone else who is willing to be named.

Background or, Not for Attribution

These phrases are interchangeable; they mean the same thing. They are not as limiting as "deep background," but they do impose certain limits on the journalist.

So what do they mean? Well, the phrase "not for attribution" defines them: you cannot specifically attribute the information to your source, but for the sake of credibility, you can provide a general description.

For instance, let's say the governor's news secretary is your source for something less serious than the check-writing story used in examples above. Let's say she tells you "on background" (or, "not for attribution") that the Governor is about to ask your city's mayor to be his lieutenant governor.

You still couldn't report it this way:

> *The governor's news secretary tells me the governor is about to ask Mayor . . .*

Or, even this way:

> *A close aide to the governor tells me the governor is about to ask Mayor . . .*

Why not? Because, although it's subjective, that kind of attribution still makes the source to easy to identify. However—and here's the difference between background and deep background—you are permitted to use your common sense and come up with a form of attribution general enough to protect the source, but specific enough to be credible. Such as:

> *A highly placed source in state government tells me the governor is about to ask Mayor . . .*

Obviously, if the governor is angered by the leak, he probably can figure out who's responsible. But in this hypothetical case, if the news secretary didn't give you the information on deep background, let alone off the record, he must not be too concerned.

There also can be another explanation, which sometimes clarifies "background" information: maybe the governor wants the news to get out, but doesn't yet want it to look like an official announcement. That's why you'll often read in reports from the nation's capital about news from, for example, "a high State Department source." That could be the secretary of state, who knows precisely what he's doing, telling reporters what he wants them to know, but avoiding direct attribution.

What's the Point?

Sometimes sources will want to put these limits on information they give you. If you want to use the information, you probably have to agree to their terms.

Making Sure You Know What to Tell and How to Tell It

Now that terms like "off the record" and "background" seem clear, let's confuse them a bit! Just because you understand them, it doesn't mean the source does. So when a story source wants to put restrictions on information to protect his or her identity, make sure you follow these four ground rules, for *your* protection:

1. When sources say something is "off the record," or "on deep background," or just "on background" or "not for attribution," always ask what they mean. They might have a different definition than yours. Countless times I've had someone tell me something was "off the record," only to learn after asking that all they meant was "not for attribution."

2. A source might start a conversation by telling you the terms he requires. If so, make sure you clarify whether he means the entire conversation, or only the first part of it. If it's only the first part, make sure you're clear on where the restriction ends.

   Or more often, a source will say at a certain stage of the interview, "Now this part is off the record," or "not for attribution" or whatever. That makes the point where the restriction ends even more unclear. It's up to you to clear it up by figuring out when the restricted part probably is finished and asking, "Are we back on the record?" or "Can I attribute this part?" or whatever.

3. Just because you're talking with someone who tells you that something has one of these restrictions on it, you don't have to agree to the terms. Simply put, you can say no, because you don't want to be handcuffed that way. Of course it might mean your source stops talking, but sometimes, when a journalist refuses to accept such restrictions, the source—who wants to get the information out—will decide to say it openly.

4. One of the ground rules is that a source must place the restriction on information *before* revealing it. In other words, if someone gives you juicy information, *then* says something like, "By the way, that was not for attribution," you can say something like, "Sorry, too late!" The game has to be played that way; otherwise, occasionally you will be saddled with restrictions on information that you would not have accepted.

The other side of the coin is, you might be dealing with someone relatively unsophisticated about privileged information and how to negotiate it, someone who doesn't know the rules. So if a source tells you after the fact that something is restricted, you do indeed have the ethical right to refuse to accept the restriction, but you also might lose the help (and possibly the friendship) of this source in the future. It's your judgment call.

Another reason to make sure you and your source are working with the same definitions: if you aren't, and the source mistakenly believes from his definition that his identity will be a secret when your definition allows you to at least partially reveal it, he might sue you. And he might win.

What's the Point?

Sometimes you must accept restrictions on information if you want the information at all. But you always have the right to say no, and to keep working other sources to find out what you've missed.

Exercises to Hold onto Your Sources _____

1. Holding an Embargo
   In essay form, what does it mean when the governor's news secretary tells you that the governor will announce his retirement from public service but tells you it is embargoed "until 3:00 tomorrow"?
   What does it mean if you break the embargo?
   When can you report the embargoed story? There are at least two answers; be thorough.

2. On the Record with Off the Record
   One source tells you "on deep background" that the fire chief is aware of dangerously frayed fire hoses but isn't demanding more money in his budget to replace them. Another source tells you the same thing "off the record." In practical terms as a reporter, what's the difference?

If you got just the "deep background" source, or just the "off the record" source, how would you report each?

3. Freedom of Choice
   In essay form, what choices do you make when a source gives you information but puts restrictions on it, like "off the record," "not for attribution," or anything else?

20

Holding onto Your Ethics

What You'll Learn

Journalistic ethics aren't just voluntary behaviors that make you feel good. No, they are necessary behaviors that enable you to conduct yourself in the best tradition of journalism in a land of liberty. Ethics empower you to maintain not just your own credibility but that of the whole news and information industry. The audience doesn't always understand journalistic ethics, but without fail, they will notice if you breach them.

You're familiar with these terms: fairness, balance, privacy, libel. It might surprise you to read this, but these and other ethical challenges to the honest practice of journalism mean different things to different people. So I won't purport to provide a single definition or application for most of them. Nor shall I lay them out with a lot of detail; several could consume a whole college course. But I will point you in short form toward what to look for when you write or report a story, so that you'll pass harmlessly by the obstacles, not stumble right into them. What you'll learn in this chapter is how to figure these things out for yourself.

What Passes for the Truth

Truth is a noble attribute, but some people might rightly bicker with your perception in a story of what's true and what's not. That's the trouble with the notion of "truth" in journalism. It's not always an indisputable reality.

Sometimes, in fact, there's more than one truth. Someone might tell you at the scene of a bad crash that the red car was weaving. But someone else might tell you it was the blue car. Who knows? Maybe both cars were weaving. Or one was only weaving to get out of the other one's way. Or maybe one witness is lying, or forgetful, or colorblind.

You'll find a more distressing example of "more than one truth" in the Middle East. If you ask an Israeli to explain how Israelis and Palestinians ended up in such a hateful conflict, he will tell you it dates back to the 1940s when Israel was created, and Palestinians fled from their homes rather than live beside the Jews. At least in part, that's evidently true. But ask a Palestinian and he'll give you a different version—that when the Jewish state was established, Jews attacked the Palestinians and kicked them out. In part, there's evidence for this version too.

240

Each side fervently believes its account of "the truth," and each has some history to back it up, which proves that sometimes truth is elusive. Sometimes it has more than one head.

A fairly recent and prominent example of "more than one truth" was the reporting Americans saw from the war in Iraq in 2003. Embedded American reporters moving with U.S. military units pretty much exclusively saw and broadcast the triumphs of the American side during that short war: tanks racing unchallenged across the desert, enemy soldiers cut down fast when they fought back, innocent Iraqi civilians given medical care and food. All true.

But in the Middle East itself, from the Arab network *Al Jazerra* and others like it, citizens saw a *different* truth: Iraqi soldiers primed to fight the invading foreigners, American prisoners of war bloody and bound, innocent Iraqi civilians mangled and burned. Also true. Just a different piece of the truth. Although people on one side of the world saw little of the other side's "truth," it would have been better if all had seen them both.

What's the Point?

As a citizen considering different sides in a conflict, you might support one side or the other. But as a journalist, you must decide whether each side's "truth" has merit, and sometimes recognize both.

No Question about Accuracy

Unlike the concept of "truth," there is no ambiguity about accuracy. Either five people are killed in a fire, or six. Either voters passed the bond issue or they didn't. Either Andrea pronounces her name as "AHN-dree-uh" or "ahn-DRAY-uh."

So this lesson is a no-brainer: if someone tells you something but you don't know if it's true or accurate, find out; otherwise, don't report it. Your source might be inadvertently mistaken or, worse, deliberately misleading you to impose his own agenda. (This happens a lot, which justifies the legendary journalistic trait of skepticism.)

Also, if you don't know something, don't guess and, obviously, don't make it up. This goes not just for facts, but for feelings, impressions ("... *most* New Yorkers are mad about ... "), and name pronunciation. Inaccuracies not only disserve the audience, but among viewers and listeners who know better, they discredit the station.

What's the Point?

It's more work to be accurate than not to be. But you know what? It's more work all around to be a good journalist than a bad one. But don't let that discourage you. It's also *much* more fulfilling.

Fairness Above All

Good ethics mean that an interview, a story, a whole show is fair, truthful and accurate. There is no excuse for doing it any other way; fairness is the foundation for all your work. Needless to say, if a story is not true and accurate, it's not fair.

But how do you decide what is fair? Truth and accuracy alone, while critical, aren't enough. To be fair, you also have to cover all sides (which sometimes means more than just two sides) that play a significant role in a debate or dispute. And you must bend over backwards to put aside your personal views when deciding who to talk to, where to put them in your piece, and what to include and exclude from the final product.

I have dealt with American Nazis, and members of the Ku Klux Klan, and Islamic fundamentalists who would turn my country into dust if they had their way. Should that affect my story? Not at all. Anyway, even if I personally despise their views, I don't have to blatantly point it out; I only have to let them speak, and expose themselves for the bigots they are. I ardently believe in what I once said to a man who complained that I'd made him look wacky: "I can't make you look wacky without your help." Neither wacky, nor racist, nor dishonest. Some day you might have to use the line yourself. Feel free.

What's the Point?

Your personal feelings, your tastes, your likes and dislikes, and your biases have no place in your news stories. Approach every story as if you have no preconceptions. It's the only way to be fair.

Different Rights to Privacy

The President of the United States doesn't have the same right to privacy that you have. Yours is better. Why? Because you are a private citizen. The president is not.

By and large, although the Constitution doesn't specifically mention it, the law has established that private citizens are entitled to privacy.

But where? In their own homes? Absolutely. If you walk up to a private citizen's front door and when she opens it, you televise her in her silly looking polka-dot pajamas without her permission, she can sue you for invasion of privacy. She'll probably win (although, as in all such cases, she probably has to demonstrate damages).

But how about videotaping and televising her while she's shopping at her neighborhood grocery store? It's not a "public" building in the sense of a government building that truly belongs to the public, but it is a place where the public is invited and, therefore, where the public has no reasonable expectation of privacy. If she's there in her silly looking polka-dot pajamas and you put her on television that way, arguably you have not invaded her privacy because she is in a public place.

On the other hand, if you're there doing a story about shoplifters, and while the narration reads, "One out of every nine shoppers is caught stealing something," you edit in a closeup of *her* (pajamas or no pajamas), she can sue you (and your station) for invasion of privacy and probably win. Damages would be obvious enough: everyone watching could have concluded that she's a shoplifter.

If you had used a generic wide shot of lots of shoppers in that last example, you would be safe; they would represent *all* shoppers. Likewise, if someone is walking down the street and ends up in a wide shot of a crowd that's used in a story, they can't do any more than complain because, like the woman in the grocery store, they are out in public and have no reasonable expectation of privacy.

Finally, private citizens who become involved in issues of public interest—whether intentionally or accidentally—are temporarily treated as newsmakers and, thus, as public figures.

Permanent public figures—like the president—are different. Whether someone is a politician, a corporate chieftain, an entertainer, a professional athlete, a big name journalist, or otherwise part of the public arena, they cannot reasonably expect the same degree of privacy as a private citizen. This is not legal advice, and you always should examine the potential legal implications, but based on experience, you can capture their images virtually anywhere except inside their homes, as long as you don't break the law, of course. That may not be fair, but it is the state of America today.

What's the Point?

Privacy is not a constitutional right, but for private citizens there is a long established right to privacy, which you as a journalist must respect, or suffer the consequences if you don't. A celebrity's right to privacy is narrower.

Benefit of the Doubt on Libel

What is libel? People sometimes think it simply means to say something about someone that isn't true. But legally it's much more specific and much more complex. To paraphrase several different dictionary definitions, libel is a false and malicious report that hurts someone's reputation or livelihood. In other words,

1. It is not accurate, *and,*
2. Whoever said it—and whoever included it in a report—didn't try to determine its accuracy, *and*
3. The subject of the report is hurt.

These standards give the journalist the benefit of the doubt, because to prove libel, an accuser must prove that all three standards are true. Our nation's courts established libel law this way because they didn't want to inhibit journalists from investigating and reporting on controversial or suspicious people or events. Libel law is designed to encourage journalistic enterprise but to discourage irresponsible enterprise.

So while you might report something that is not accurate *and* that hurts the subject of the story, if you can show that you made an honest effort to determine its accuracy (even though obviously you failed), you might have trouble sleeping at night but you cannot be convicted of libel. Likewise, if your report is inaccurate and you didn't even try to find out, but the subject of the story cannot prove that she was hurt by it, you're not guilty of libel (although you *ought* to have trouble sleeping at night). Of course, if the subject of a story suffers damage from your report and sues you for libel but you can prove that the report was accurate, then you will suffer no legal consequence.

One more thing that's important to understand. If you do a television or radio news story, and libel is committed by someone speaking in a sound bite, you are not off the hook. Look back at the second qualification of libel: "Whoever said it—*and whoever included it in a report*—didn't try to determine its accuracy." So it doesn't matter whether you actually wrote it or said it. If you broadcast it and it's libelous, you may be found guilty.

By the way, you'll note that I write only about libel and not about slander, even though you think they're synonymous. In a way, they are: both words mean that someone's reputation or standing has been hurt. But libel typically applies to something said or written in a public setting (including a broadcast); slander typically applies only to something said in a private setting.

What's the Point?

Needless to say, you don't want to broadcast anything libelous. But you have considerable, some say excessive, latitude before libel is committed. Your obligation is not to abuse it.

Staging for the Stage

If you're producing a television entertainment program, you can ask your actors and actresses to repeat a scene as many times as you need to get it right. In news, you can't. What this means is, you *cannot* ask someone to reenact a spontaneous action because you missed it the first time, or to do something that substantively illustrates the story you're telling, if they wouldn't otherwise do it if you hadn't asked.

Examples? I can think of three good ones over the years—*bad* ones, actually—from my own network:

An American diplomat was arrested for espionage. The government alleged that in exchange for intelligence, Soviet agents had given him money at a suburban Washington shopping mall. Although ABC News hadn't been at the mall to videotape the alleged exchange, it staged it in a re–creation, blurring the picture so the characters—two ABC News employees—couldn't be identified. The unethical reenactment was uncovered. Some people were embarrassed; others lost their jobs. They hadn't known for certain if, let alone how, the money was transferred; the reenactment was only a guess, not a fact. Although the diplomat ultimately was convicted, the television footage and ensuing controversy could have prejudiced his trial and helped him go free.

A reporter and camera crew got a tip about a police raid on a drug house. But they got there too late to see the first law enforcement team break through the door. So they asked the agents to stage it, in other words, to do it again. Did the same agents participate who did it the first time? Did they do it the same way the second time as they did the first, or did they show more bravado, or less unjustified force, because the camera was rolling? The video that viewers saw may have communicated the general look of the raid, but it was fiction, not fact, and should not have gone on the air.

A camera crew was riding all night with two police officers on patrol, and wanted a shot of the police car racing through the dark streets with its emergency lights flashing, but it was a quiet night and there wasn't a single urgent call. So they asked the officers to stage one by running through an intersection, against a red traffic light. They complied, although because it wasn't a real emergency call, they didn't activate the siren. Sadly, a woman on the cross street drove legally through the intersection. The police car, staging something for journalists, killed her.

And finally, an experience of my own:

After the Soviet invasion of Afghanistan, the British government "recalled" its ambassador from the capital, Kabul. This is the diplomatic equivalent of formally protesting a country's behavior. The Queen's representative was to fly out on a Friday, but because my colleagues from the British network ITN wanted to air the story of his departure on the very day he'd leave, they went to his official residence on Thursday and asked him to stage the departure, so they could ship the footage in time for Friday air. Allied with ITN and knowing I could use the footage in my own piece, I tagged along, and began to notice troubling details. The ambassador was wearing a suit, whereas the next day he would dress casually for the long trip. He got into his sedan on its left side but the ITN crew asked him to get in on the right side for better lighting, and he complied. Although his wife would be leaving with him the next day, she didn't bother participating for the phony shoot. All told, the British network's staged video tape was no better than a scene shot in Hollywood for a fictional film. They used it anyway. I'm proud to say, we didn't.

As with so many other rules about which you have read in this book, the rule about staging also has an exception. If you are doing a story or part of a story about someone, and you need another shot or two over which to do a VO, you can ask the subject to walk down the sidewalk or to work at her desk or to do something benign that doesn't allow any substantive change in the story's outcome.

What's the Point?

Questions about staging require good judgment, but if you don't feel qualified to judge, you really don't have to. Just draw the line at the bottom and don't stage anything. Period!

Gifts Worth Too Much

Once, after touring an electronics factory in eastern Europe, the factory director tried to give me a little keychain with the company's symbol attached to it. It was just a gesture of goodwill on his part, something he offered to all visitors, the equivalent of a pen with a company's logo, or a water bottle with a name printed on it. It probably wasn't worth a dollar.

But muttering some stupid logic, I gave it back to him. My moral code as a journalist said, don't accept gifts, for if you do, it might create the impression in the giver's mind that you now are indebted to him, and in the viewer's mind that you have been bought.

Unfortunately, the factory director tried to put the keychain back in my hand, and I put it back in his. He was hurt, I was embarrassed. No one in his right mind would think this cheap little keychain was a bribe, but I had drawn the line at the bottom.

That night, because the whole visit had ended so awkwardly, I called ABC's vice president in charge of such things and asked if I had acted wrong, and the policy that emerged from our talk was, "You can accept the price of lunch, but not the price of dinner."

What he meant was, don't take any gift so valuable that the giver might conceivably think you're in his pocket. Or valuable enough to give the audience even the appearance of impropriety.

I relate the story this way because there is no hard and fast rule, nor uniformity amongst news organizations on what kind of gift is appropriate and what kind is not. Some will draw the line at the very bottom, others will put a dollar figure on what you can accept, and others will just tell you to use your best judgment.

It's not that hard. Today, I would accept the keychain. Or even a lunch. But nothing more. When I moved to ABC's bureau in Denver, a ski pass came in the mail, unsolicited, good for two free days at every ski resort in Colorado. I love to ski, and would have loved to have used the pass, but I cut it in two parts and threw it away. What would have happened if I used it, then had to report one day on a gondola falling to the ground, killing four skiers trapped inside? How would it look if, even though I believed it, I reported that the ski resort, somehow, was not at fault? Someone could accuse me of failing to fully investigate the resort's culpability because I had been skiing there for free.

Imagine you have a steak and champagne dinner at a politician's expense, then have to report on charges that he was embezzling money. Or what if you take a free trip on an airline, then get assigned to report on the cause of the fatal crash of one of its planes? Use your head, maintain your integrity, and those questions won't come up.

What's the Point?

It goes without saying that you must never report a story, or report a story a particular way, because someone has given you something to do so. But the rule about gifts goes further: you must never put yourself in the position of even appearing to report something because you've been bribed. You also don't want to feel like you owe a favor to the gift giver. We report to the public. The public must trust us.

Checkbook Journalism

The rule about gifts cuts the other way, too. You must never pay anyone (or even ask anyone) to say something a certain way. If you request someone's participation in a story and they only agree to participate if they're paid, walk away. As you just read, you operate on the foundation of the public's trust.

But what about paying someone on a piecemeal basis for his time, or energy, or expertise? Here, frankly, there are two standards. When working in the United States, unless it's someone regularly featured as a consultant, you don't pay, and there are no exceptions. Stations and networks will pay expert consultants to appear from time to time when the subject of their expertise becomes newsworthy—military and intelligence experts in time of war, for instance—but then, they are working in the capacity of a journalist. When you simply approach someone with a request to do an interview, or explain a topic, or take you on a tour of a site in the news, either he does it for free or you find someone else. It's the only way for everyone to be sure that someone isn't altering a story because you've given them money.

Overseas, regrettably, the practice is different. European journalists typically provide an "honorarium" to experts who help them produce their stories. Over the years, American journalists working overseas have "gone along to get along." It's not our proudest practice, but sometimes it's the only way to assure the expert's assistance. If you find yourself in such a situation, satisfy yourself that the honorarium merely wins you cooperation, not compliance.

What's the Point?

Just as money shouldn't influence your coverage, don't influence your sources with money.

Covering the Disorder, Not Creating It

Once, I caused a small riot. We were covering nighttime antiwar protests outside a Republican nominating convention in Miami, and I turned on the light I was holding for the camera crew. Before it went on, the protesters were just shouting. After it went on, they started throwing things, and the police responded by barging into the crowd, and it got ugly. The protesters who threw things broke the law and deserved to be arrested, but the light had been their invitation. Could anybody directly blame me? No. Did I blame myself? Yes.

But at least that was just a stupid mistake. Another time, during a riot against the British military presence in Northern Ireland, I saw a photographer deliberately incite a protester to throw something and, what's worse, he gave the protester the rock to throw. That's unethical on the face of it, but although I had nothing to do with the photographer's actions, indirectly I became a victim.

At about three o'clock that next morning, despite the riots, a milkman and his son, dedicated to their customers, made their usual rounds in their three–wheeled electric milk cart. A rioter hit them with a homemade gas bomb. Panicked by the fire, the milkman swerved and hit a tree. He and his son died in the flames. My crew and I were right around the corner, and when we heard the crash we ran in that direction, getting there before the police. That led the police to accuse *us* of inciting a rioter to attack the milk cart so we could get dramatic video tape. We were arrested and detained until we could prove that we weren't guilty, although we still were denounced the next day in the British parliament for the death of the milkman and his son.

What's the Point?

This lesson is short and to the point: you don't make the news, you only cover it. Don't do anything to violate that!

However, this doesn't mean that when you're covering a story and someone needs lifesaving help, you shouldn't stop what you're doing as a journalist and do something helpful as a citizen. It only means you should try not to stimulate or otherwise affect the outcome of a story if human life or precious property aren't at stake.

When You Don't Have to Treat Everyone Equally

You used to hear politicians or issue advocates demand coverage on TV or radio station because of the "Equal Time Rule." The FCC (Federal Communications Commission) *used* to require all news programs that gave air time to one candidate or advocate to give "equal time" to the opposition. But the Equal Time Rule for news and information broadcasts was discontinued.

It still applies to entertainment programs. If a sitcom or a late night show has a declared candidate on for a cameo appearance, it must find a way to provide equal time for other candidates for the same office. But newscasts, magazine shows, talk shows, even the tabloid gossip shows are immune.

You only need to know this in case anyone ever demands "equal time." Of course, you do want to be fair to all significant announced candidates and advocacy organizations during a political campaign.

What's the Point?

Being fair during a campaign is the right thing to do, but from the standpoint of broadcast law, it's not a requirement.

How Free Is Information?

There are so-called "sunshine laws" at almost all levels of government to insure that the conduct of any government official, or committee, or agency, cannot escape public scrutiny. At the federal level, it's called the Freedom of Information law.

Such laws typically apply to government records, which means if you want to examine employment profiles at a state agency to see if it's hiring ex-felons, or to see the transcript of a city council committee that met behind closed doors, with exceptions you'll read in a moment, you're entitled to do so.

This doesn't mean though that government bureaucrats (or high-ranking officials) will make it easy for you. Some aren't fully aware of the public's rights under sunshine laws, others just don't want you snooping around, and still others have something to hide and won't submit to sunshine laws without a fight. The good news is, although it consumes time and money, if you go to court, you'll usually win.

When won't you? When you demand records that usually are exempt from sunshine laws, which fall into three categories:

1. Records that pertain to pending legal prosecution, which might be compromised by publicity.
2. Records that might reveal matters of personal privacy, which falls beyond the scope of sunshine laws.
3. Records that might jeopardize national security. Federal agencies have been known to cite national security concerns for withholding records when such concerns have been bogus. It's always up to you to decide when to pick a fight.

Lastly, sunshine laws at all levels of government apply *only* to government. They don't apply to private businesses, although if you need information about publicly-held companies that sell stock and therefore are subject to federal regulators like the SEC (Securities and Exchange Commission), or companies subject to oversight by agencies such as the FCC (Federal Communications Commission) or the FAA (Federal Aviation Administration), you can get your hands on the records that those government agencies keep.

What's the Point?

Acting on the public's behalf, you have certain rights. Know them. Be prepared to fight for them.

Our Ethical Foundations

As journalists, why do we have the rights we have? Because we are citizens of the United States of America. We are citizens of the Constitution, and beneficiaries of its First Amendment, which is about the nation's citizens, not just its "press." By this stage of your education, you should know what the First Amendment says. But to make sure you refresh yourself, I won't tell you here; as the first exercise at the end of this chapter, you'll have to look it up.

You'll also have to look up two particular codes of ethics for journalists. There are several, and even some news organizations have their own. But like different word definitions in different dictionaries, different codes of ethics are remarkably similar.

Whether in print or in broadcast, whether in radio or in television news, and whether working behind the scenes or identified to the audience, your responsibilities to be fair and balanced, truthful and accurate, respectful and honest, and both cautious and aggressive, are the same.

Exercises to Reinforce Your Ethics _____

1. **The First Amendment**
   Find it. Write it up. Turn it in. And most important, learn it. Without it, you can't be a journalist in America.

2. **The Codes of Ethics**
   Both the Radio and Television News Directors Association, and the Society of Professional Journalists, have codes of ethics worth learning, and following. Find both. Then write a sentence summarizing each standard that both codes have in common.

21

Holding onto Your Dream

What You'll Learn

It's probably hard for you to figure out right now how you're going to get from where you are today—studying broadcast journalism—to actually practicing broadcast journalism. And no wonder; there is no prescribed "perfect" path.

Some veterans will tell you to go off to a small station in a small market where you'll write, report, shoot, edit, anchor, and sweep the floor at the end of the night. Then, if it's too small for you, work your way up to someplace bigger.

Some will tell you to get an entry-level job (like "gopher," which really means "go for" this and "go for" that) at a station in a bigger market, put one hundred percent of your energy, personality, and initiative into your work, and once your superiors take notice, you'll win promotion to higher-level jobs there.

Some will tell you the best place to start your career in broadcasting is in print, because then you'll learn the pure craft of information gathering and written storytelling before adulterating it with the demands of picture and sound.

And some will say you need expertise in the areas of people's lives that you cannot acquire in journalism school or at a TV or radio station, big or small. And by the way, what about journalism school? You'll find conflicting opinions on the value of that, too.

In this chapter, you won't learn about the "right" way or the "wrong" way to become and to be a broadcast journalist, because there is no right or wrong way. Instead, you'll learn of the possibilities, with a few recommendations thrown in to enhance your resume and your skills.

How to Get There

Internships. They're the single best way to stand out from the crowd when you're competing for your first job in broadcasting. When a news director is comparing job applicants, and you've been an intern but the other top competitor hasn't, the news director at least can be confident that you probably know the lingo and won't likely trip over the tripod.

That's how I ended up with ABC News. After an internship in the news department at KGO-TV in San Francisco, I went to graduate school in Chicago. ABC News was looking for someone to fill a temporary five-month position in its bureau there. Of all the students in the graduate broadcast journalism program, only two of us ever had set foot in a working television newsroom. The other guy had a lot more experience than I had, and they offered him the job, but he decided to return to his hometown where a permanent job awaited. I got the next nod. I still tripped over a tripod or two and had to fake my way through the lingo I still didn't know, but the internship got me in the door. It was up to me to succeed, of course, once I got that far. It'll be the same for you.

There are several other good reasons to seek an internship.

Learning

Different stations have their interns do different jobs. You might get to do research, write readers for the anchor, operate equipment, dispatch crews, conduct interviews, shoot video, contact guests, or actually report.

In big markets, however, where editorial and technical jobs are unionized, an intern might only get to *watch* the professionals doing their work. But while there is no substitute for actually doing a job, even merely watching is worthwhile. You can ask questions. You can make suggestions. You can absorb the processes the professionals follow.

Exposure

The people running the newsroom are exposed to you and your talent. Of course, if they're not impressed, you have no future there. But if they are, then when your internship is complete and an opening comes up, you might have the inside track.

Networking

This simply means getting to know people. Maybe it's someone in the top ranks at your station. Or someone at another station who you get to know while tagging along with a news team covering stories. Or someone in politics, or business, or culture, who likes what they see and hear when they deal with you as an intern.

Networking also loosely means having an "ear to the ground," in other words, being in a professional environment where you're probably privy to information about jobs and opportunities at other stations, possibly in other markets, before word spreads.

College Credits

As with so many other parts of life, internships have their downside. Namely, typically you don't get paid. (If you're asked to do work that a paid staffer otherwise would be doing, familiarize yourself with state and federal law. Depending on what you're asked to do, it might say you must be paid.) If you get an unpaid internship but still have to earn money, you'll have to work extra hours elsewhere to get along.

And, when you're an intern, you probably have to do some of the "grunt" work. If you're with a camera crew, it might mean carrying the gear. If you're in the newsroom, it might mean looking up telephone numbers. Or clipping articles from newspapers. Or making coffee. But it's all worth doing. It's a practical education. And a foot in the door.

And, if it's approved by your school, it's worth college credits. Internship directors and counselors in many college and university journalism programs can usually tell you what's available, what's required, and how to apply.

An "official" internship, where the newsroom experience helps you fulfill your school's requirements, is best. But any credible internship, if it's a learning experience, is useful.

What's the Point?

Internships are invaluable. Apply for several. Hope to get one.

What to Take to Get There

I can't count how many times I've been asked, "What courses should I take to do what you did?" I also can't count how many different opinions I've heard from others in this business—journalism professors and practitioners—who try to answer. You'll hear many opinions because no single approach proves to be uniquely superior or uniquely successful.

One school of thought says, focus on courses in journalism. That way, you'll already know how to shoot and write and construct a story. There's no reason to specialize in a particular subject, because you'll have to be a jack of *all* trades.

Another school of thought says, focus on the subjects that will qualify you to write and report about them as a journalist. Like science, medicine, economics, politics, business, law, sports, and meteorology. There's no reason to learn the specific methods of journalism, because if you bring a broad background to the task, you'll pick up the processes easily enough by just working in a newsroom.

My school of thought says, combine the two. On the one hand, your journalism courses will give you the skills a news director wants when you apply for your first job. You'll be a better writer, a better interviewer, a better producer, a better technician. You'll be familiar at least with how a story is produced and how a newsroom works, and probably more.

On the other hand, if you only learn to write and report but don't know much of anything about the subjects about which you'll be *required* to write and report, you won't be much use to anybody. So don't focus exclusively on journalism, but also don't ignore it.

What's the Point?

You want to be well rounded for two reasons. First, to be good at your job. Second, to get that job. Someone with broad interests *and* journalistic skills more likely will be a top candidate.

Once You've Gotten There

If I ran a newsroom today, I'd want all my journalists to work to the standards of this book. But it's a dream. Nor is it necessary. Other books and other professors will teach some journalistic practices differently. Just as well, only differently.

That's why the lesson that's important to remember above all others is this: although basic principles shouldn't change from newsroom to newsroom, styles should, and do. All TV and radio stations want to present the news, but the style with which each presents it—the style of writing, shooting, editing, interviewing, and prioritizing what to cover and how to show it—is what sets each one apart.

So whether you learn about broadcast journalism from this and other college courses, or you pick it up from your first news director, you can safely predict that your *second* news director will want you to do some things—probably a lot of things—differently. What you have to do is, go with the flow. At least you start with an advantage: you already know one good way to do things, if not more.

You start with another advantage too: you know it's not a "nine-to-five" job. Sometimes that's because you work on an early morning broadcast and get up in the middle of the night. Sometimes it's because you work on a post–prime time broadcast and work 'til late at night. Sometimes it's because you're on a story that starts in the middle of the night and carries you all the way into the next night! That's what coffee is for.

What's the Point?

Each news director, each executive producer, each *boss* you encounter may have a different way of doing things, and try to break you of some of the habits you carry into his newsroom. Don't resist. As I've tried to emphasize throughout this book, there's more than one good way to do most things in journalism. But they're all fun, as long as you can get that cup of coffee.

And While You're There

Everyone who contributes to the final look, sound, and content of a newscast is a journalist. The job title might be assignment editor, graphic artist, or sound technician, but every job with input to the broadcast has the same goal: to deliver a clear, concise, full news show.

As such, no matter what kind of position you hope to fill at a station, you will be working as a journalist, and this book will be a useful guide for your performance. Furthermore, no matter what kind of position you hope to fill, you might change your mind.

Feel free to do that. You could get your first job and discover that instead of writing, you prefer shooting. Or that you love the adrenalin rush of the assignment editor's job more than the show producer's job. Or, vice versa.

You also might find that you prefer print to broadcast, or that you only can get a *job* in print, not broadcast. Nothing wrong with that, either. Obviously, the style and tools you'd use are vastly different, but the principles don't change, because no matter what the medium is, journalism is journalism.

What's the Point?

Those who talk into microphones aren't the only journalists in a newsroom. Nor are they the only ones having fun. Journalism—at any level, in any medium—is one of the most interesting, challenging, diverse, rewarding jobs around. You can be a part of it. You'll be the envy of your friends.

Exercises to Fulfill Your Dream _____

1. Write a hundred words (no more) on the value of internships.

2. Choose a station where you'd like to be an intern. Research your school's requirements, and the station's. This must include the right contact people to whom you'll apply and to whom your teachers and counselors can send letters of recommendation.

3. Choose a mentor who'll be willing to work with you, then after getting your instructor's approval, create a resume with your mentor's help that you can include in your search for either an internship or your first job at a radio or television station.

4. Describe in a hundred words (no more) the best curriculum for you to pursue to work as a broadcast journalist.

5. In a hundred words (no more), describe what you think—at this point in your education—you want to do in journalism.

Index